Political Writings

Political Writings

Jean-François Lyotard

Translated by Bill Readings and Kevin Paul

University of Minnesota Press
Minneapolis

Chapters 1-7 originally appeared in *Tombeau de l'intellectuel et autres papiers,* Editions Galilée, Paris, 1984; chapter 8 originally appeared as "Lettre morte" in *Journal des Etudiants de la Sorbonne*, 1964; chapter 9 originally appeared as "Projet pour une Charte" in *Dérive á partir de Marx et Freud.* Christian Bourgois Editeur, Paris, 1973; chapter 10 originally appeared as "Nanterre, ici, maintenant" in *Dérive á partir de Marx et Freud.* Christian Bourgois Editeur, Paris, 1973; chapter 11 originally appeared as "le 23 mars" in *Dérive á partir de Marx et Freud.* Christian Bourgois Editeur, Paris, 1973; chapter 12 originally appeared as "Sur le Départment de psychanalyse de Vincennes" in *Les Temps Modernes*, 1974; chapter 13 originally appeared as "L'endurance et la profession" in *Critique*, 1978, and the English translation originally appeared in *Yale French Studies* 63 (1982), reprinted by permission; chapter 14 originally appeared as "Ersiegerungen" in *Journal des Etudiants du Graduiertenkolleg, Siegen,* West Germany, 1989; chapter 15 originally appeared as "Nés en 1925" in *Les Temps Modernes,* 1948; chapter 16 originally appeared as "Tribune sans tribun" in *Education 2000*, 1978; chapter 17 originally appeared as "Oikos" in *Oekologie im Endspiel,* Fink Verlag, Munich, 1989; chapter 18 originally appeared as "Ligne générale" in *Amnesty International*, 1990; chapter 19 originally appeared in *Politics, Theory and Contemporary Culture,* ed. Mark Poster, 1992, © Columbia University Press, New York, reprinted by permission of the publisher; chapter 20 originally appeared as "La culpabilité allemande" in *L'Age Nouveau*, 1948; chapter 21 originally appeared as "Apropos de *Heidegger et 'les juifs'* " in *Passagen Verlag*, 1988; chapter 22 originally appeared as "La mainmise" in *Autres Temps,* 1989; chapter 23 originally appeared as "L'Europe, les Juifs et le livre" in *Libération*, 1990; chapters 24-34 originally appeared in *La Guerre des Algériens,* Editions Galilée, Paris, 1989.

Published by the University of Minnesota Press
2037 University Avenue Southeast, Minneapolis, MN 55455-3092
Printed in the United States of America on acid-free paper

Library of Congress Cataloging-in-Publication Data

Lyotard, Jean François.
[Selections. English. 1993]
Political writings / Jean-François Lyotard ; translated by Bill Readings with Kevin Paul Geiman, foreword by Bill Readings.
p. cm.
Includes index.
ISBN 0-8166-2043-1 (acid free)
ISBN 0-8166-2045-8 (pbk. : acid free)
1. Politics and literature. I. Title.
PN51.L94 1993
844'.914—dc20 92-44863
CIP

The University of Minnesota is an
equal-opportunity educator and employer.

Contents

IV. More "jews"

V. Algerians

Abbreviations

ALN Armée de libération nationale (Algerian National Liberation Army)

The military arm of the FLN from 1954 to 1962, the National Liberation Army was in the forefront of the struggle for Algerian independence. Many political leaders, such as Boumedienne, rose to prominence through the army.

ANP Armée nationale populaire (Algerian People's Army)

This organization replaced the ALN as the official Algerian military establishment in 1962. It was known as the Guardian of the Revolution, and it remained loyal to Ben Bella during the postindependence divisions of 1965.

CCE Comité de coordination et d'exécution (Executive Coordinating Committee)

In August 1956 the internal leadership of the FLN established a formal policy-making body to synchronize the movement's political and military activities. The five-member CCE was the executive of the CNRA, which had 34 members.

CGT Confédération générale du travail

The French Communist Trade Union Confederation, a group of unions controlled by the French Communist party. In 1956 the FLN ordered all Algerians to leave the French trade unions and formed the UGTA. The leader of the CGT in 1968 was Georges Séguy.

CNRA Conseil national de la révolution algérienne (National Council of the Algerian Revolution

Thirty-four member policy-making body founded by the FLN in August 1956. In 1962 the CNRA adopted a series of policies for an independent Algeria known as the Tripoli program. This program called for agrarian reform and nationalizations. It was opposed by Ben Khedda of the GPRA.

CRUA Comité révolutionnaire d'unité et d'action

The prototype of the CNRA, the CRUA came into being in 1954 as a grouping of Algerian revolutionaries committed to the armed struggle. Largely drawn from the revolutionary "committee of 22," its membership included Ben Bella.

CSP Comité de salut public (Committee of Public Safety)

The name adopted by a group of right-wing French colonists, led by Generals Massu and Salan, who opposed Algerian independence.

FLN Front de libération nationale (Algerian National Liberation Front)

Algerian independence movement formed in 1954, which came to power under Ben Bella's leadership in the one-party postindependence state of Algeria in 1962. The war of independence was launched by Frontist guerrillas on November 1, 1954, and the Front remained the independence group most directly identified with the war.

GG Gouvernement général

The official title of the French command in Algiers.

GPRA Gouvernement provisoire de la république algérienne

The provisional government of the Algerian republic was set up by the FLN during the war of independence and negotiated the 1962 Evian agreements with France. Based in Tunis, this government-in-exile was headed by Abbas and included Ben Khedda.

JC Jeunesse communiste (Young Communists)

The communist youth movement in France.

MNA Mouvement national algérien (Algerian National Movement)

An independence movement opposed to the FLN, founded by Messali soon after the revolution began. The MNA had influence among Algerian workers in France.

MTLD Mouvement pour le triomphe des libertés démocratiques

The movement for the triumph of democratic liberties, also known as the centralists, was founded before the revolution and led by Messali. Committed to unequivocal independence, it opposed Abbas's integrationist program. Its newspaper was *El Maghrib el Arabi*.

MRP Mouvement républicain populaire (Popular Front)

The coalition of communists, socialists, and Christian democrats, led by Léon Blum, that ruled France from 1944 to 1947.

OAS Organisation armée secrète (Secret Army Organization)

A terrorist group of right-wing vigilantes opposed to Algerian independence. Founded by Pierre Sergent, it came to light in the putsch of 1961.

OS Organisation spéciale (Special Organization)

The clandestine organization for armed resistance to French occupation in Algeria, formed in 1947 by Aït Ahmed when the authorities suppressed political protest. Later led by Ben Bella, it developed into the ALN.

PCA Parti communiste algérien (Algerian Communist party)

Led by Messali, the PCA never belonged to the FLN coalition.

PCF Parti communiste français (French Communist party)

Led by Secretary General Thorez during the Algerian war. Valdeck Rochet took over upon the death of Thorez in 1964.

PDI Parti démocratique de l'indépendance (Istiqlal)

The Moroccan Democratic Independence party was formed in 1944 and won independence in 1955. Its newspaper was called *Al-Istiqlal.*

PPA Parti du peuple algérien (Algerian People's Party)

The prewar party led by Messali that became the MTLD around 1946.

PRS Parti de la révolution socialiste (Algerian Party of the Socialist Revolution)

Founded by Mohamed Boudiaf immediately after independence in 1962 and based in Morocco, the PRS was opposed to the GPRA government.

PS Parti socialiste (French Socialist party)

PSA Parti socialiste autonome

In 1958 a group of socialists split off from the SFIO, in opposition to SFIO leader Guy Mollet, who was supporting de Gaulle's return to power. In 1959 Mendès-France joined the PSA, which later merged with other groups to form the Unified Socialist party.

RPF Rassemblement du peuple français

Gaullist group from 1947 to 1952.

SAU Sections administratives urbaines

French colonial administrative classifications for Algerian towns and cities.

SAS Sections administratives spéciales

French colonial administrative classification for areas of political turbulence.

SFIO Section française de l'Internationale ouvrière

The French section of the workers' International became the

present Socialist party in 1969. SFIO leader Guy Mollet became French premier in 1956.

SNE Sup Syndicat national de l'enseignement supérieur

The French university teachers' union, led in 1968 by Alain Geismar.

UDMA Union démocratique du Manifeste algérien (Democratic Union of the Algerian Manifesto)

Founded by Abbas in 1948, the UDMA maintained "friendly neutrality" during the first year of the war of independence, afterwards supporting the FLN. A liberal bourgeois party, the UDMA formally joined the FLN in 1956. Its newspaper was *Egalité: La République Algérienne.*

UEC Union d'étudiants communistes (French Communist Students' Union)

UGEMA Union générale des étudiants musulmans algériens (General Union of Algerian Muslim Students)

Formed by the FLN in 1955 as an autonomous student wing of the party, the group changed its name to Union nationale des étudiants algériens in 1963.

UGT Union générale des travailleurs (French General Workers' Union)

Noncommunist trade union in France.

UGTA Union générale des travailleurs algériens (Algerian General Union of Workers)

Formed in 1956, when the CGT was no longer politically viable, after the FLN broke with the PCF.

UGTT Union générale des travailleurs tunisiens (Tunisian General Workers' Union)

Broke away from the CGT in 1946 under the leadership of Hached. The UGTT cooperated closely with the Néo-Destour party after Hached was murdered by colonist vigilantes in the early 1950s; Ben Salah took over the leadership.

UGS Union de la gauche socialiste (Union of the Socialist Left)

UNR Union pour la nouvelle république

Gaullist party from 1958 to 1967, afterwards called the UDR (Union pour la défense de la république, and later Union des démocrats pour la république). Chaban-Delmers was president of the party in 1968–69.

USRAF Union pour le salut et le renouveau de l'Algérie française

A precursor of the CSP, this organization was founded by General Massu after the riots of French settlers on May 13, 1958, in Algiers to represent the interests of the *pieds-noirs*.

USTA Union des syndicats des travailleurs algériens

When the UGTA split off from the communist CGT in 1956, the CGT in Algeria reacted by forming itself into an autonomous group and changing its name to the USTA.

USTT Union de syndicats de travailleurs tunisiens

When the UGTT split off from the communist CGT in 1945, the CGT in Tunisia reacted by becoming autonomous and changing its name to the USTT.

UTM Union des travailleurs marocains (Moroccan Workers' Union)

Independent Moroccan workers' union, led by Mahjoub ben Seddik.

Foreword
The End of the Political
Bill Readings

Biography and Engagement

". . . the impasse between militant delirium and skepticism"
"March 23"

Spanning more than thirty years of political activity, this collection of texts by a single individual might seem to call out for a biographical narrative to accompany it. For all its insistence on historical analysis, the political left has always relished hagiography, since the individual as moral exemplum performs the problematic theoretical reconciliation between historical or economic determinism and individual action, sketches a politics for the present conjuncture. Politics, for contemporary Marxism, thus names the presence of historical forces as a field of possibilities. Individuals, by their political actions, actualize history correctly or incorrectly. Despite our vaunted suspicion of the liberal humanist "subject," we still want heroic narratives. "Men do not make history under circumstances chosen by themselves," certainly, but they still make themselves as examples of the historical process.[1]

The writings collected here certainly provide a useful empirical corrective to charges that poststructuralism is an evasion of politics, or that Lyotard's account of the postmodern condition is the product of blissful ignorance of the postcolonial question. Yet any discussion of the formative influences of the Second World War, the complex fragmentations of the postwar French left, the challenge of the Algerian War to the social fabric of France, the role and treatment of intellectuals in the French media, the persistence of anti-Semitism in French society, or the political role of the university during and since the events of May 1968 would obscure far more than it would clarify. Such themes and events appear in these texts; indeed, their absence would be surprising. Algeria is not Lyotard's Spanish Civil War, however, or even Sartre's Algeria. That is to say, Algeria offers Lyotard no way to pretend that he can occupy the position of the other and engage in heroic combat by proxy, as foot soldier, journalist, or strategist. His account of the anti-imperialist struggle is not that of an epistemological imperialist ready to speak in the name of others, eager to realize himself through the process of self-immolation or self-emiseration. Lyotard knows that engaged intellectuals do not "lose themselves" as common soldiers or simple reporters but rather find themselves thereby, as the selfless consciousness of history itself. Relinquishing this pretension, he writes not of "the Algerian War" but of "the Algerians' war"—a war that is not his, cannot be his, but that nonetheless calls out to him, demands a testimony that can never be adequate, a response that can never redeem his debt or obligation.

Thus, Lyotard's political writing can never add up, can never achieve the status of a settlement of accounts, a settled or established account, a biography. As Lyotard himself remarks, revolution is not a matter of bookkeeping: even if history will have proved him right in arguing against the common leftist assumption of the universal validity of Marxist analysis in anticolonial struggles,[2] the solace of hindsight can only betray what is most political, and most tenuous, in these writings. Their politics lies in a fragile and fugitive attention to events, to the unforeseeable solidarity of the oppressed and the unimaginable imagination of militants. No historical forces, not even an indomitable and ahistorical popular will, can account for inexplicable mass demonstrations in Algeria or civil disobediences without a political program in the Paris of 1968. Such events seem to occur in flagrant disregard of possible origins or likely outcomes, as eruptions of an affective enthusiasm that ignores cognitive explanation and classification, including appeals to "the human spirit."[3] We give these events names or dates that function as names. "1968" functions as a name in that it exceeds historical accounting: it is not a year that stands out in history so much as a name that marks the failure of historical consciousness to reduce temporality to a regulated succession or rhythm. The names of such events are rigid designators of their specificity, they mark the very fact that we cannot determine their historical or political significance: these names indicate referents whose meaning is yet to be determined, that evoke a work of political discussion in order to invent the criteria by which they may be judged.

Politics, in Lyotard's writings, is a sense of astonishment that anything can happen at all, given the crushing weight of the capitalist economy and the institutions of the modern state on the one hand, and the party and union bureaucracies on the other. Any politics that seeks to predict and organize resistance and critique can only serve to strengthen the state, given that capitalism does not suffer from contradictions so much as profit from them. In an advanced capitalist democracy, the union organization, with its patrons and bosses, does not simply repeatedly fail the workers, it turns their very resistance into a locus of alienation in that the worker has access to his or her strength only insofar as it is mediated by a representational system. The lineaments of this process become clear when the unions are directly integrated into the state, as in the old Soviet Union. Then bureaucracy rather than the cash nexus becomes the locus of expropriation: in each case the workers' strength is no longer their own; it is returned to them as illusory representation, whether as wages or as Red Square parades.

And yet, despite the capacity of systems of political representation to absorb and channel energies, things happen; unpredictable resistances occur. A political writing must preserve a sense of wonder at these happenings, if it is not to fall into either chiliastic militancy or disillusioned skepticism. Militant psychosis denies the world in favor of an interior certainty, and dooms itself to heroic failure—dooms itself in that each failure serves only to bolster that certainty. Each act of the Baader-Meinhof group provided the West German state with a pretext for reinforcing the police as the repressive apparatus of "liberal capitalist democracy," and the group hailed each defeat as a victory, as a further revelation of the true nature of capitalism, a step on the road to terminal crisis—right up to the point at which one of the group managed the remarkable feat of shooting himself in the back of the head in a West German prison. The cynical skeptic is the obverse of this coin, the one who finds in each failure a confirmation of the utter loss of political hope, in each success an illusion and a betrayal. Despair masks itself as "realism." Neither militant nor cynic has anything to learn; neither can listen. Lyotard's political writing is a struggle to listen, to hear a politics that cannot speak the language of the political.

Herein lies another reason for the inappropriateness of biographical narrative for this least Hegelian of thinkers. Narratives of heroic struggle or growing disillusion can only replay the binary opposition between militant and skeptic that structures the postwar or cold war period, the very opposition against which all of Lyotard's political writing struggles, to a greater or lesser degree.

The writings in this collection are not organized chronologically. In Lyotard's case, to trace the shift from his membership in Socialism or Barbarism through his participation in the events of May 1968 and on to an analysis of what he has called "the postmodern condition" (whether the process is presented as a growing despair and loss of commitment or as a growing refinement of the terms of political analysis) would be to return these writings to the very order of political discourse against which they struggle, at which they scream and laugh. No balance sheet of positions taken can do justice to his politics of writing, since these texts are written in a revolutionary time: the noncumulative time of minoritarian struggles, which resist history, refuse the dialectic of imperial time that seeks to transform them into oppositional forces, or to erase them altogether.

Finally, intellectual biography is disallowed by Lyotard's refusal to be an intellectual, to represent or incarnate an authority, any authority, which marks him as not merely a member of a minority but as a minoritarian thinker, carrying on a politics that is devoid of all totalitarian vocation. A politics, that is, that looks very unlike what we are used to, and a politics that will require more detailed introduction.

Debt Crisis and Modern Political Thought

The present volume groups essays and articles around topics that are not simply political "issues." Each marks a field in which the terms of political action and thought have come into crisis. The essays and interviews grouped under the title "Big Brothers," with its allusion to the Orwellian state portrayed in *1984*, focus on the problem of authority in political writing. As such, they generalize the question of the role and function of intellectuals raised in the section of that name. How is one to write, speak, or act politically without presuming an authority, implicitly practicing the kind of totalitarian injustice for which Lyotard and Deleuze criticize Lacan in "Concerning the Vincennes Psychoanalytic Department"? The notion of authority presumes the capacity to say what is right or good, to issue prescriptions as to the nature of justice that are based upon determinate or describable criteria. And that presumption is the first step toward totalitarianism and terror, since difference is precluded right from the start. One may argue over the determination of criteria, but once a sufficient consensus has been reached, the suppression of the minority can begin. In contrast, Lyotard argues for a minoritarian politics, a politics that does not presume to establish an alternative authority in political matters. He refuses the notion that the political can be a matter of cognitive description (and thus of determinate judgments), arguing instead for politics as an uncertain process of indeterminate judgment. Justice must not seek to be justified once and for all, must not seek to become authoritative. Rather than trying to say what the political is or should be, to determine the identity of the political, Lyotard insists upon a politics of difference. In this sense, Lyotard's political writings do not attempt to write the political but to engage a politics of writing that will not assume the fixity of authority, will not seek the "last word" characteristic of a Big Brother.

The students of whom Lyotard writes are not simply intellectuals in waiting. Their function in the events of May 1968 is crucially that of refusal, a refusal to understand their intellectual activity as a process of training that would assign them a role within the state, an insistence that they do not know what kind of people they may be, that further study is required. The students are not simply heroic militants: their militancy challenges the representational claim of democracy, the claim that in a liberal democracy society achieves exhaustive representation, reflects itself to itself. The students motivate a society to rebel *against its own elected representatives*. They do so in the name of an uncertainty about who they are, not in the name of militant certainty. Students enact the sense in which we are and are not part of society; we always function in society before we understand what it means to do so, and we do so until death.

The social predicament of modernity that students expose is one of difference (there are others) and of temporal nonequivalence (deferral). Born too soon, without knowledge, and yet born too late to live that knowledge except as tradition received from elsewhere, students name the temporal predicament of modernity. On the one hand, too soon: they are born into culture, but they still have to learn to speak its language. On the other hand, too late: the culture they are born into precedes them, and they cannot make its anteriority their own, they can only handle the fragments of its language. Students remind us that neither nostalgia nor education can settle accounts with culture as tradition and betrayal: we are handed over to culture even as it is handed to us. Modernism tries to forget this predicament in two ways: by the *conservatism* that says that we can live the tradition (that it is not too late) and by the *progressive modernism* that says we can make an entirely fresh start (that we are not incomplete, we can teach ourselves).

In each case, reactionaries and progressives (of both left and right) talk about culture as if it ought to be, or is, synonymous with society. Reactionaries say that culture ought to provide the model for society, that we should live in a world of high culture, or of organic villages. Culture should determine society. Progressives tend to say that culture is society, or it is ideological illusion. The self-definition of the human community should define the model of our being-together. "We" can make our own salvation. Socially displaced by the strange temporality of education, students provide a critique of the possibility that society might represent itself to itself, might define itself through the autonomous exercise of its own will, the presumption on which the claim to authority made by modern representative democracy is based. As "*Ersiegerungen*" points out, the modernist project of autonomy and universal communicability is not provisionally but fundamentally incomplete: no authority can terminate the pedagogic relation, no knowledge can save us (from) thinking.

A similar sense of debt and obligation to tradition as undermining the Enlightenment claim to freedom through knowledge underpins Lyotard's writing on the "jews." Lyotard's writings on Judaism are not those of an adept, nor are they the product of the nostalgia of a would-be convert. No such conversion is possible (this is not an *alternative* to Christianity). The "jews" (who are not simply empirical Jewish people) mark a limit to the modern European idea of humanity: resolutely marginal, they refuse to join the universal human race and they cling to a tradition founded on respect for the unpresentable, for the impossibility of Enlightenment. Authority issues from a position that cannot be occupied by the subject; it is heteronomous. These people simply refuse to become autonomous political subjects. Integration or extermination, the options offered to "jews" by the modern enlightened state, are revealed in their full horror by the event named "Auschwitz," which brings the Enlightenment project of history as the rational process of realizing the essential autonomy of the human race to an acknowledgment of its irrationality and inhumanity. Auschwitz names a debt from which European humanity cannot be freed, an obligation of atonement that must not be historically rationalized as one event among others in European history. It names the injustice of understanding history as a project of liberating humanity from the past, from tradition, from obligation to the other.

The war of the Algerians is not primarily important to Lyotard as an instance of nationalist struggle for self-determination. The Algerians, he repeatedly insists, are not simply fighting for the right to do to themselves what the French have done to them. Rather, the bloody process of decolonization marks a limit to a modernist and imperialist philosophy of historical progress that is common, under diverse forms, to both left and right. As an affirmation of the local or the particular, the Algerian war throws the universalist pretensions of the nation-state into crisis: the struggle is not merely over whether French colonists or native Algerians should direct the development of the state and society in Algeria. What counts in these writings is the presentation of a war against the presumed neutrality of "progress" and "development," a struggle not to become the representatives of a process of "universal" human development (capitalist *or* communist) that has been defined in Europe.

Politics and the State: No Salvation

> *Marxism, the last shoot stemming from both the Enlightenment and Christianity, seems to have lost all its critical power.*
>
> "The Wall, the Gulf, and the Sun"

This resistance to modernist universalism is part of Lyotard's wider argument against what may be called the politics of redemption. By this term I mean the understanding of politics as the ordering of the political so as to achieve a redeemed society, liberated from historical necessity. The Christians promise liberation by the Messiah, the Enlightenment proclaims the capacity of rational thought and acquired knowledge to make "man" the master of "his" world and realize mankind's essential freedom, Marxism argues that the process of history will fulfill itself as the proletariat comes to incarnate human consciousness of its species-being as essentially laboring. In each case, a proper determination of the nature of the political can bring history to an end, redeem humanity from necessity.

Lyotard's political writings mark a troubled disengagement from the politics of redemption. He speaks of "depoliticization" when he is writing on Algeria, of "antipolitics" in reference to May 1968, of a minoritarian judaism distinct from imperial history, and elsewhere of paganism and postmodernism. These are all names for the attempt to take a distance from the Enlightenment model of politics as the site of a secular redemption (which is summarized most succinctly in "Tomb of the Intellectual" and "The Wall, the Gulf, and the Sun"). It is characteristic of modernity for politics to be understood as naming the mode of interaction between history and the contemporary. Yet, once one no longer believes that history will save us through political action by producing a transcendent, liberated, and empowered subject, how is one to do anything but despair? These political writings demand that this question should be introduced.

In the note appended to his writings on Algeria, Lyotard refers to a "depoliticization": the loss of belief in an alternative political truth that will authoritatively legitimate oppositional critique.[4] This loss of faith in salvation is actualized in the rise of the modern bureaucratic state as an essentially unipolar society. In place of the clash of workers and bosses comes a system that offers to internalize such conflicts. This is not simply a matter of setting up industrial relations tribunals. The "machine" of which Lyotard speaks in "Dead Letter" is an early figure for the complicity between capitalism and the nation-state, a complicity in which the dual functions of expropriation and administration carried out by the French in Algeria provided an object lesson. Lenin is correct to argue that imperialism is the highest stage of capitalism in that the administrative role is not a feudal hangover, a duty of care; it is the reformulation of the social bond as an autonomous and unipolar system of representation. As capitalism becomes a global system, power appears as administration not coercion, managerial rather than directly oppressive.

If we sketch the lineaments of the bleakest picture that Lyotard provides, then the primary relation of subjects is to a state in which they participate only at the price of becoming operatives. The emergence of the state thus marks a terminal point for political thought, and it is against this backdrop that politics must be rethought. Rather than the political question being what kind of state can establish the just society and realize human destiny, the positioning of the state as the unifying horizon for all political representations becomes the stumbling block for a just politics. Consumerism is merely one symptom of this process of the almost complete internalization and reconsumption of the product of the system. That is to say, consumerism is less of an ideological falsification of well-being (bread and circuses) than a mark that no benefit exterior to the system can be imagined, no benefit that would not in its term be subject to cost/benefit analysis (was that vacation a good buy?). The state marks a certain triumph of capitalism, of capitalism as an energetics that seeks to synthesize a profit from differences by reducing them to accountable variations within a homogeneous mode of representation (money). The state does not simply extend the cash nexus, it analogizes its indifferent operation into all aspects of social life. Within this representational system, tribunals regulate social tensions in terms of quantifiable denominators of cost/benefit analysis: money, time in jail, quality time, information exchange, and so forth. The unipolar state is the terminus of modernity as the progressive integration of all possibilities as *representable* for and by the state. The Western state replaces command with communication as the governing ideology of representational consensus. Development and management replace expropriation in its raw form: the social control of capital in liberal democracies is no more than the subjugation of all wealth and power to these twin exigencies of the system.

By contrast, the weakness of socialist central planning lies in its failure to understand the autonomy of the bureaucratic system, its stubborn clinging to the unrealized promise of a society beyond the state. Hence the Marxist version of the state is too inflexible to become all-encompassing: critical energies cannot be harnessed for the improvement of the system's functioning. On the other hand, the unipolar Western state, by presuming the intertranslatability of political forces, turns almost all resistance into a source of energy. All dissidence can be expressed, provided that it allows itself to be represented. Politics ends once the state becomes the sole site where the political is managed, an end in itself. "The Wall, the Gulf, and the Sun" notes the extension of this process to international politics, whereby conflict is internalized under the horizon of the extraterrestrial.

The politics of Lyotard's writings lies in their attempt to rethink the terms of resistance, to find a way to think against a state that has no outside, that seeks always to realize itself as the state of things. As Lyotard notes in his critique of the capitalist-bureaucratic system in his writings on May 1968, the unions have themselves become an apparatus for the governing of the labor force within that system.[5] Lyotard's abiding distrust of the role of the party is not simply a matter of historical betrayals, of the persistence of Stalinism in France. The cynical calculations of the French and Algerian

Communist parties in seeking to preserve French influence in Algeria as a conduit for their own role is merely a symptom of the more general complicity of radical organizations with the systems they claim to oppose. The party remains entirely within the political structure of representation in that it treats the workers that it claims to represent as nothing but the mute referent of its own discourse. Attacking the *politics of representation* rather than *political representations*, Lyotard argues against the pretension to speak in the name of others as the cornerstone of injustice, be it liberal or totalitarian.

Intellectuals: Speaking for Others

> *For a long time, in the West, philosophers have been exposed to the temptation of the role of the intellectual, they have been tempted to turn themselves into the representatives of an authority. And there are not many, since Plato, over twenty-five hundred years, who have not succumbed to this temptation. It seems to me that Lyotard would like to belong to this minority; that's what he told me to tell you.*
>
> "A Podium without a Podium"

Lyotard's problem with speaking in the name of others, which runs throughout these texts, has little to do with modesty or shyness. Rather, it is a matter of the pragmatics of discursive legitimation. To pretend to speak *for* the oppressed is to objectify them once more, to make them the referent of one's own discourse. The argument with the oppressor then concerns the nature of the referent, but not its position in relation to discourse.

This might sound like the prelude to an argument for autonomy, for letting people speak for themselves (at times in the writings on Algeria it seems that way). However, it is more radically an argument against discursive legitimation as such. First, because, as "The Grip" points out, the dream of discursive autonomy is itself founded on a forgetting of debt and obligation to the other. To presume that all people can in principle speak for themselves is a double victimization: it assumes the speaker's access to discourse and it assumes that the speaker is inherently a potential modern subject. Second, whether one is speaking for oneself or for another, the problem lies in the authority assumed in speaking for, in the name of . . . Hence the problem is not simply one of paternalism, but of the presumption to authority in politics.

This is the root of Lyotard's attack on intellectuals, experts, and big brothers. The intellectual is exiled from the particular in order to reach the universal, who is a citizen of the universe, who speaks to everyone and to no one in particular:

> It seems to me that "intellectuals" are . . . thinkers who situate themselves in the position of man, humanity, the nation, the people, the proletariat, the creature, or some such entity, that is, who identify themselves with a subject endowed with a universal value so as to describe and analyze a situation or condition from this point of view and to prescribe what ought to be done in order for this subject to realize itself or at least in order for its realization to progress. The "intellectuals" address each individual insofar as he or she is the repository or the embryo of this entity. ("Tomb of the Intellectual")

The intellectual, as a modernist creature, rationalizes history by means of abstraction, constructing a grand narrative of the liberation of a subject as self-realization. The end of history is thus the realization of mankind as essentially free from ignorance (Enlightenment), essentially capable of providing for material needs in a free market (capitalism), or essentially laboring (Marxism). Actual events are merely the raw materials for a metadiscursive reflection upon the progress of this narrative of self-realization. Apart from the exile of metalanguage as pure alienation, Lyotard insists that there is another kind of exile—the exile of a Europe whose nationals "emigrate right where they are, become indeterminate" so as to be neither "good villagers" nor "the talented messengers [great communicators?] that the megalopolis claims for its own" ("*Ersiegerungen*"). Doing this is a process of "working through our rootlessness," identifying a margin that is not defined by reference to the center, a local exile that is not a rooted dwelling, for all its locality.

This rejection of intellectual authority is perhaps the most difficult thing to preserve in Lyotard's thinking: does not all writing, even his, contain a de facto presumption to speak authoritatively? So what does it mean to appear on television ("A Podium without a Podium") to announce, in a voice divided from one's image, that one is not an intellectual, that one does not pretend to competence and authority in matters of philosophy, that there should be no such competence in such mundane matters as those philosophy treats (love, work, society, health, beauty, justice, etc.)? Lyotard insists that he is not an expert, even if he seems to play one on television. He has no authority to recommend any panacea. Authority would be a legitimate competence to determine meaning or value in those mundane philosophical matters that make up everyday life. And in the name of that competence, that privileged access to the referent, discourse is legitimated: this is the meaning of the referent, for any and all addressees. To speak for others in politics is the pretension to speak for all, to achieve a discourse that is proof against pragmatics. And in the discursive pragmatics of this phrasing we have a little domination effect in miniature: the speaker effaces the addressee, legitimating himself or herself only in relation to the referent and the signification attached to it. This effect becomes terroristic at the point where addressee and referent are the same: when the intellectual (speaker) is telling x (addressee) what is good (signification) for x (referent). Insofar as the determination of the referent's signification is presumed to be authoritative, the addressee can only speak in his or her turn *in conformity with* that description, as the referent of the intellectual's discourse. The problem of speaking for others, in their name, is more generally the problem of the claim to exclusive authority over effects of reference, the claim to determine a given political meaning that serves to eradicate the possibility of politics.

These writings owe their politics to their persistent refusal to privilege political meaning—a finality external to political pragmatics—or even to historicize political *effects*. To historicize a political effect is to translate pragmatics into a language of meaning. As I have remarked in attempting to resist the temptation of biography, the historical perspective is the means by which the intellectual can determine the meaning of political events. This is the root of Lyotard's refusal, in "March 23," to write a history book on the events of May 1968, his insistence on an "antihistory" as the only way to speak on the day after the movement of March 22. No external standard will permit political calculation: there is no universal language of political meaning in which the signification of all referents can be authoritatively determined. Rather, politics is the struggle to witness to the dissensus among the different languages that political discourse seeks to homogenize.

An Endless Politics

The nature of this struggle shifts in the course of Lyotard's writings: the far leftist appeal to spontaneous popular resistance comes to be replaced by a focus on judgment and witness. Resistance becomes less a mode of redemption, a metaphysics that counterposes desire, poetry, or popular will to dominant representations, than a form of attention, a minor process[6] of reading or listening that evokes an unaccountable or intractable differend with representation, "which forbids any reconciliation of the parties in the idiom of either one of them" ("The Differend"). In "Dead Letter," we might still think that poetry can save us from the machine. In the writings on May 1968, it seems that desire can breach the dominant mode of discursive representation, erupt in a way that cannot be channelled by the capitalist-bureaucratic state. The turn to Judaism and to the differend decisively rejects the possibility of an alternative epistemological ground for political critique, shifts resistance away from oppositionality to difference. Politics becomes a matter of justice, of handling differences, rather than of establishing truth or even countertruth.[7]

Thus, giving up a redemptive politics means ceasing to believe that the political can be a locus of healing, of solutions. The end of the political as the site where humankind works out its meaning or destiny means that politics will not come to an end. This loss of faith only gives rise to cynical inactivity for those who remain within the perspective of redemption. Lyotard's vitriolic critiques of the state, the party, and "big politics" in general can thus be linked to the philosophical rejection of a politics based on models of the perfect society (be they Plato's or Marx's) that is familiar from *Just Gaming*.[8] What is perhaps more pointed in these writings than in *Just Gaming* is a sense of how those models work (in the lives of workers, the colonized, and young people) and how those oppressed by political models can at times resist them without recourse to other, supposedly better, models. Modeling, for all its glamour, is always exploitative.

It is exploitative because the political model remains pious, religious in its promise of a hereafter: submit to your bosses in the factory, the home, or the party now, and all will be well later on. All will be well because politics will have come to an end. What Lyotard's writings, on the contrary, promulgate is not so much the heroic militancy of a refusal to submit as a refusal to think that politics will come to an end. The time of "big politics," the idea of the political as the site where humanity struggles to define its destiny and realize its meaning, may well have passed. That is what Lyotard means by "depoliticization": humankind's representation of itself to itself is no longer primarily political, the business of a party or a state. But this is not because politics has stopped; it is precisely because we no longer believe that it will ever come to an end, that it will ever fulfill that self-representation. Once politics is no longer the sphere in which meaning is to be worked out, politics ceases to be the search for an identity, a redemptive significance that might lie behind or beyond the activities of everyday life. Rather, politics is the attempt to handle conflicts that admit of no resolution, to think justice in relation to conflict and difference.

Thus Marxism is to be honored for its evocation of the differend of exploitation that underlies the supposed equity of the wage-labor transaction, for realizing that labor is not bought or exchanged but enslaved in the capitalist system. Capitalist exchange, as Lyotard does not cease to point out, victimizes by virtue of the presumption of exchangeability that underlies its representational system. The worker becomes, for him- or herself, a unit of value in the system of the other. Yet for Lyotard, alienation is not reducible to an ideological falsification, a flawed representation. Indeed, it is the Marxist desire to identify alienation as a reversible ideological distortion that grounds its pious faith in the possibility of emancipation. The problem lies with the understanding of politics as the struggle *for*, rather than against, representation. A minoritarian politics does not seek to take its place in big politics, to gain representation in parliament, for example. The minoritarian, the "jew," the gypsy, and the native American insist upon their differend with the representational system of parliamentary politics as such. They respect external authorities (Yahweh, tradition, ancestors, future generations, etc.), they do not seek to speak for themselves as autonomous subjects communicating with other autonomous subjects, they seek to respond to those authorities. Their refusal of parliament is not made in the name of a better kind of parliament that might include everyone in a larger consensus, but in order to testify to their differend with the Western discourse of universal humanity, with the rule of representation in which silence equals death. The differend announces itself by a heard silence, the sense that something is trying to be said that cannot be phrased. The speechless witness of the Auschwitz survivor, which insists that the *Shoah* be remembered *as unspeakable*, imposes a refusal of the communicational ideology of political modernity. The events to which these writings witness are political insofar as they displace representational systems in this way.

The possibility of politics lies in actions and desires that are sensible only as *heard silences*, traces of radical dissensus within modes and structures of political representation, social communication, or economic accounting. Lyotard's displacement of modernity is an insistence that these differences are not accidentally but structurally repressed by the modernist drive to transparency in representation, communication, and accounting, by the dream of a self-regulating autonomy.

The difficult question is how to take a distance from modernist pieties without presuming to escape the predicament of modernity for either a new modernity or a return to the premodern, without counterposing a pious nostalgia for the grounded experience of a home, of dwelling, of premodernist rootedness (Heidegger). Nor is Lyotard aiming at the critical detachment, the transvalued cynicism, of a postmodern cool (Baudrillard). Here, political writing is a matter of thinking modernity against modernism, against attempts to render the predicament of modernity the locus of a determinate historical project for the realization of a universal subject.

And these writings insistently remind us that emancipation (Kant's "man's emergence from his self-incurred immaturity") is nothing other than alienation in its purest form, the identification of freedom with self-domination, which is also the terrorization of all those who do not participate in saying "we."[9] As "The General Line" reminds us, there is a "no-man's land," like the "grip" of the debt to an unthinkable Other by which we are preceded, that haunts and prevents any such attempt to reduce the subject to a pure point of self-consciousness. Rather than counter partial alienation with a total (and thus transparent) alienation, Lyotard argues that humanity does not have an origin that it can grasp so as to become fully self-conscious, an empowered identity. Humanity does not have a birthright over which it might once more exercise control, be it a human nature or an essential human difference from nature (culture). Rather, Lyotard speaks of the soul (and of psychoanalysis, the analysis of the soul) to name a deep uncertainty about the position of the human between nature and culture, between heteronomous tradition and autonomy, between the inhuman and the human. The Freudian unconscious is crucial here, once the attempt to historicize it through identification with the working class has been abandoned.[10] What Lyotard realizes is that the repressed does not return in historical time, and thus cannot be assigned a determinate signification. With the end of redemption and a sense of the radical intractability of differends, we come closer to a feminist than to a Marxist politics, given that feminism insists upon sexual difference without seeking to *resolve* it.[11] Gender difference imposes a differend; we are obligated by a difference that we cannot master. Testifying to this difference does not mean overcoming it by achieving communication between the genders, it means an alert or respectful acknowledgment of the impossibility and necessity of exchange, around a differend that is sensed but that cannot be expressed in a shared idiom, over which no final agreement can be reached. The obligation to remain alert to and respectful of voices that we cannot hear clearly cannot be lifted. That is the condition of politics, of the struggle to handle differends justly. As Lyotard remarks, "Something like this occurred in 1968, and has occurred in the women's movement for ten years . . . There are other cases" ("The Differend"). There will be other cases, and they will demand other political moves, if we are to seek to do them justice. Readers of these political writings will find no authoritative maxims here to protect them from facing that obligation.

Part I
Intellectuals

1

Tomb of the Intellectual

(1983)

The spokesperson of the socialist government calls on "the intellectuals" to open the debate on the "transformation" France requires in order to "catch up" in economic and social matters. He specifies, however, that he would like "concrete involvement in thinking" rather than "big names talking publicly about engagement."[1]

What exactly does he mean by "intellectuals"? His appeal is really an appeal for ideas people, experts, decision makers. Of course it is an appeal for intelligences, but for intelligences who take on or will have to take on administrative, economic, social, and cultural responsibilities, or for intelligences who at least debate or will debate the aforementioned "transformation" without losing sight of these responsibilities. Yet it seems to me that "intellectuals" are more like thinkers who situate themselves in the position of man, humanity, the nation, the people, the proletariat, the creature, or some such entity. That is to say, they are thinkers who identify themselves with a subject endowed with a universal value so as to describe and analyze a situation or a condition from this point of view and to prescribe what ought to be done in order for this subject to realize itself, or at least in order for its realization to progress. The "intellectuals" address each individual insofar as each is the repository or the embryo of this entity. Their statements refer to and arise from the individual according to the same rule. The responsibility of "intellectuals" is inseparable from the (shared) idea of a universal subject. It alone can give Voltaire, Zola, Péguy, Sartre (to stay within the confines of France) the authority that has been accorded to them.

Max Gallo's appeal thus suffers from a confusion of responsibilities. He ignores the dissociations that are the basic principle of the task of intelligence, and that also to some extent ground the de facto divisions between professions today.

New technologies, essentially linked to the technosciences of language, along with the concentration of civil, economic, social, and military administrations, have changed the nature of intermediary and higher occupational tasks and have attracted numerous thinkers trained in the hard sciences, high technology, and the human sciences.

These new cadres are not intellectuals as such. The professional exercise of their intelligence is not directed toward the fullest possible embodiment of the universal subject in the domain of their competence, but to the achievement of the best possible performance in that domain. This performance is defined by the best input/output (cost/benefit) ratio relative to an operation. It is a technical criterion in the fullest sense (including financing, time gained or lost, the evaluation of the operation by a public, etc.). Thinkers engaged in such responsibilities can and probably must be led to invent new mechanisms. In this sense they assuredly investigate what works best in their domains. But they question neither the limits of these domains nor the nature of "performance," in the way that a subject that has a vocation to universality necessarily does. They accept the received compartmentalization of realities and the received criterion for the evaluation of actions.

I am simplifying, obviously. The proliferation of new technologies continually destabilizes this compartmentalization. But the fact remains that when a writer, an artist, a scholar, or a philosopher takes on this kind of responsibility, she or he accepts ipso facto the conditions of that responsibility: the need to get results in the assigned domain. The same thing goes for cultural tasks. One directs a cultural center, a department in the culture ministry, one participates in a committee granting aid to the arts: whether one is a great dramatist or a great painter, as someone in charge of culture one has to stick to a completely different kind of task than that of "creation." The very idea of cultural activity, of cultural "stimulation," presupposes that the addressee (the public, the user) lacks knowledge, taste, sensibility, lacks the means of expression and needs to be educated. In the first place, the public has to be won over, seduced, and so forth (unlike what takes place in teaching). Success in the management of culture is determined in principle in terms of results, in terms of changes in the behavior of addressees that are judged to be positive. The problem of quantifying these results is another question.

The only responsibility of artists, writers, or philosophers as such is a responsibility toward the question What is painting, writing, thought? If anyone says to them, "Your work is for the most part unintelligible," they have the right, they have the duty, not to take any notice of the objection. Their addressee is not the public and, I would say, is not even the "community" of artists, writers, and so forth. To tell the truth, they do not know who their addressee is, and this is what it is to be an artist, a writer, and so forth: to throw a "message" out into the void. Nor do they have any better idea of who their judge is, because in doing what they do, they also question the accepted criteria of judgment in painting, literature, and so forth. And the same goes for the limits that define recognized domains, genres, and disciplines. Let us say that they experiment. They in no way seek to cultivate, educate, or train anyone at all. Anything that pushes them to locate their activities within the game quite rightly appears as unacceptable.

All the same, they are not "intellectuals." They do not need to identify with a universal subject and take on the responsibilities of the human community in order to take on responsibility for "creation." (In inverted commas to protest against the connotations of Christian theology and romantic aesthetics that remain attached to this word. Will we ever find the proper term to designate an activity that is essentially dispossessed and dispossessing?) On the contrary, the revolution in theoretical physics achieved by Einstein and the Danes has helped to disrupt the modern idea of a universal subject (and an object) of knowledge. The Futurists' investigations were of course adapted to an ideology, that of fascism, but it should be acknowledged that fascism was not an indispensable element in those investigations. When Apollinaire writes that artists nowadays should make themselves inhuman, he clearly means that avant-garde movements are not initiated by the "intellectuals," who are too human. *Return from the USSR* is the work of an "intellectual" (or perhaps a citizen-writer), *The Counterfeiters* the work of a "creator"; to judge the two books in the same light because they are by the same author would be a denial of justice to each of them. The link between the two is not a weak one; it simply does not exist.

Although the same person can indeed fill two or three functions—indeed, cases of this have been observed (Malraux, for example)—these functions are not any less heterogenous to each other in all their aspects. Nor is this the end of the matter. This person is also a citizen who enjoys the rights and exercises the responsibilities of everyday citizens. These responsibilities concern the question, What is the best mode of coexistence and how can it be achieved? This question differs completely from those that govern the activity of an intellectual, of a cadre or of a "creator." Nonetheless, it also requires the activity of intelligence.

But of course the assumption of responsibilities concerning the idea of a universal subject or concerning administrative, cultural, or other decisions, or even concerning "creative" activity, does not lend any particular authority to the holder of these responsibilities when it come to his or her task as a citizen. For nothing proves that optimal performance defines the best mode of coexistence or even contributes to it. Nor that "creativity" for its part is beneficial to the civic community or that "creators" have particular insights to communicate to that community. Nor, finally, that the point of view of universality is appropriate to the elaboration and resolution of the questions posed to a citizen of a particular country at a particular moment.

There is still always a great temptation to put the renown earned in the exercise of one of these responsibilities to the service of another. It is probably this kind of transfer that people in general, and Max Gallo in particular, expect from the "intellectuals." It is in effect this kind of transfer that characterizes intellectuals as such. This encroachment only ceases to be a confusion and an unjustified usurpation on one condition: that a universalizing thought, the only one the "intellectual" can take pride in, can arrange the different responsibilities to which I have referred in relation to each other in a system or at least according to a common purpose. Now it is precisely this totalizing unity, this universality, that thought has lacked since at least the middle of the twentieth century.

To put it bluntly, one can be an "intellectual" without dishonor only if the wrong lies entirely on one side, if the victims are victims and the torturers inexcusable, if in the world of names that forms our history, some at least shine like pure ideas, spotless (Frederick II for Kant). It was in this sense that Marx denounced the "pure and simple wrong" done to the worker by the condition of wage slavery. His indictment was authorized by a universal subject to come, which would organize all the aforementioned responsibilities, including those of the thinker, to a single end, the emancipation of the proletariat. The Paris Commune was the (almost) transparent name that embodied this end. This authority has disappeared, not only because of the real nature of the USSR, a representative appointed by the emancipated proletariat, but primarily because the signs that could legitimate the thought of such a subject have become more and more hard to find. Judge for yourselves: the most important of these signs, perhaps the only one, in Marx's eyes as for the Bolsheviks, was the international solidarity of the workers . . .

The same goes for the thought of the Enlightenment, which has animated liberal politics for a century. It has become obsolete. One can judge its condition by considering the state of education, which was its strong point, in the most advanced societies. The "intellectuals" who made up the *Aufklärer* and their nineteenth-century heirs thought that propagating education would strengthen the freedom of the citizen, would get rid of political sectarianism, would hinder wars. Today no one expects teaching, which is discredited everywhere, to train more enlightened citizens—only professionals who perform better. Such is the officially formulated objective of French reform of undergraduate education. Ignorance is no longer a tort, and the acquisition of knowledge is a professional qualification that promises a better salary.

There ought no longer to be "intellectuals," and if there are any, it is because they are blind to this new fact in Western history since the eighteenth century: there is no universal subject-victim, appearing in reality, in whose name thought could draw up an indictment that would be at the same time a "conception of the world" (look for names). Even "the most disadvantaged," whose point of view Sartre sought to espouse in order to guide himself through the labyrinth of injustices, was only, when all is said and done, a negative, anonymous, and empirical entity. I am not saying that there is no need to get involved in the fate of the most disadvantaged: ethical and civic responsibility demand that one should. But this point of view only allows defensive and local interventions. Extended beyond such interventions, it can mislead thought as it misled Sartre's.

Max Gallo will not find what he is looking for. What he is looking for belongs to another age. My conclusion is not, however, that painters paint, that philosophers philosophize, that scientists do research, that managers manage, that the organizers cultivate, and that politicians (of whom I did not speak on purpose, so as not to embarrass Max Gallo) do politics. My conclusion is rather "optimistic" in principle, even if it seems to be "pessimistic" in fact (but these notions themselves come from the Enlightenment). The decline, perhaps the ruin, of the universal idea can free thought and life from totalizing obsessions. The multiplicity of responsibilities, and their independence (their incompatibility), oblige and will oblige those who take on those responsibilities, small or great, to be flexible, tolerant, and svelte. These qualities will cease to be the contrary of rigor, honesty, and force; they will be their signs. Intelligences do not fall silent, they do not withdraw into their beloved work, they try to live up to this new responsibility, which renders the "intellectuals" troublesome, impossible: the responsibility to distinguish intelligence from the paranoia that gave rise to "modernity."

2
The Differend
(1982)

The socialists' victory did not thrill me.[1] I said to myself: perhaps they lied during their campaign and will behave like good children in following the same line as Raymond Barre—increasing public spending on "social" programs by 3 percent of the gross national product, an increase to be covered by the national debt, a little inflation, income tax, and every available means of protecting employers. Thus by 1988 or 1995, the international competitiveness of French firms will not be seriously weakened, and at the same time society's problems will remain unchanged. Or perhaps they did not lie to their electors, and they are going to introduce a neo-Keynesian economic program, a "welfare state" with a dash of self-management; given both the international structure of production and the market and the already low level of productive investment that currently exists, the socialists will clash head-on with hostile owners and managers of capital, they will have to give up after two years, once they have lost the confidence of their electoral constituency, and the hour of Jacques Chirac will have come.[2]

Yet I was wrong. Rather than adopting either policy wholeheartedly, they have gone in for a little of both, and the result will be the algebraic equation of certain advantages and disadvantages inherent in the two policies.

These calculations are not, and never were, the product of disillusionment. Their logic is that of capital. After thirty years of expansion, it has entered a new phase of overcapitalization, with both the customary effects and some new ones, which has given rise to both the usual remedies and some attempts at new ones. Among the habitual remedies, war, the most effective of them all, seems to have taken a new lease on life in Washington and Moscow, for different but complementary reasons. The logic of capital is essentially the logic of *Capital*, without its dialectical framework. By this I do not mean that there are no contradictions in the functioning of the capitalist economy but only that nothing results from these contradictions that signifies or announces the obsolescence of capitalism.

To move to true socialism, to an economy freed from the law of value, it is not enough merely to find the contradictions produced by that law unbearable; you have to recognize them for what they are and want to uproot them. This consciousness and this will are called the subject of history, the proletariat, in the Marxist tradition. Now, after a hundred years of its great moment, the history of the revolutionary movement has provided ample proof that this subject has not arisen, and it is reasonable to think that it will not arise.

One might as well say that there is no global alternative to capitalism, no alternative within the framework of a dialectical thought and a revolutionary politics, that is. It follows that in the coming crisis the stake will not be socialism (humanity taking control of its ends and its means) but the extension of capitalist relations of production to countries currently under bureaucratic control.

This is not to say that there is no society that can contradict the logic of capital. The success of the socialists in France is a proof of its reality. For Valéry Giscard d'Estaing and Raymond Barre, authentic figures of capital, this society was only a moment in the reproduction of capital, the moment of the restructuring of the useful labor force and hence exclusively one of productive consumption. It happens that this society is also the constitutional sovereign, and that it has persecuted those who despised it. But what does the sovereign want, by way of respect?

The counselors of the sovereign soon came to find it capricious. It wants everything all at once. To give it what we can, let's reform. In this way, the absence of the suspicion of contempt for the monarch one serves allows one to assume the monarch's role. But there is no way of despising the sovereign people nor of replacing it if one thinks that it does not exist. Universal suffrage does not imply the universal subject, but exactly the contrary. Society is traversed by conflicts of interest that oppose "social partners"; the sovereign ballot box indicates in which partner's favor these conflicts should be settled. This system, which has become a banality, gives reformist politics its material.

But there is something else. "Society," as one says, is inhabited by differends. I would say that there is a differend between two parties when the "settlement" of the conflict that opposes them appears in the idiom of one of them while the tort from which the other suffers cannot signify itself in this idiom. Contracts and agreements between economic partners do not prevent—on the contrary they presuppose—that the workers (or their representatives) have had to and will have to speak of their labor (and make their labor speak) as if it were the temporary cession of a commodity of which they were the owners. Even when they discuss whether the conditions of this cession are just or unjust and when they act so as to modify those conditions, they must always keep quiet about the fact that their labor is no such cession (and not only because they cannot do otherwise).[3]

With the logic of *Capital*, the aspect of Marxism that remains alive is, at least, this sense of the differend, which forbids any reconciliation of the parties in the idiom of either one of them. Something like this occurred in 1968, and has occurred in the women's movement for ten years, and the differend underlies the question of the immigrant workers. There are other cases.

The intelligentsia is not sparing with its support, its advice, its participation in the new power. It certainly has an activity of reform to accomplish, as is already apparent in matters of culture, justice, teaching, and research. Rightly or wrongly (in what idiom would one debate it?), I believe that the activities of thought have another vocation: that of bearing witness to differends.

When a Samuel Beckett writes his books without caring whether they are understood, when a Jerome Lindon dares to publish them, and when the ministry passes a law that allows one to find them in bookstores, this is how a testimony to the differend in literature can find its addressees. The same thing holds, mutatis mutandis, for a painter, a filmmaker, a musician, a philosopher, a dramatist, a scientist. This is not to say that they need not bother themselves with the means of reaching their addressees, and hence need not take part in the working out of a "cultural policy" (a terrifying expression, all the same). They should not forget, however, that politics is only business and culture is only tradition unless both of them are worked over by a sense of the differend, which, moreover, is nobody's special prerogative.

3

For a Cultural Nonpolicy

(1981)

1. The "fact" is that the Socialist party dominates French political institutions.[1] But the direction that it will impose upon the activities of the country, in the context of an extremely tight world market, is not a "fact." A possibly significant part of the electoral majority expects the restoration of the welfare state by the Socialist party. Yet Keynesianism is simply impossible in the present state of imperialism. And there is no organized political movement on the international scale that provides an alternative to imperialism, as thirty years of the world history of communisms teaches us. The new regime in France is an alternation within the framework of international capitalism. Thus it must follow the neoliberal policy of supporting competitive sectors of activity, which allow foreign trade to be balanced and the currency to be defended, while providing some satisfaction to the social strata that elected it. Thus I expect this satisfaction to be meager.

2. You seem to accept it as a "fact" that the new government has a "cultural policy." The institution of cultural policy has its historic horizon in the century (1880-1970) in which large political parties, organized in a military-industrial fashion, fought over the "masses" (that is, classes broken up by the development of industrial capitalism) with a view to winning the battle against decadence (imputed to this or that enemy, according to the case). "Culture" is the mind considered as a component of the forces at work in this battle. With cultural policy, the mind passes into the domain of the political bureaus and ministerial cabinets. This "strategy making" begins with German social democrats at the end of the nineteenth century. It continues (according to contrary but homogenous modalities) with the "cultural policies" of fascism, nazism, Stalinism, Francoism, Castroism, Maoism. At the end of this century of party-states, it would be intelligent, it would be something new, to put an end to this institution. It consecrates the decadence of the mind that it is supposed to combat: it subordinates all its activities to the production of an identity, whether national, historical, popular, class, or of

blood, or one composed of a little of each. Now, the mind has nothing to do with this fixing upon a figure of this kind, even that of humanity. (The pilgrimage to the Pantheon was disturbing, in this respect, as was its staging [*mise en scène*] on television. Not all that different from that summit of cultural narcissism, the Paris-Paris exhibition.)

3. Of course, capitalism also has its "policy" for culture, which is no less alienating for being more insidious. It selects the activities of the mind according to criteria of good performance: the value of a book is judged by its sales figures, the value of a curriculum by the number of students registered, the value of a television program by the ratings, of a scientific invention by its technological spin-offs, and so forth. It doesn't take a massive institution to counter this process—a few laws or decrees concerning key points, those at which the law of the market threatens to submerge the freedom of the mind (the law on the unitary pricing [*prix unique*] of books is one such defense), suffice. And this mechanism should not discourage investment, but attract it, not by offering the hope of profit, but by appealing to a motive that seems sadly foreign to French owners and managers of capital (unlike their peers elsewhere): the glory that can be added to their name by the foundation of an institute, a chair, a public lecture, a scholarship, a society, an endowment, a cultural center. Here too, new and more encouraging legislation is to be desired.

4. You seem to admit as a "fact" that "intellectuals," and others, are professionals who have to make their claims count. But a profession sells a product or a service that can be defined by its use, and hence can in principle be assessed. The legitimacy of its claims can be measured by this yardstick. The activities of someone in the theater or the cinema, of a writer, a comedian, a scholar, even of a teacher, cannot be measured in this way, especially nowadays. His or her "culture"—since Joyce, Cage, Frampton, Duchamp, Bohr, Artaud, May 1968—belongs more to the capacity to question and experiment with his or her activities than to make them conform to received and transmissible paradigms. This "culture" has never been so "philosophical." Now not only would Socrates fail before the CSCU,[2] he would have difficulty obtaining funds for the project. How does one evaluate the utility of the service provided by a question or a proposition? If there is a claim to be made, it is that "intellectuals" and others should be allowed the freedom to question all their activities. It is not their task, but that of the legislative body, to determine the percentage of the gross national product that ought to be devoted to financing them. This percentage will in any case be insufficient because the mind is infinity. But it matters that local "cultural" collectives (the university, the school, the laboratory, the museum, the theater,

the conservatory, etc.; without prejudice to the redefinition of local entities) should also have the freedom to question the use to be made of the funding corresponding to the "budget" accorded by public authorities (and of the funds it may obtain from private sources). An arrangement that might favor such independence would perhaps be that the authority distributing the funds should itself be local (regional, for example, in the framework of decentralization). The region's accounting office would check the use made of these funds (only to see that there was no embezzlement). I am not an administrator; here I have in mind what ought to serve as a model of this cultural nonpolicy: the constant, brilliant, and popular initiatives of the Italian municipalities and local groups concerning the activities of the mind.

4
New Technologies
(1982)

1. The question of industrial strategies appropriate to the present situation must be fully asked. The variables at work are not only technology, industrial production, and the economic crisis. The very notion that each has an *impact* on the other is still too crude.

2. The human universe concerned is that of the most developed societies. As for the question asked (the impact of new technologies on industrial strategies in the context of the crisis),[1] this universe can be characterized *grosso modo* as one governed by a mixed economy of a strong technoscientific character. This characterization allows identification of four domains in which the variables pertinent to our question are to be found: the scientific, the technical, the economic, and that of the state.

3. Each of these domains, which is closely interwoven with the others, is distinguished only insofar as each domain is governed by a different Idea:[2] the scientific is governed by the Idea of the best knowledge, the technical by that of optimum performance (the best input/output ratio), the economic by the Idea of the highest wealth, the state by the Idea of the best being-together.[3] Each of these Ideas is an absolute toward which one has to work. The Idea has a regulatory function for the discourses and actions occurring in each of the aforementioned domains.

4. The responsibilities incurred by agents in the various domains differ. Einstein has a responsibility to knowledge, Roosevelt has a responsibility in relation to being-together, Rockefeller has a responsibility in relation to wealth, Wiener has a responsibility in relation to performance. Their phrases and their acts ask to be evaluated according to the criterion that corresponds to the regulatory Idea of their proper domain.[4]

5. In the present epoch, science and technology combine to form contempo-

rary technoscience. In technoscience, technology plays the role of furnishing the proof of scientific arguments: it allows one to say of a scientific utterance that claims to be true, "here is a case of it." The result of this is a profound transformation in the nature of knowledge. Truth is subjected to more and more sophisticated means of "falsifying" scientific utterances.

6. The economic domain (that is, capital) and the domain of the state combine (essentially in order to get out of the second great crisis of overcapitalization in the 1930s). The result is the contemporary mixed economy with its giant national and multinational firms, and the banker states, clients, and bosses.

7. On the basis of this double combination, technoscience falls under the hegemony of the states and the companies: "military," space, nuclear, biological, linguistic, and sociopsychological budgets. This subordination develops in the United States during the Second World War and in the world during the periods of reconstruction and rapid expansion.

8. The aforementioned regulatory Ideas are then grouped into a vast complex: to know in order to be able to perform; to be able to perform in order to be rich; to be rich in order to be together well, to be able to perform, to know. Industrial strategies are then incorporated without question into the functioning of closed systems governed by autoregulatory mechanisms of feedback and foreseeable growth. It is possible to believe that humanity is in the process of emerging from economic prehistory.

9. This is the way in which the reconstruction of national or zonal economies took place after the Second World War. It came to an end around 1955, to be supplanted by regular rapid growth over a twenty-year period. At that time, the world market reconstituted itself, to be finally glutted by an enormous accumulation of capital. Overcapitalization brought with it a fall in the incentive to invest, in the middle of the seventies, to which were added the energy crisis and a crisis in the complex of regulatory Ideas during the sixties, which asked, What is the end of knowledge? This is the question of scientists, students, and teachers. Must one seek to perform at the price of the destruction of "nature" or the environment? Is good being-together possible in the closed system of labor and consumption?

10. What is called the impact of the new technologies intervened in the context of these destabilizations, in this uncertainty over regulatory Ideas.

11. Essentially, the new technologies concern language. They are in continu-

ity with prior technologies in that they substitute automata for natural agents (humans, animals, etc.). They are different in that the substitution bears on sequences previously carried out by the higher nervous centers (cortex). They suppose the analysis of operating sequences, their encoding into artificial languages, the constitution of artificial memories, the training of automata obeying orders given in this language.

12. Language treated in this way is informational: it is made up of messages going from a sender to a receiver, both of whom are in possession of the same code (with or without translation). Information occurs only when the message responds to a question issued in the first place by the current addressee. The question is formulated in binary terms (yes or no, 1/0). The information is evaluated in terms of probability (between 1 and 0). It can be calculated. Its cost can be figured. Science, technology, and economy find a common measure of knowledge, power, and price in information.

13. This recentering of the three domains around the informational paradigm occurs mainly in terms of the following aspects:

- —the intrinsic exteriorization of knowledge in relation to the knower: the introduction of fragmented activities and strongly hierarchized organization in research, and the laboratory become industrial workshop;
- —an increased technological component in the formation of knowledge: the new machines (particle accelerators, supercomputers, electronic telescopes, lasers), their servants, their schedules of availability, the tasks of management, and the new kinds of research they require;
- —the spread of automata to the so-called tertiary sectors of production: the "elevation" of qualifications (new métiers), specialization in the tasks of the "employees," of the "inferior and average ranks of management," of the "ideas people" and "decision makers";
- —the multiplication of commodities with integrated automata and, more generally, with an integrated language (the logical language of microprocessors) used in both production and consumption.

14. Certain effects of "informatization" can be noted in each of the three domains:

14.1. There is an increased concentration in the means of the production of knowledge. This is in principle compatible with their decentralization. To respond to this concentration, an increased intervention of the states or large firms or both in the production of knowledge is foreseeable and already observable. For example, just calculate the research budget of the developed countries. Considerable amounts of capital are frozen in investments in long-term research materials whose obsolescence is difficult to calculate.

14.2. In the technosocial domain, we see technological unemployment, the extension of the average training time of the work force, increases in its cost, the reorganization of the curriculum according to criteria of performance rather than of culture, and a reduction in the length of necessary working time. There are costs inherent in this set of effects—an increased devaluation of productive labor occurs.

14.3. A slow transformation can be observed in the relationship to wealth. The issue of "statutory surplus value" linked to the consumer society declines along with the demand for objects associated with this way of life. Objects of all technological levels that allow and encourage the individual initiative of the user become of interest: computer and information-processing games, for example, or questions posed to "home terminals." Dispersal of the horizons of everyday life.

15. As for state control, the technologies of language touch its domain in regard to all aspects of its responsibility for the Idea of being-together: the multiplication of organizations for management and administration (ministers, agencies, missions); the constitution of memories (files, archives, etc.); the relationship to the new media; and so forth. The important fact is this: in handling language, the new technologies directly handle the social bond, being-together. They make it more independent of traditional regulation by institutions, and more directly affected by knowledge, technology, and the marketplace. Confidence in the establishment and in the representatives of the institution (notables, parties, syndicates, ideologies, etc.) declines. The values that are associated with the institutions also decline. A certain cultural availability, and a curiosity for experimentation, perhaps increase. One can hope, at least, for some advance in material culture (be it only in the form of a search for "quality") and perhaps even in the culture of the individual will (a slow recession in the "welfare" mentality).

16. In this respect, state control encounters a considerable challenge. It is not asked to induce faith, to reinforce existing units (ideological, social, etc.), but to advance material culture and the culture of the mind and will.

Example 1: The monopolies of state control are perceived as obstacles to initiative or opacities in communicational exchange (free radio stations, autonomy of the universities, experiments in uncontrolled fields of research).

Example 2: Cultural policies are not expected to be conceived on the model of totalitarianisms (German social democracy of the end of the nineteenth century, communism, nazism, etc.), but on the model of allowing free experimentation. There is a simultaneous need for less state (totalitarian) and more state (public service).

17. What can industrial strategy be in this technological context and in that of the crisis?[5] It would be necessary to direct efforts not only toward the high-tech sectors, but also toward the high-tech sectors of high tech. By this I mean not only to multiply the applications of the informational treatment of language, but also to support research on the postinformational treatment of language.

For example, R. Thom writes, "An order contains no information." Informational treatment only takes into account phrases that describe a "reality." But language contains many other families of phrases that obey different regimes and require other methods of analysis. For example, the four Ideas initially cited are not descriptions of realities, but regulatory Ideas (containing a prescription). It would moreover be necessary to find a way to give citizens the means of calculating the "costs" of the ideas they cherish: "If you want this, then these are the implications." This study would have to be undertaken at the highest level of complexity (the economic, fiscal, social, familial, and even the affective cost).

As for the crisis, once the energy problem has been resolved, the potential "market" opened by the new technologies is immense, because language is potentially an infinity of phrases, even if it is true that each of the language machines contains on average little invested capital. But the niche, so to speak, that French industries would have to occupy would be that of enlarging and making more complex the treatment of language (postinformational and postcommunicational)—for example, the analysis, the formalization, the committing to memory of persuasive rhetorics, of "musics," of inscriptions of movement (kineographic techniques, such as kinetic holography), and so forth. Hence, a strategy of patents and sophisticated equipment "ready to use" that would have to go alongside a politics of a concerted reduction in the legal working day on an international scale.

5

Wittgenstein "After"

(1983)

One can love a thought. One is not for all that a specialist in this thought, nor capable of explaining it to others. One does not make of it a profession or a vocation. It is "only" a feeling. A feeling is like a phrase waiting to be formulated. One feels that one is thinking (even if only a little) "after" this thought. One must, one will have to, link onto it. One tries to find a way. This "after" is not yet fixed. What is certain is that this thought will be taken into account, and one will be accountable to it.

These linkages have always occurred. They mark out paths of affinity, which become fixed in traditions. Aristotle thinks "after" the Sophists, Kant after the crisis of Leibnizian rationalism and of the grounding of law, after Hume and Rousseau. Wittgenstein is a solitary thinker. Of course, he thinks "after" Frege, Russell, logical positivism, and no doubt after Schopenhauer and Spengler. But his solitude is marked in that he also thinks "after" himself. The publication of the *Tractatus* in 1921 announced a brilliant philosopher of logic and mathematics. Published two years after his death, in 1953, the *Investigations* witness to the fact that he had taken another direction. It is easy to see that the *Investigations* link onto the *Tractatus*, but the manner of their linkage could not have been foreseen. Russell is dropped; Wittgenstein links onto Wittgenstein, with some inclination to disavow the latter (the earlier Wittgenstein, that is). A solitude that isn't concerned about "the oeuvre." What comes after displaces what preceded it.

He is not solitary because he ignores the world and his time, but rather because he does not ignore them. It is often those who think in groups who ignore them. Groups serve this purpose. But the finest listening requires some silence, a screening of large numbers of "well known" things by minuscule worries. From his hut in Norway, his cottage in Ireland, his room in Trinity College, Cambridge, where he gives a course, if one can call it that, to five or six students, but also from the trenches in the Dolomites in 1917 and the Newcastle medical laboratory in 1943, this Viennese from the beginning of the century continues to sense the malaise of his time. Nietzsche had thought that it was a sickness of the will. But Wittgenstein is a republican, like Kant. Like Kant, he thinks that the time is diseased by language. Kant did not know capitalism, however, while Wittgenstein has been immersed in it.

The examination of language games, just like the critique of the faculties, identifies and reinforces the separation of language from itself. There is no unity to language; there are islands of language, each of them ruled by a different regime, untranslatable into the others. This dispersion is good in itself, and ought to be respected. It is deadly when one phrase regime prevails over the others. " 'Language (or thought) is something unique'—this proves to be a superstition (*not* a mistake!), itself produced by grammatical illusions" (*Investigations*, §110). This superstition, which Kant called transcendental illusion, did not stop the *Aufklärer*[1] from hoping that human history might have universal emancipation as its final goal, a goal to which philosophy contributes. For Wittgenstein, this malaise has no foreseeable remedy. It is linked to the hegemony of industrial technoscience, whose age is perhaps "the beginning of the end for humanity" (*Culture and Value,* 56), and whose " 'cultural' expressions are such things as set theory and behaviorist psychology. In this situation, philosophy can do nothing on its own, the sickness that gives rise to its problems can only be cured by a change in ways of living and thinking" (*Foundations of Mathematics*, II, 23). And if he had to choose, "I am by no means sure that I should prefer a continuation of my work by others to a change in the way people live which would make all these questions superfluous" (*Culture and Value*, 61).

The reflection of the *Tractatus*, which bears on the nature of logical and mathematical language, works by means of a philosophical metaphor that is, in the final analysis, fairly classical. Language is an image of the world; the world is represented in it (but the images of events that form propositions are themselves events, and language is part of the world). Thus, there is a "mirror": the elements of language and the elements of reality are organized according to an analogous structure. Knowledge can be grounded on the basis of this presupposition. But it encounters two limits. The most immediate one is that one cannot express what makes propositions possible (the structural analogy between the world and language) by means of a logical or mathematical proposition. The other inexpressible element, at the greatest distance from the mirror, is ethical, aesthetic, or theological (perhaps political) value. *You ought* is not a proposition; it is not the image of a state of affairs. The meaning of life is not in the world: "ethics is transcendental," "God does not reveal himself *in* the world" (*Tractatus*).

In the *Tractatus*, silence protects the languages of value against the claims of knowledge. In the subsequent investigations, silence disconnects the phrases of ordinary language and reveals their import. In ordinary language, a multiplicity of phrases obeys different regimes. Giving someone an order does not have either the same stakes or the same rules for success as describing a landscape to him or her, telling him or her a story, providing the blueprint of a piece of machinery, or promising him or her something. Each set (or family) of phrases brings specific pressures to bear on the interlocutors, which push them to make phrase linkages in one way rather than another. In principle, "after" any given phrase, any phrase whatsoever may occur. If this is not generally the case, if some linkages are more expected than others, it is because rules for making linkages have been fixed and learned under the aegis of tradition. These rules may or may not be known to the participants, as in many games. Each of these families, whose limits, as the name indicates, are fluid, can be compared to a kind of game. Games do not have many common traits among them; a move made in bridge cannot be "translated" into a move made in tennis. The same goes for phrases, which are moves in language games: one does not "translate" a mathematical proof into a narration. Translation is itself a language game.

Mourning for the unity of language—a certain "joy" in the description of its strengths and its weaknesses, the refusal to have recourse to metaphysical entities like finality, the will to power, or even *thought*—ought to make Wittgenstein familiar to us. Writers, in the Mallarmean ambience of the crisis of letters, carried out a task that was of course not analogous or even convergent, yet which was not entirely alien to this: perhaps we should call it related. I know few works so useful for understanding Wittgenstein as Gertrude Stein's *How to Write.*

The major difference no doubt lies in the persistence of an ultimately empiricist notion of language use in Wittgenstein's writing. In these terms, people make use of language. They play at it. The fact that they do not know all the rules of the various language games has no impact on this anthropological assumption.

After Wittgenstein, the first task is that of overcoming this humanist obstacle to the analysis of phrase regimes, to make philosophy inhuman. Humanity is not the user of language, nor even its guardian; there is no more one subject than there is one language. Phrases situate names and pronouns (or their equivalent) in the universes they present. Philosophy is a discourse that has as its rule the search for its rule (and that of other discourses), a discourse in which phrases thus try themselves out without rules and link themselves guided only by amazement at the fact that everything has not been said, that a new phrase occurs, that it is not the case that nothing happens.

Secondly, the implications of this inhumanity for the question of the "social bond" remain to be analyzed. It should be easily understood that the principal difficulty is neither that of the state nor of "civil society," as is often thought, but consists in the functioning of capital, which is a regime of linking phrases far more supple and far more "inhuman" (oppressive, if you will) than any political or social regime. Wages, profits, funds for payment and credit, investment, growth and recession, the money market: it would indeed be interesting to analyze these objects as moves or rules proceeding from various language games. And what if capital were a multiform way of dominating time, of linking?

6
Intellectual Fashions
(1983)

From the classical age to our own day, intellectual fashions have had their institutions: courts, salons, newspapers, journals, the electronic media. These are not means of diffusing ideas or works. Words or turns of phrase (rhetorics) that summarize, crystallize, but above all symbolize these ideas and these works are put into circulation there at high frequency, at an exceptional level of agitation. These are passwords. But where do they let you pass? They are loaded with symbolic value: the community that exchanges them recognizes itself by means of them, not because of their meaning, but thanks to their fiduciary value, their power to make distinctions.

From the princely or royal courts to the journals, the manifestos, the avant-garde publications, from the Renaissance to today, this fiduciary value of fashionable words has charged its inflection. The credit that fashionable words lend procures a mercantile power, not just an ideological or political one. The editors, the movie producers, the television directors, the newspaper editors, if not the "authors" of these ideas, make money out of the fashions in words. Mercantile exchange penetrates what is called culture, and imposes its rule of optimal difference. People speculate on the gaps between ways of thinking (of speaking) just as they do on those between ways of dressing, between modes of production, or between currencies. The difference in value that results from the gap consists in a gain of time. You have to move faster than the rest, be the first to furnish the words (the clothes, the currencies) that allow the community that adopts them to differentiate itself for a moment. One fulfills a desire for difference, and at the same time one destroys difference. The life of passwords is ephemeral.

Intellectual fashions presuppose the desire to be different from the rest in thinking. Common culture, if it ever existed, is not enough. It differentiates itself into subcultures, which focus themselves into currents, families of thought, sects, villages. The vitality of municipal governments in Italy is eminently suited to these rivalries. Keeping up. At the limit you can die for the latest word—dandyism. The Peloponnesian War was perhaps the effect of fashions: people died for the glory of the name of the city and its eponyms. Fashion makes terms that signify ideas (sign, structure, pragmatics) count as proper names. But this rivalry only takes place on the basis of a common culture in which difference is valued. There is agreement that this discordance, if not this discord, is desirable. There is consensus on an interest in dissensus. Each village is made up of a unified people, the "intellectual class."

The opposition of the modern to the classical is not chronological. The classical is not the ancient. Modernity is a temporal manner, like a kind of table manners or manner of thinking. It does not consist only in a particular attention paid to the future rather than to tradition. The perspective is classical, and there is a tradition of the new (understood as innovation). The modern is a feeling for the event as such, impromptu, imminent, urgent, disarming knowledge and even consciousness. The event is an absolute performative: it happens. Fashion is affirmed by the desire to be the event.

As soon as it happens, it ceases to be an event, it becomes a piece of information, which circulates and which loses its destabilizing force. The detective novel makes crime the paradigm of the event, time's surprise.

Fashion has an affinity with aesthetics. The latter develops in the middle of the nineteenth century at the same time as poetics declines. The value of the work is determined by its evaluation by its addressees (the "public"), and not by the respect that the sender (author, artist, thinker) displays for the rules of the genre. Taste ceases to be a common sensibility fixed by rules. The community of taste is appealed to only as a horizon of universality. When one says "this is beautiful," one means everyone ought to find this work beautiful, just, and so forth. Fashion in matters of thought, at least of theory, means that even the works that place truth at stake (and that in principle elicit arguments) fall under the regime of feeling and its undisputed sharing. But this sharing has to remain minoritarian and elitist.

This requirement of minority is essential to modernity. Modernity consists in working at the limits of what was thought to be generally accepted, in thought as in the arts, in the sciences, in matters of technology, and in politics. A modern painter is a painter for whom the nature of painting is at stake in the picture he or she is making. Philosophy, at least as critique, has probably always been modern. This work of testing limits also bears the name of the avant-garde. In the contemporary epoch, fashions often shield themselves with the title of the avant-garde. This is not always accurate. Sometimes it is. The right to bear this name can be judged on the basis of the disruption resulting from critical activity in thought. It may well be the case that one has to wait a long time to find out whether the title of avant-garde is deserved.

7
A Svelte Appendix to the Postmodern Question
(1982)

A few remarks, devoid of theoretical pretensions, and in no particular order.[1]

One hears talk everywhere that the great problem of society today is that of the state. This is a mistake, and a serious one. The problem that overshadows all others, including that of the contemporary state, is that of capital.

Capitalism is one of the names of modernity. It presupposes the investment of the desire for the infinite in an instance already designated by Descartes (and perhaps by Augustine, the first modern), that of the will. Literary and artistic romanticism believed in struggling against this realist, bourgeois, shopkeeper's interpretation of will as infinite enrichment. But capitalism has been able to subordinate to itself the infinite desire for knowledge that animates the sciences, and to submit its achievements to its own criterion of technicity: the rule of performance that requires the endless optimalization of the cost/benefit (input/output) ratio. And romanticism was thrown back, still alive, into the culture of nostalgia (Baudelaire's "the world is going to end," and Benjamin's commentaries) while capitalism became, has become, a figure that is not "economic," not "sociological," but metaphysical. In capitalism, infinity is posed as that which is not yet determined, as that which the will must indefinitely dominate and appropriate. It bears the names of cosmos, of energy. It gives rise to research and development. It has to be conquered, to be turned into the means to an end, and this end is the glory of the will, a glory that is itself infinite. In this sense, capital is the real romanticism.

What strikes one when one returns to Europe from the United States is a bankruptcy of will, at least along the lines of this figure. The "socialist" countries also suffer from this anemia. Willing as infinite strength and as the infinity of "realization" cannot find its instance in a state, which uses up will in order to maintain itself as if it were a finality. The expansion of the will requires only minimal institutions. Capitalism does not love order; the state loves it. The finality of capitalism is not a technical, social, or political creation built according to rule, its aesthetic is not that of the beautiful but of the sublime, its poetics is that of the genius: capitalist creation does not bend to rules, it invents them.

Everything Benjamin describes as "loss of aura," aesthetic of "shock," destruction of taste and experience is the effect of this will that cares little or nothing for rules. Traditions, statutes, objects, locations freighted with an individual and a collective past, accepted legitimacies, classical images of the world and of humanity, even when they are preserved, are preserved only as a means to an end: the glory of the will.

Marx understood all this very well, notably in the *Manifesto*. He tried to show where the figure of capitalism undid itself. He did not think of it as a figure, but as a thermodynamic system. And he showed that (1) it could not control its heat source, the labor force; (2) it did not control the gap between this source and the heat sink (the increase in value of production); and (3) it was going to exhaust its heat source.

Capitalism is, more properly, a figure. As a system, capitalism has as its heat source not the labor force but energy in general, physics (the system is not isolated). As figure, capitalism derives its force from the Idea of infinity. It can appear in human experience as the desire for money, the desire for power, or the desire for novelty. And all this can seem very ugly, very disquieting. But these desires are the anthropological translation of something that is ontologically the "instantiation" of infinity in the will.

This "instantiation" does not take place according to social class. Social classes are not pertinent ontological categories. There is no class that incarnates and monopolizes the infinity of the will. When I say "capitalism," I do not mean the owners or the managers of capital. There are thousands of examples that show their resistance to willing, even technological willing. The same goes for the workers. It is a transcendental illusion to confuse what belongs to the order of ideas of reason (ontology) with what belongs to the order of concepts of the understanding (sociology). This illusion has produced both bureaucratic states, in particular, and all states.

When German (or American) philosophers today speak of the neoirrationalism of French thought, when Habermas gives lessons in progressive thought to Derrida and Foucault in the name of the project of modernity, they are seriously mistaken about what is at issue in modernity. The issue was not and is not (for modernity has not come to an end), the Enlightenment pure and simple, it was and is the insinuation of will into reason. Kant spoke of a drive of reason to go beyond experience, and he understood philosophy anthropologically as a *Drang*, as an impulse to fight, to create differends (*Streiten*).

And let's think a little more about the ambiguity of the aesthetics of a Diderot, divided between the neoclassicism of his theory of "relations" and the postmodernism of his writing in the *Salons*, in *Jacques*, and in the *Neveu de Rameau*.[2] The Schlegels were not fooled by it. They knew that the problem was precisely not that of consensus (of Habermasian *Diskurs*), but that of the unpresentable, of the unexpected force of the Idea, of the event as the presentation of an unknown phrase, initially unacceptable and then accepted because tried out. The Enlightenment was hand in glove with preromanticism.

The decisive feature of what is called the postindustrial (Touraine, Bell), is that the infinity of the will invades language itself. The big deal of the past twenty years, to speak in the extremely dull phraseology of political economy and historical periodization, has been the transformation of language into a productive commodity. This takes two forms. First, phrases are considered as messages, to be encoded, decoded, transmitted, and arranged (packaged), reproduced, preserved, kept accessible (memories), combined and concluded (calculations), opposed (games, conflicts, cybernetics). Second, the unit of measurement—which is also a unit of price—is established: information. The effects of the penetration of capitalism into language are only beginning. Under the guise of an extension of markets and a new industrial strategy, the coming century is that of the investment of the desire for infinity, according to the criterion of optimum performance, in matters of language.

Language is the whole social bond (money is only an aspect of language, the accountable aspect, payment and credit, at any rate a play on differences of place or time). This investment of the desire for the infinite in language is thus going to destabilize the living creations of social life itself. It is a mistake to be afraid of an alienation occurring. The concept of alienation comes from Christian theology and also from the philosophy of nature. But god and nature have to give way as figures of infinity. We are not alienated by either the telephone or the television as means (media). We will not be alienated by the language machines. The only danger is if the will hands them over to states whose only concern is their own survival, that is, a need to create belief. But it is not alienation if the human gives way to a complex and aleatory assembly of (innumerable) program-transforming messages (Stourdzé). The messages are themselves only metastable states of information, subject to catastrophes.

In speaking of the idea of postmodernity, I situate myself in this context. And in this context I say that our role as thinkers is to deepen what language there is, to critique the shallow notion of information, to reveal an irremediable opacity within language itself. Language is not an "instrument of communication," it is a highly complex archipelago formed of domains of phrases, phrases from such different regimes that one cannot translate a phrase from one regime (a descriptive, for example) into a phrase from another (an evaluative, a prescriptive). It is in this sense that Thom writes "an order contains no information." All the investigations of the scientific, literary, and artistic avant-gardes over the past century have headed in this direction, the discovery of the incommensurability of the phrase regimes amongst them.

The criterion of optimal performance, in this light, seems to be a serious invalidation of the possibilities of language. Freud, Duchamp, Bohr, Gertrude Stein, but before them Rabelais and Sterne, are postmoderns in that they stress paradoxes, which always attest the incommensurability of which I am speaking. In this way they find themselves closest to the capacity and the practice of ordinary language.

As for what you call the French philosophy of recent years, if it has been postmodern in some way, this is because it has also stressed incommensurabilities, through its reflection on the deconstruction of writing (Derrida), on the disorder of discourse (Foucault), on the epistemological paradox (Serres), on alterity (Lévinas), on the effect of meaning by nomadic encounter (Deleuze).

When one reads Adorno *now*—above all texts like *Aesthetic Theory*, *Negative Dialectics*, and *Minima Moralia*—with these names in mind, one senses the element of an anticipation of the postmodern in his thought, even though it is still largely reticent, or refused.

What pushes him to this refusal is the political question. For if what I am roughly and quickly describing as postmodern here is accurate, what then of justice? Does what I say lead one to advocate the politics of neoliberalism? I do not think so in the least. It is itself an illusion. The reality is concentration into industrial, social, and financial empires served by the states and the political classes. But it is beginning to appear, on the one hand, that these monopolitical monsters do not always perform optimally and that they can act as hindrances to the will (what we used to call barbarism);[3] on the other hand, it seems that labor in the nineteenth-century sense is what must be suppressed, and by other means than unemployment. Stendhal already said at the beginning of the nineteenth century that the ideal is no longer the physical force of ancient peoples; it is flexibility, speed, metamorphic capacity (one goes to the ball in the evening, and one wages war the next day at dawn). Svelteness,[4] wakefulness, a Zen and an Italian term. It is most of all a quality of language, because it takes very little energy to create the new (Einstein in Zurich). The language machines are not expensive. This fact already makes the economists desperate: they tell us that the machines will not soak up the enormous overcapitalization with which we are burdened at the end of a period of expansion. This is probably the case. Thus the infinity of the will must come to terms with svelteness: much less "working," much more learning, knowing, inventing, circulating. Justice in politics lies in pushing in this direction. (It will indeed be necessary one day to reach an international accord on the concerted reduction of labor time without a loss of purchasing power.)

Part II
Students

8
Dead Letter
(1962)

Even if the number of classrooms, assistants, conference leaders, and professors were to be increased, even if the profession were better paid, I hope we would continue to hear the question asked of us, students and teachers, by life at the Sorbonne, by work in the university: What is culture? How is it present here?

The great secret need by which students and teachers are preoccupied is not a desire for an increase in the number of classrooms, for a reduction in the student-teacher ratio, for better financial incentives for teaching, or for official recognition of the dignity of learning. We could still work in cramped conditions, in anonymity, in poverty, unrecognized. The fellahs who learn to read and write in the underground forces have nothing, not even "qualified" teachers; they have a desire to understand their life and the world, and the desire to live up to this desire.

Culture is lending an ear to what strives to be said, culture is giving a voice to those who do not have a voice and who seek one. This voice is not only discursive; it can be, it has been, dancing and painting, building and sculpture.

Historically, culture is a particular way of being in fundamental situations: birth, death, love, work, giving birth, being embodied, growing old, speaking. People have to be born, to die, and so forth, and a people arises in response to these tasks, to these calls, as it understands them. This understanding, this listening, and the resonance that is granted it, is at the same time what a people is, its understanding of itself, its being-together. Culture is not a system of meanings attributed to fundamental situations on the basis of conventions, a project, or a contract; it is the being-there that is people.

By the same token, it is not an activity separated from other activities, but only their "common sense."[1] There is and there ought to be as much culture in what the West has split off and ignored under the titles of "sexuality" and "labor" as there is in a sonata or a totem pole. The nature of a response to the call of rest, of hunger, the way in which certain appeals are not heard at all—all that is culture. Even when the working out of the meaning that is common to all activities develops into a differentiated reflection, it is (as one sees in certain archaic cultures) the elderly who are in charge of it, not because they are no longer good for anything else, not because they are placed outside the community, but because they are in the community as the result of the community, having already had to respond to almost all of the situations of culture and now occupied with preparing themselves for the last of them.

Inhabiting all the relations of a people to the world and to itself, all of its understanding and all of its work, culture is simply existence accepted as meaningful. In culture there is no work (in the sense of an activity whose purpose, as production or consumption, lies outside of itself), nor is there religiosity either (as the delegation to an Other of the task of giving order to life and death), and there is not even art undertaken as an exercise of expression. Similarly, there are no cultivated and uncultivated activities. There is no need to bear witness to the fact that there is a culture and to its nature by specific rites or solemnities set apart. All of life is this witness.

This weight of meaning in activity is present in *L'île nue*, in *Come Back, Africa*, in the tattered rags of living culture dispersed around the Mediterranean basin and elsewhere, in black music, in the topography of old Amsterdam.

We are essentially cut off from it. In our society sign and signification, activity and culture, living and understanding, are dissociated. Responses to fundamental situations lie on one side of this divide; the meaning of these situations and these answers is sought on the other side. But the answers cannot be answers, cannot correspond to a call, because this call is sought elsewhere, because meaning becomes the object of a question and this question becomes the object of a special activity ("culture").

On the one hand, activities devoid of meaning are organized according to the model of the machine, a model whose purpose lies outside itself, which does not question that purpose. A mechanistic economy, whose principle is the search for an optimal relation between expenditure and production, is imposed as the rule of all activities: procreating, which has now become the technology of parturition, aims to produce at will, with the least possible wasted expenditure, a child that is viable in all desirable respects. Working becomes the carrying out of operations, subjected to imperatives of time and even of norms foreign to its content, ultimately dictated by the axiom (which manages the "managers" in the first place) that "economic" society is a machine and ought to obey the rule of the best possible cost/benefit ratio, for all types of results and investments. Love provides the occasion for the establishment of a technology by means of which affectivity and sexuality, once isolated, can be engaged in according to the same principle: seduction and eroticism, left to themselves, seek the best return on one's feeling for and one's enjoyment of the other. In the practice of sport, being embodied is split off as a particular situation and worked on by specific exercises according to the same general economy. Recreation and rest, eating and dwelling are similarly mechanized.

Each of these activities become machines has an apparatus assigned to it that is made up of specialists qualified to guarantee its optimal functioning. This apparatus has in its turn to obey the rule of optimal balance. Thus a new apparatus is set up to ensure the functioning of the preceding one. The machines are superimposed on one another in a hierarchy. Their reason is always elsewhere. Death itself has become only the death of others.

The people as a common attention to situations, as the understanding of itself, is destroyed. Its particular way of being-there is ground up in the uniformly mechanistic organization. Sociality and personality succumb at the same time.

On the other hand, culture is no longer a practice of listening and responding to the call of fundamental situations in everyday life. Displaced from everyday life, set on one side in special activities, what can culture hear, with what can it correspond? At the Sorbonne one does not procreate, one does not love, one is not a body, one neither eats nor dies, one does not work (in the sense of the workshop). The mind alone seems to be able to earn the right of entry; but the mind is simply the meaning of what is left behind at the door, left outside.

When the mind and life are divorced, the intellectual is the one who cultivates the mind, who cultivates the meaning of life without life itself. But, just as answering without understanding is blind and ends up reducing itself to a technologism that seeks its reason in itself alone, so too devoting oneself to understanding in general as a vocation without being able to answer in specific situations is vain. The mind is nothing except meaning received and revealed in the situations and the answers of which life is made up. Intellectuals cannot carry out the task imposed on them: to witness for the mind. The mind that they look after has left life, their lives, behind.

Let us nonetheless enter into the place where culture is cultivated. Once activities have been stripped of their common sense, the reason that culture nonetheless seeks to provide for them can only unify them externally, in a supplementary discourse. This discourse is no longer the thing itself—male and female according to the promptings of the flesh, the worker and his or her work in the movement of their reciprocal creation, and so forth—that speaks in the gestures, in the silences, and in the words of love, of labor, and so on. Rather, it is an established discourse *about* love, labor, and so forth. No one who is in love joins the banquet of the philosophers; Alcibiades would be forced to leave. Speaking does not let what is going on speak itself; rather it confers meaning (*sens*) on non-sense. Degenerate versions of Marxism and existentialism lend their names to the leading theme: Man is the creature who makes and who makes himself.

Culture grapples with the question of what there is to say. A cultural activity would gather and preserve the sense that activities have abandoned. But if there is non-sense outside the university, there cannot be sense within. Modern life does not expect to receive its reason from the professors, however willing they may be to provide it. No appeal to this culture comes from a labor force exhausted in factories and offices, from the loneliness of women with all modern conveniences around two p.m. behind the windows of their dormitory suburbs, from the disenchantment of young people in black leather leaning up against Formica counters, from the useless elderly, from a childhood made up of rejection. No reason can make this humanity accept itself, still less make it like itself, for what it is.

The Faculty does not have the vocation of responding to the real problem of culture, to the meaning of life: life does not invoke the Faculty as its potential guide toward its truth.[2] That which is cultivated between our walls, the culture that has a Faculty dedicated to it, is made up of the arts and the human sciences, two versions of humanity, the one given in the "humanities," the other in "anthropology," something that is quite different from the understanding and expression of the contemporary world.

The humanities mould a model of mankind that arose in the Renaissance once Christianity was no longer capable of understanding its world and responding to it, when the cultural void that developed more or less accepted the raisons d'être that the Greeks had supplied in earlier times for the question already evident in the first tragedians and the first philosophers: according to what reason is there something to live and die for? The person of the humanities is first of all the sage who seeks to set himself or herself in agreement with a wise world, in metaphysics, in ethics, in politics, in aesthetics, in gymnastics, this reason that dialogues with the reason in being. It is this wisdom that lends speech in the university its well-balanced syntax. This wisdom also serves as a guide for the judgments that the university pronounces against the modern malaise, and as a shield against the intrusion of disharmony and violence into the interior of the university. It is in the name of this wisdom that eclecticism of truths and pluralism in opinions are held to be fundamental values. It is this very same wisdom that authorizes the traditional relation of professorial authority in which a knowledge is professed from the seat of authority, a knowledge whose disciplined acquisition has coincided with the degrees by which its holder has ascended to that chair.

But because the *humanitas* cultivated here is not the spirit of these times, acquiring such a knowledge requires that it be taught to ignore actual situations; welcoming liberalism supposes ignorance of the universal constraint exercised over real activities; to invoke the order of the mind is to revoke the spirit of a disordered reality; to discourse according to the melodic rule is to make a vain challenge to ears prepared for the silence of words and the fury of sounds. The sages produced by the course of unlearning that constitutes such studies can only be called "academicians," they can only hear their peers, can only be heard by them. If they go out into the streets, it is to proclaim the values they profess, the values that were professed to them. But how might the freedom of which the university declares itself to be the guardian find an echo in the factories and the offices, in the barracks, the prisons, the hospitals, on the building sites, where the tumultuous silence of constraint reigns?

If so many students fail to get their degrees, it is useless to blame this on their lack of financial means, or on a decline in their abilities. It does make sense to attribute their quitting to the impossible condition created for them by the discordance between the questions that humanity asks itself through them and the answers that the humanities supply to those questions.

But given the failings of the Faculty of Letters, we now have a Faculty of Human Sciences. An effort seems to be made to hear modern humanity. Has humanism not caught up with its times by becoming anthropology? Economics, sociology, and psychology have been authorized. The new student generation, if it has difficulty in cultivating classical *humanitas*, seems to nourish a realistic affection for the science of humanity.

From being retrospective, culture becomes "forward-looking." University parlance accommodates the words, as strange as barbarian gems, with which the new knowledge surrounds previously unexpressed phenomena: psychodrama, introjection, test groups, acculturation, transfer. Industrial labor, religiosity in boardinghouses, adolescent crisis, neuroses and psychoses, paleo- and neotechnologies, poles of development and kinship structures, film studies—all enter the portals of the university. The mandarins give way to research and intervention; the Sorbonne seems to take a footing in the city once more. Seminars and working groups give rise to a new pedagogy in which exchange between generations, the dialogue between researchers, and collective expression situate the knowledge that exposes itself there.

Just as the person whom the study of letters aimed to develop was manifest, so the person prepared by anthropology is unexpressed. The human sciences are waiting for their formulation. But this can only be a counter-metaphysics: historical science frees itself of the philosophy of history, social science relegates Marxism and all the -isms to the storeroom, psychology has freed itself of the traditional presuppositions of humanism, ethnology puts Greco-Christian wisdom in its place, even psychoanalysis suspects Freudian generalizations of metaphysics.

Yet do the activities that are worn down and kept on a leash by specialized apparatuses in society, the activities that are stripped of the power to resonate, find their speech in the new "culture"? They are talked about, but this discourse does not make these activities more significant for those who carry them out, these activities "do not say any more to them," even if their agents were to speak in person[3] (because the interview is also one of these new methods). Anthropology cannot be the culture of a life whose elements are all subjected to the rule of technological discourse alone.

The intervention of anthropology into life does not give the latter the unity of a meaning. Of course it is not blinded by the obsolete model of humanity that cuts the study of letters off from reality. However, it is hostile or powerless to hear the question that is asked in the world, "What do we live for?" which is the question of culture. Scattered across the multiple sectors of life, sectors that it accepts as so many special fields for study and intervention, anthropology seeks an alibi for its deafness and myopia in its dignity as a science. But science in modern practice does not propose that its object should call upon it to respond: it sets out its object as a mere thing and works on it according to a mechanical strategy, the same one that operates on activities in actual society. Thus the science of humanity, however pure the intentions of its protagonists, is destined to endow the social apparatuses with a supplement of power in offering them the means of an increased mechanization of the activities they seek to regulate. There is no need for the industrial sociologist or the psychotechnician to be *corrupted* in order for psychosocial "culture" to be incorporated into the strategy that corporate leadership uses on the workers, any more than there was for the scientific and technical inventions of the nineteenth century, so profitable to the organization of the technological oppression of labor, to be directly stimulated by that oppression. It is enough for the results of research, whether technical or anthropological, to be inspired by the same principle that rules society: the aim of all activity is to reach optimal equilibrium between cost and benefit. Anthropology merely brings new refinements to the application of this rule, which is that of our unculture.

Leaving the shelter of letters to seek refuge in the science of humanity no doubt provides some renewal for the Faculty, but at the price of eluding the cultural task once more. Besides its own specialists (the professors), the Sorbonne will train the thinkers of a labor camp that is suited to the model by which modern institutions tend to organize life and thought. The unthought question in the grind of the technical world, the question that the absurdity of the extermination camps first brought into the open—What meaning is there in existing?—is a question that resounds for everyone, Monday morning and Saturday night, that reveals the emptiness of "civilization" in all of its industrial flashiness. We should not expect academics and experts on mankind to answer it or even to hear it as produced by anything other than a metaphysical anxiety, although it is in reality the only serious, vital, everyday question.

The repression that culture undergoes does not necessarily take the form of a gun held to the university's head by a totalitarian state. Police measures are not required for the oppression of the only "faculty" that is essential to culture, the faculty of listening to and saying what asks to be heard and said; all it takes is for ears to be deaf and words to be lacking. The failure of university discourse to embrace the desire for meaning, for values to be embodied in activities, and for a reconstitution of community is not a recent phenomenon—did the Sorbonne, for example, hear or express the paroxysm of this desire a century ago during the Paris Commune?

But what is happening today is that this desire—which is everywhere, in the everyday resistance of the workers to increased rhythms of work and of soldiers to orders, in the "irrational" stubbornness of the Aveyron miners, in last year's Belgian strikes, in the generalized sabotage of the mechanistic organization by which apparatuses throughout the world try to suppress the resonance of actions and activities—this desire, which is the only desire for a culture that there is, cannot find the words to express itself. Not only is literature a separate occupation more incapable than ever of lending its own words to this desire; politics, for its part, is so cautious that no significant political organization whose speech and gestures could make this desire reverberate exists anywhere in the modern world.

The activity of speaking is itself subject to the mechanistic model. Speech is no longer the activity that lets what demands to be said be spoken (poetry). It is an operation performed on what are now called "listeners" in order to make them do and say whatever conforms to the plans of the apparatus that regulates their activity (strategy). Speaking is only the instrument of operations, be these working (instructions), consuming (advertising), or voting (propaganda). Thus the identity of meaning and speech is overcome. The meaning of language also lies elsewhere, in constraint, nowhere.

Cultural desire is the desire to put an end to the exile of meaning as external to activities. It is at the same time the desire to put an end to the exile of activities as estranged from their sense. Its instrument cannot be the university, which dwells in this very exile, and is the product of it. Nor can speech alone be its instrument. Now we must look for the acts in which this desire is already silently present; we must hear in these acts the call of a sense, a call that has no truck with the operational world but that is nevertheless utterly contemporary; we must make the call ring out, at the cost of transgressing (destroying) the apparatuses that stifle it; we must find the ways to make it ring out, the opportunities and the means. That is what it means to take culture literally.

9
Preamble to a Charter
(1968)

The starting point of our struggle at Nanterre was a refusal of the Fouchet reforms (November 1967)[1] and the practical affirmation of the right to political expression in the faculty (March 22, 1968, onward). Henceforth, social reality and the university's function in relation to it will be subjected to permanent criticism and contestation. Our task will have to be that of displacing [*détourner*][2] the entire institution of the university as fully as possible from the functions to which it is restricted by both the ruling class and its own deeply internalized repressions, in order to turn it into a place for working out the means of the critical understanding and expression of reality. The resumption of classes at Nanterre in 1968 will not be a return to normal; normality was cultural oppression. Our task is not simply to "make the faculty work" (for whom, to what ends?) but to criticize, to deconstruct the institution, to determine the orientation we want to give to our work, to develop a program for this work, and to realize it.

I. May 1968

1. The crisis that began in May 1968 is not a "crisis"; it ushers us into a new period of history. Critique and struggle target and disrupt not only the political regime but also the social system, and not only capitalist private property but also the organization of life as a whole, all of the "values" that modern societies, be they from the West or the East, utilize or fabricate, impose or insinuate, to defuse desire. To fail to see this is to fail to understand anything about our movement: the spirit that shook the nation to the point of creating a power vacuum was not about claiming rights within society. This is not a will for political renewal but the desire for something different, the desire for another society, for different relations between people. The force of this desire shook the edifice of exploitation, oppression, and alienation; it struck fear into the hearts of all the individuals, organizations, and

parties with an immediate or a distant interest in power; and it was this force that they used every possible means to repress. They couldn't manage it.

2. The political oppression of the citizen and the socioeconomic exploitation of labor were denounced in word and deed. But the movement attacked cultural alienation with the same vigor. Thus it extended revolutionary critique across the entire domain over which the modern ruling classes had established their grip. In the university, critique addressed the exteriority of knowledge to life, its connivance with power, along with the persistence of hierarchical relations. In society, critique attacked the monopolization of knowledge by a single social class, the mercantilization and the deproblematization of the information distributed to other classes, the provision of cultural objects that favor identifications that are not under the subject's control and hence are controllable by the powers that be, and the exclusion of the laboring classes from the means of understanding and expression. What the movement wants to destroy is the separation of culture from social experience (the division between intellectual and manual labor) along with the separation between decision making and practice (the division between managers and operatives), and, finally, the denigration and recuperation of creative forces.

3. Our critique is not only verbal; it is critical-practical. It involves the offensive blockage of the institution of the university and its diversion [*détournement*] to revolutionary ends, it involves physical combat against the so-called order, transgressions. Through its form of struggle, the movement makes manifest the weakness of the system as a whole. It revives the workers' struggle that had been absorbed and deadened by the verbal and legal forms imposed by the system. The movement affirms the freedom to speak equally, mockery of the hierarchy, the courage to submit all questions to open debate, the destruction of enforced isolation, encounter, and initiative, against the continuing violence of oppression in businesses, in leisure, in families, in the establishments of so-called education. Our violence consists in reestablishing expressive speech and gesture; our opponents' violence consists in repressing them. To try to prosecute our violence in the courts is quite simply laughable.

4. The radical and practical character of this critique finds an echo among the workers, particularly the young. Protest is beginning to leave the ghetto of the university; the critique of cultural alienation is beginning to join up with the critique of socioeconomic exploitation and political oppression once again. An embryonic alliance is forming between the workers' and the students' struggles. It is weak with respect to the adversary that has to be fought; it is formidable if one compares it to the isolation and the hopelessness that reigned in the class struggle before May 1968.

5. The future of the current revolution depends entirely on the strengthening of the alliance between students and workers. The students bring their denunciation of culture and values to the struggle. Isolated, their critique will be recuperated by the system: the ruling class can always enjoy the cultural revolution as spectacle. The workers bring their experience and their denunciation of exploitation to the struggle; isolated, and in the absence of a revolutionary party, their struggle ceases to challenge the system and merely makes claims within it. In modern society, where technical development increases the importance of intellectual labor, the student is no longer a young bourgeois bohemian but is an element of the social forces of production in training. That is why the student's desertion from the ruling-class camp can assume a decisive importance.

6. In order to achieve this alliance, the movement ought not to let itself be intimidated by slander, wherever it comes from; above all it ought not to let itself be disarmed from within by self-censorship. That we are called provocateurs and adventurers wouldn't deserve a moment's attention were it not that the insult hides a very dangerous attempt to cut the student movement off from the workers' movement and to keep the workers within the established social and political order. We must reply by consolidating our alliance with the workers on the basis of a critique of this "order" as a whole. But alliance is not subordination, neither that of the workers to the students, nor even that of the students to the workers. The student movement has brought a dimension to the revolution that the workers' movement, such as it is, had lost; the student movement is something more than a trigger in the class struggle—it is a constitutive element of it, both in theory and in practice. For the problem actually posed by modern societies is not only how to get rid of the boss as the owner of capital, but also how to overcome the separation between managers and operatives. By placing this problem in the foreground, the student movement has demonstrated that this aspect of the revolutionary program, which constitutes socialism's most radical content, is the only effective reply to the contradictions of modern societies.

II. The Faculty

1. The faculty is not an independent institution dedicated to the elaboration and transmission of a knowledge in itself. A society such as ours, which can only continue to exist by ceaselessly aiming at the complete integration of all of its functions, is not able to maintain a zone of free knowledge and free expression within itself. The faculty stands at the center of two major operations mounted against the means of understanding and expression: the operations of defusing and recuperation. The defusing of the means of understanding and expression is carried out by the faculty of dead letters; their

recuperation is the task of the faculty of human relations.[3] The former diverts intelligence and inventiveness away from praxis toward the fetishization of finished works, of the past, of that which is established; the latter employs the same intelligence and inventiveness in the conditioning of the work force and the raising of its output. The work of defusing produces the scholar; the work of recuperation produces the expert. The imagination of the ruling class cannot come up with anything more innovative than to make the faculty produce experts rather than scholars. That was the Fouchet plan.

2. Not only are the means of understanding and expression the preserve of a few people: *by virtue of this very limitation* they cease to be means of intelligence and creation. They become a closed-off culture, shut up in either delight or efficiency, led astray. The fact is that expression and intelligence are most often destined to trace their path outside the university. It would be useless to democratize entry into the university if the alienation of the mind that reigns inside it were to remain intact. The faculty must become a place where tools and works are forged.

3. The university will not, of course, be revolutionary; whatever we may be able to do here can and will be recuperated by the powers that be, until society as a whole is reconstructed differently. Yet the task to be carried out in the faculty is not merely one of vulgar reformism. We have to impose institutions and modes of teaching and research that allow the critical comprehension of reality in all its forms and the liberation of the power of expression. We must not leave the carrying out of these reforms to the powers that be and to their allies, the moderate teachers and students. They would simply not carry out any reforms, and their failure would put us straight back in the old university system. The distinction would not always get made between the critique of a university judged to be inadequate because it is *not adapted* to the requirements of modern capitalism and the critique of a university judged inadequate precisely because it would *remain adapted* to these requirements, and contestation would continue to be confused with reformism. The movement would be led to shut itself up in the sphere of the university instead of fighting alongside the workers. It would slip backward. Basically, it would be recuperated.

4. In grappling not only with political oppression and socioeconomic exploitation but also with cultural alienation, the movement has revealed that repression is not only a matter of police brutality or electoral fiddling, nor even exclusively a matter of pressure on wage earners and on the rhythms of work. Rather, it slides into the content and the forms of culture, of the culture that the ruling class diffuses through television, the press, social clubs, package holidays, the cinema, and magazines just as much as through university culture. In particular, it appears that at the heart of the cultural relation (in society, distributor / cultural product / consumer; in the university,

teacher / knowledge / student), repressive systems that are much more archaic than those of class society and that feed the repressive systems of class society are in operation. The drama of desire and its repression, of fear and the reactionary search for security, form the silent province in which the ruling classes work more and more openly in order to maintain their domination, and this is the level that our critique must reach if it is to be true. The truth is what transforms; it alone is revolutionary; with it alone there is no compromise. We must try to be the salt of truth in the wound of alienation.

5. We must keep the pedagogical relation as a whole open, offered to critical consciousness. The teacher/pupil relation ought to be permanently protected against both a falling back into the old hierarchic magisterial relation and the demagogy that proposes a symmetry between the teacher and the pupil, as well as against the training of the pupil as a mere expert/counselor. Knowledge must also be ceaselessly kept from reverting back into a known thing. The splitting apart of knowledge (for example, into departments and into specialities in the faculty) must also be disrupted, and the purposes of knowledge must be the object of a permanent indictment: in this society, knowledge is constantly compromised with power.

6. Those who fear the politicizing of teaching and hope that serious work will be possible in this faculty should be completely reassured. We too fear the politicizing of the university by Fouchet or Otoli; we too want true work, that is, the work of truth. We have no catechism to be recited, no dogma to insinuate, no conviction to suggest. We want the questions that are asked of humanity to be asked and to continue to be asked in all the seminars, workshops, and commissions of the faculty.

7. The projects that are presented here arise from this spirit. They have no other aim than to consolidate the conquests of May 1968 at the most advanced point attained by the movement. In particular, we affirm that we will concede nothing on the following points:

—freedom of expression and political assembly in the faculty;
—participation by both students and teachers in all bodies; and
—common student-teacher electoral lists.

10
Nanterre, Here, Now
(1970)

The style of intervention of these groups, like the general context in which they operate—at Assas, from an extreme-right ideology, elsewhere, under the pretext of a pseudo revolutionary phraseology—makes them auxiliaries of big capital. It is thus a union question of first importance that there be no ambiguity on this point: all the teachers' and students' unions ought to condemn such practices publicly and unite their efforts to make them impossible. We condemn all commando acts using violence against the teachers, the students, and the ensemble of the personnel. Our union struggle is supported by the large majority in the universities; it can only progress in the struggle of ideas and persuasion. . . . The armed gangs that attack the militants ought to be dissolved.

Georges Innocent, secretary general of the National Union of University Teachers (SNE Sup.), communiqué of February 14, 1970

The following text takes up the ideas that I was supposed to put forward in the meeting against the repression, organized by the union minorities of the SNI, the SNES, and the SNE Sup,[1] as well as by the researchers' union. It was not possible for me to speak, the security marshals having taken it upon themselves to throw out a small group of "troublemakers" (among whose number were three teachers suspended by the ministry) who chanted, "We want our money back, we want our money back"—which was relevant since the meetings are theatrical spectacles and this one was not particularly good. I had to leave in turn, on my own initiative. The repression had entered the meeting. This banal incident is full of meaning, and this meaning is the same that emanates from the affairs of Nanterre.

Spring 1969: the next-to-last appearance of the cops on the Nanterre campus happens "calmly." For several days the faculty of letters [building] has been surrounded by a cordon of riot police spaced five meters apart as if on parade, while the guardians of the peace formed a line at each entrance. Cops and secret police disguised as "strong-armed attendants" were removed right before the university elections following indignant protests and a hunger strike.

February-March 1970: the first cops that appear on the "normalized" [banalisé] *campus serve as a target. Friday and Monday, as soon as the cops penetrate the interior of the campus, they are greeted by projectiles thrown by the students. Tuesday, March 5, at 3:30 p.m., 1,500 agitators leave the faculty [building], and several go looking for the cops outside the campus. For three hours the cops will try to occupy the terrain but will be driven back beyond the buildings. Not only did the students cause the "normalization" of the campus to fail, they also took back the campus space.*[2]

There is no question that the repression has intensified. But such a superficial effect is not the right place from which to begin an analysis of what is happening at Nanterre. At the least, it is necessary to *reverse* the apparent facts: repression is itself a riposte, and it is the movement that has seized and for the moment holds the initiative, at least in the milieu of the university. Everything that participates in the system (in the increased reproduction of capital, Eastern as well as Western) works together to suppress the slow, subterranean, worldwide push that is visibly shaking the sites where teaching takes place, but that is also rocking the sites of production (even though it is a thousand times crushed, anesthetized, paralyzed, led astray, threatened). This critique is not at all mysterious in origin: it proceeds from the fact that activities and institutions previously sheltered from the requirement for the increased reproduction of capital are now under orders to operate as simple moments in the circuit of this reproduction. This is especially the case for the so-called educational and teaching function.

7:00 p.m.: the (senseless) order to withdraw to the university cafeteria circulates among the students. It will be little obeyed. The students leave the fac[ulty building] at once. The cops who had left the campus receive permission to charge back onto a campus deserted by the majority of the students: the beatings begin.

They are most violent at the exit to the cafeteria, once the students have been forced to evacuate the building. After they had switched off the lights, the cops saturated the building with tear gas (and other) grenades.

It is absolutely necessary to identify very precisely the point of insertion of the so-called student movement into the subterranean system that constitutes the entire "reason" of our societies. This point of insertion occurs with the inevitable subordination of both the "contents" of culture and the pedagogical relation to the sole operative categories of capital: production and consumption. Not only are there no "armed gangs," it is not enough to say that there is a crisis in our culture. Why has this crisis occurred, if not because traditional cultural values, relics of all kinds (to cite a few at random: the predominance of a university discourse and freedoms characteristic of the Middle Ages, the Napoleonic hierarchy, the secularism and neutrality of the Third Republic) combined in the university practice, are being annihilated by capitalism? The system ends up by devouring everything that is outside it; the "despair of young people" is the despair of the M-C-C-M cycle.[3] The so-called student movement draws its life from the void created by the domination of capital. Such is its inevitability.

This void spreads its chill within the walls of the faculties. Most of the teachers *and the students* prefer not to see it. Almost all that is said, almost all that *we* think, on the subject of this so-called teaching crisis (but that nevertheless obliges *Le Monde* to open a strange wavering column on "leftist" agitation alongside the university page), is motivated as a defense against anxiety. When the folks of the Autonomous Union pose the problem of the faculty of Nanterre in terms of "the freedom and security of individuals" against "armed gangs" (motion read by J. Beaujeu to the Transitional Council of February 20, 1970, the same council that voted to open the campus to the police), it is of course a maneuver at one level ("In the event that the Transitional Management Council did not support them," it says at the end of the motion, "they [the members of the union] would immediately begin an administrative strike"). In truth, however, this is a *displacement* that allows the anxiety provoked by teaching under present conditions to be disguised as the fear of being attacked with iron bars. The old political phraseology fulfills the same role: when the individuals or the groups that take initiatives are judged to be irresponsible adventurers, they are compared to organizations that, in their seriousness, their continuity, their order, and their numbers claim to be able to cover up this vacuum of meaning. The solemn banalities of the Trotskyists constitute attempts at a counterinvestment that might ward off the fear of *what is to be done?*[4]

"A request was brought before the room-assignment commission: a group of students asks for the allocation of a room on the ground floor, type C13, from 5:00 to 7:00 p.m. every evening and on Saturday from 2:00 to 5:00 p.m., for cultural activities. These involved organizing supervised

studies for the young North Africans of the shantytown. The Commission on Room Assignments remarks that the faculty would in no way be the place for activities that concern primary education."

Transitional Management Council of the Nanterre Faculty, session of February 20, 1970, official minutes

Politics, too, is an institution. Fringe group politics is a miniaturized institution. There is no difference between the security stewards [*service d'ordre*] of the March 16 meeting and those of the "Communist" party; the question of whether keeping "order" is a service does not always get asked. The question is not even that of knowing *what* order is at stake, that is, the question of the signified of the institution. The question is that of the *form* taken by the presence of order, of the relation there is between the people to whom one renders this "service" (of keeping order) and this order. This relation is mediated, bureaucratized, abstract, preserved in the very form in which we inherit it from our adversaries. The same goes for political discourse: there, too, a phraseology is handed down to us and we reproduce it faithfully. We let our relation to our political activity and to our comrades be mediated by an institutionalized *form* of speech. This institution most obviously consists of placing this speech once and for all in the mouth of a great dead man: Marx or Lenin or Trotsky or Mao (he may not be dead, but he is oriental—the Bajazet of politics). Thus the symbolic Father continues, under various imaginary costumes, to govern our words and our acts; thus the question of power among our own ranks is always stifled, always displaced into the question of the power facing us. A first victory would be to manage to speak of these affairs without "talking politics."

M. Touzard: How long might it take to transform the faculty domain into the public domain?
M. Beaujeu: An interministerial agreement would be necessary.
M. Francés:[5]

Transitional Management Council of the Nanterre Faculty, session of February 20, 1970, official minutes

On Friday, February 27, the police patrol the paths of the university area in force. Clashes. On Monday and Tuesday, March 2 and 3, confrontations and scuffles between Parisian police and both mobile guards (who try to hold these paths) and the students (who occupy the buildings of Law and Letters). At 7:00 p.m., the forces of "order" have abandoned the terrain and the students attack a group of police in the parking lot close to the railroad. In the classrooms, the ground is strewn with chairs without legs, broken glass, and water that has been spread to counteract tear gas; barricades are set up all the way to the ceiling behind the entrances, seminar tables are pushed up against the windows as shields; on the terraces the same system of protection, accumulation of diverse materials. On the campus, cars with slashed tires, and so on. All very familiar.

> *"What no one has said is that from March 4 on, the withdrawal (of the police forces) was requested by the commanders of the police themselves. ... What we know too is that our colleagues had decided either not to get out of their police vans, or to exceed all their orders, if the playacting of March 2 and 3 began again. ... In the future, we have decided to insist that, for requisitions of this kind, staff representatives be in a position to discuss the means of deployment and above all the conditions of employment of personnel. If this is not the case, we reserve the right to issue any and all union orders appropriate to the situation."*
>
> G. Monate, secretary general of the Autonomous Federation of Police Unions

> *A student on the roof of the faculty. A cop close to the buildings. Exchanges of projectiles. Verbal exchange:*
> *"Go to hell, your father is minister!"*
> *"Then why do you obey him, asshole?"*

At the initial level, a classical analysis can be provided: 1969 was a year of restoration and even of revenge. And at this level, everything holds together perfectly: de Gaulle and his Gaullists are bent on winning over some of the wage earners, teachers, and students to their regime by means of participationist policy. They refuse to bow before the offensive of the owners of capital who, since June 1968, have expatriated their piles of money so that its return may be made conditional on the return of a repressive government. The Gaullists accept the challenge of the referendum and are beaten by the campaign of the capitalists. For the National Education Ministry, the defeat of this tendency meant the downfall of Faure.[6]

> *The professors are nonexistent and scared to death (those in the faculty, of course, not those involved in the action). They no longer exist in the eyes of the students. Poorly displaced anxieties: in an ethnology classroom, while fifty or so students supply those on the roofs with tables, chairs, and other utensils, a flabbergasted and totally ignored prof implores: "Please, leave a few of them, save something . . . "*

All the pontiffs, successful or unsuccessful mandarins, prepare with bitterness, not to mention sheer stupidity, to cross swords with the people who had made them tremble in May. The minister makes Faurist declarations while issuing guarantees and signing warrants like an anti-Faurist. The truth is that he is in deep trouble: the return to ancient university practices is no longer appropriate to the "expansion" required to facilitate the circulation of capital. Where to gain support? There is hardly anything promising apart from the participationist line of the union organizations controlled by the "Communist" party and the sincere reformism of a few professors. But here again, things are not so easy: the "communists" or their fellow travelers have taken over leadership positions in the teachers' unions and even in the establishment administrations. This may well be all to the good, but after all, it is still the *Communist party*! The CDR[7] complains about infiltration, but even if he wanted to, Guichard cannot reply to them as Faure did: he has no de Gaulle. Overall the reformist line is a razor's edge, occupied by two or three individuals, like

> *Students and cops fight. Hundreds of persons massed on the other side of the railroad watch the spectacle all afternoon. They will not come to rejoin us. It will not occur to the students to point their sound system toward them.*

Ricoeur. Insisting on the university's right to elbow room easily wins the re-establishment of its prerogatives. This is not in the interest of the system (an interest that is Faurist), it is the indulgence of the system's particular passion for the university. In the Transitional Council of Nanterre, this passion rules: the leftists boycotted last year's elections (refusing the reintegration of the movement within the system); there are elected "communists" in the UER [departmental] councils, but few of them represent their UER[8] in the Faculty Council; the elected students practice absenteeism. If you were a person of the right, you would have said to yourself, "A good opportunity to have done with the troublemakers, with the armed gangs, with the longhairs."

> *The cops driven back sideways to building E throw grenades at the students at the junction of the two faculty buildings. The grenades are picked up and thrown back; when they fall smoking they are stamped out. When the cops charge, the students withdraw and counterattack. The view from the buildings of Nanterre shows clearly that, provided the students do not retreat, the cops retreat.*

Yet, simultaneously, these troublemakers in effect provided the pretext for such an offensive, and this is exactly what the "moderate leftists" (also called "legal leftists") reproach them for. Around the faculty of Nanterre there are housing projects, a shantytown, and factories. Since May, the General Workers' Union (CGT) has actively sought to eliminate the militant leftist workers, to stifle criticism of its objectives and its modes of action. It should in fact be noted that never in the social history of this country has the union organization been confronted by such a significant element on its left. It is in the tradition of the "Communist" party to extend the hand of friendship to its right and to smash heads to its left (as Althusser would say, this is a "relic" of the Stalinist epoch), while all the time identifying those to the right with those to its left in its discourses. That is not particularly difficult to grasp, but it is nothing new either. We should perhaps examine the events themselves instead.

From around the end of January, leftist militants have been carrying out a campaign against increases in the Métro fares at the Marcel Sembat, Billancourt, and Pont de Sèvres stations, which serve the workshops of Renault at Billancourt. The campaign consists in encouraging a boycott of ticket punching *on the spot*, so that thousands of workers get out without paying. An embarrassing situation for the Métro unions. At the beginning of March, this campaign against the price increases shifts to the inside of the Renault company; the committee for the company, where the CGT is in the majority, had just raised the canteen prices. There are collisions and clashes at the Métro entrances and at the entrances to the canteen. The "communist" and assimilated press unleash their fury; for example, on February 14, the CGT Renault union calls on "the workers of the Renault factories to intervene massively to bring to their senses the fascist-Maoist gangs, which try to agitate the working class at the doors of the factories and the faculties and which profit from a troubling complicity." This complicity appears in the fact that several militants who took part in the Métro campaign are accused and condemned to fines and prison sentences (suspended, it is true . . .).

The "rowdies," as Séguy says (he is not compliant, but he gets an hour on the air with Descamps on Europe 1 on March 5), decide to not let the "communists" and their allies distribute their defamatory press inside the campus.[9] Tuesday, February 10 (and/or Wednesday the 11th—witnesses disagree), the "communist" students who arrive at the university cafeteria are "kidnapped" one by one (I'm citing *La cause du peuple*, no. 17, February 21, which itself places inverted commas around *kidnapped*) and called to account for the defamation of the Maoists by the "communist" party press. "They were thrown out with a boot up the backside" declared the Maoist paper, not beating around the bush. On February 11, a fairly large (40 to 60) group of "communists" (the Union of "Communist" Students and "Communist" Youth and/or CGT) cleaned the hallways of the faculty of letters, destroying the posters and propaganda material of the *Gauche proletarienne* and *Vive la revolution*; several militants from these organizations were attacked and wounded. It seems that the next day at noon, the secretary of the section of the CGT syndicate of administrative personnel was expelled from the university cafeteria. In the afternoon, a Union of "Communist" Students group with helmets and clubs posted itself in the faculty of law, expecting an attack from the Maoists; a small group of CGT members stood ready to intervene, outside. The equally "armed" leftists did not consider themselves to be in a good tactical position and did not attack; the "communists" left (after having struck a militant of the Law Student's Action Committee who was working in a classroom and sent him to the hospital), and the battle took place in the parking lot in front of the university library. There were wounded on both sides; a CGT militant had several skull fractures (it seems that he had acted as if he were aiming his car at his adversaries, and that he had been pulled out of it by them and beaten violently).

René Rémond, in the Council of February 24, drew a black picture of the "insecurity" that reigned throughout the university area and even in the classrooms of the faculty: break-ins, thefts, armed attacks, squatting in rooms, "young Arabs," "North African adolescents." The unofficial crèche that had been installed without authorization in an (empty) room of the faculty was considered by the reporter to be one of the crimes against common law. University opinion was really outraged: sticking blindly to the effects, it could not see that behind Rémond's picture there is Beaujeu's motion, that behind the "violence" something else was playing itself out that actually had nothing to do with the university as such. Even Kant did not dream of charging the sansculottes with infractions of common law, nor Hegel the soldiers

In order to remove a speedily built barricade from the alley in front of the law building, the cops use an armored bulldozer. At the same time it lets small groups of cops advance toward the sports ground, protecting them from the bombardments from the terrace of the law building. Finally, the driver tries to play skittles with the students, but the students dodge the bulldozer and reciprocate: they pursue it and smash its side-view mirrors and several side windows to pieces, but without managing to reach the driver, who is protected by a thick grille. The students only just fail in the attempt to unbalance and tip over the bulldozer, which does not return to the campus.

of Jena. The good souls who pose the problem of university "agitation" in terms of violence are not very far removed from the regime that intends to place the university within the jurisdiction of common law.

What happened next happened of its own accord: the Autonomous Union, the restoration party, strengthened by general disapproval and encouraged by the active anti-Maoist campaign of the "Communist" party, managed to have the streets of the campus opened to the police in the Council of February 20. This time, the coalition seemed general. Even the Communist League thought it worthwhile to equate "communists" and Maoists in its disapproval: these affronts, it writes (*Le Monde*, February 18), are the deed of "heirs of Stalinism, who want to make fratricidal practices arise again within the workers' movement." This little maneuver emerged from the meeting of March 6 on the campus and above all from that of March 18 at the Mutualité (in which the communists participated along with the Convention of Republican Institutions and the Socialist party); mostly, what emerged was the eternal delay of the Trotskyists.

Thus everything seemed settled, and the handful of itinerant anarchists seemed to have nothing left to do but go off elsewhere. The reader will have understood without my saying it that, given the atmosphere of restorationist lethargy characteristic of the life of the faculty since the beginning of classes in October, it seemed certain that the student body would give up its solidarity with these maniacs. On March 3, however, the third day of the opening of the campus, after a general assembly in room B2 stuffed to bursting point, a thousand students took to the "street" to demonstrate against the presence of the police; and when the police, attacked at the Porte de la Folie, tried to occupy the campus they received jeers and projectiles from almost the entire student body, who had retrenched and sealed themselves inside the buildings.

I am not praising either activism or violence.

Note rather that on three occasions, it was the movement (in this instance essentially some Maoists with whom, moreover, I do not find myself in agreement, as I will explain in a moment) that took the initiative: the campaign in the Métro, the campaign against press insults, the active refusal to accept opening the campus to the police. In this last case, any analysis such as "the students fought because the polices forces paraded" must be rejected. Quite the opposite occurred: on the March 3, the police did not

> *In response to the beatings echoing from the terrace of the law building come the slogans chanted from all the floors of the faculty buildings— "This is only the beginning, let's keep fighting," "Cops off campus"— accompanied by banging of fists against the windows and of boards against the metal window frames. A chanted noise, unified on the off beat that picks up again and breaks over the cops who beat on their shields in time to their chanting: "This is only the beginning, let's keep fighting," "Students S.S."*

show themselves on the campus; it was the students who went looking for them and forced them to withdraw, using the tactical advantage lent to them by the "extraterritoriality" of the university buildings. The fury of the police and their explosion in front of the university cafeteria at the end of the day have no other cause. What matters here is not physical violence, but initiative. Initiative always presents itself as a transgression. In the Métro, a double transgression, both of the ticket booth where one should pay and of the public space in which one should not speak to one's neighbors; at the university cafeteria, transgression of the "freedom of the press"; on March

3, transgression of the plans decided on by the Faculty Council. And likewise in the factories and in offices, transgression of the plans decided on by the union.

This transgression is not offered, but carried out. This is the immense difference between the movement and the fringe groups [*groupuscules*]. The latter remain within the order of discourse; *all verbalized transgressions can be absorbed by the system*; the system incorporates a purely verbal critique within itself. Any word can be said around a committee table, can be made the object of a negotiation, of an arbitration. The transgression in deed can only scandalize; it constitutes a nonrecuperable critique; it makes a hole in the system; it installs, for an instant, a region in which relations are not *mediated* by the Métro ticket, by the ideology of the newspaper, by the university institution. A potentiality arises in the field of social experience. Talk arises again in the Salle des Pas Perdus at Saint-Lazare, in the homes of the immigrant workers.

"Political action implies a calculated use of violence, in which the chances of success are weighed," said Paul Ricoeur in a recent speech (*Le Monde*, March 13, 1970). Let's not get ironic about his own talents as a calculator, since the minister's response to his letter of resignation (*Le Monde*, March 18) is lesson enough concerning this "politics." The activity I'm trying to describe is obviously in flagrant contradiction of the "politics" of Guichard and Ricoeur. The latter is precisely a nonpolitics. It consists in defining "success" by a ridiculous quantitative change within the institution: a 3 percent increase in salaries spread out over a year; *n* percent of students admitted to university councils; at least four grades per semester to establish a unit of value for continuous assessment [*contrôle*];[10] three minutes allowed in each working period to go to the washroom; a supposed fourth week of paid vacation; and so forth. "Successes" immediately annihilated by the infallible logic of the system, which has no need to calculate the use it makes of violence and contents itself with calculating the use made of capital; its basic violence consists in this equation: anything whatsoever = potential capital. This is the whole secret of the quantitative character of "successes": accounting is necessary, and it is the whole secret of their eminently transitory character that relative surplus value must be created.

What is called violence (which is never exploitation or alienation) is relegated to the position of an occasional complement to dialogue in this "politics": a partner leaves the committee room and signals his troops to exercise some "violence." Thus it is that the Transitional Council of Nanterre-Letters ordered a two-day strike on December 3 and 4, 1969, to obtain extra credits for activities; a strike suspended, moreover, at the end of one day because "at the end of a working meeting marked by a great cordiality, where (he had) been able to measure the respect accorded to our opinions" (circular signed Paul Ricoeur and dated December 3), the dean thought he could resume cooperation with the directors of the ministry. Very little violence, very sanitized; it has as its model the two-hour strikes, the revolving stoppages, the "days of action," the motions, the delegations, and other bullshit with which the unions have amused the workers for decades. This "violence" is the other of discourse, but within discourse; it is the death of words, but as a simple moment of language; it allows the crude dialogue between leaders to pass as a class dialectic; it is reality become a simple appendix of the bureaucracy, an alibi that is only an alibi, the supposed cross that in fact adorns the rose the managers wear in their buttonholes. It is critique recuperated, Hegelianized, hermeneuticized.

The struggle at Nanterre is not "political": it in no way aims to seize power in its present form, even political power. It is even less interested in introducing new interlocutors to the conference table. Its reach extends beyond the regime and the surface on which it pretends to act and invites us to join in discussion. The struggle directly attacks the *system*. In the sphere of the university, attacking the system cannot mean demanding supplementary credits or a "democratization" of teaching or an increase in the number of scholarships. The university belongs to the system insofar as the system is capitalist and bureaucratic. That it is capitalist does not mean that it belongs to a few large trusts (preferably foreign), but that now and then the system forces the university to function like an organization for the production of a

The cops take up positions in front of the buildings. The law faculty building comes out first: posted on the large terrace that encircles the building, behind a minibarricade set up in front of the entrance, the students force the cops to retreat. But doing this, the cops come within range of projectiles thrown from the buildings of the faculty of letters: caught between lines of fire, they have to retreat once more. At this moment, the campus is not simply opened to the police; the cops transform it into a theater of operations. They destroy a palisade to gain a few meters of space, the bulldozer brought as a reinforcement passes over the lawn as if it were waste ground and smashes in a car that blocks its retreat, the grenades thrown against the facade break the windows to reach the students. The transformation of the faculty grows. To reach the upper floors you have to move behind the barricades that protect against the various projectiles thrown by the cops who are posted under the canopies that cover the entrance to the buildings. The terraces are more and more crowded, the tables are pulled out of the rooms to protect the occupants of the terraces from direct hits by grenades, while the chairs lose their legs at an accelerated rate. Driven back beyond the buildings, the cops are harassed by the students who have reoccupied the parterre until 7:00 p.m.

qualified labor force: "If the nation spends so much money and makes so many efforts for its university, it is to have a youth that works, that is serious and useful. Such are the object and the aim of the university" (Georges Pompidou, speech of March 13).

The university is the bureaucratic offspring of the bureaucratic system because it is the institution that gives access to all the other institutions. If you want a place in the system, you must have a quality label. No employment without a diploma, however small it is (if it doesn't work, it is because you are Portuguese, Algerian, or African). Hence proceeds the importance of the control of knowledge. How do you get your diploma? By accepting the division and presentation of subjects as they are currently taught; by accepting the discipline of institutions and the discipline of the pedagogical relationship. Functions of the teacher: to consume cultural contents in order to produce cultural contents that can be consumed by the students; to produce salable students (consumable labor force). Function of the students: to consume contents (with an eye to exams, to academic competition); to consume along with them the pedagogical forms that prefigure professional and social hierarchies. What the teachers are completely unconscious of, though the students sometimes perceive it, is that the only value that governs the real functioning of the teaching establishments is the same that operates openly at the surface of society: produce and consume no matter what, in ever-increasing quantity.

It becomes difficult to ignore, now, that the transmission of knowledge is at the same time the affirmation of the hierarchy and that it allows the preservation in people's minds of respect for powers exterior to teaching, the preservation of the power of capital. In relation to this, the dividing line does not lie between students and teachers, nor between progressives and conservatives. It cannot appear on the surface of the institutions, nor in the form of traditional political organizations.

The real critique of the system can only take place (at least at the moment, and for the foreseeable future) through interventions of the *here and now* kind, decided on and managed by those who make it. The critique of capitalism and of its university in meetings, even if they take place in the teaching establishments, is immediately digested by the system. The organization and its discourse, even if they are revolutionary in their signified, are made of the same stuff as the objects of their criticism. This is where Maoism (I am only speaking of the Maoism we see in France) remains in its way highly ideological: if not always in its organizational forms, in any case in its discursive position. I have seen the Maoist film on Flins 1968–69: a propaganda film, identical in its procedure, in its relation to the spectator, to the improbable CGT film on May 1968.[11] Listen to Geismar speak from the podium of the March 16, 1970, meeting: encoded language, full of stilted phrases, a real stomach turner.[12] Perhaps worse: in attacking the "communists" for their revisionism, the Maoists cover up the essential element, which is the critique of bureaucracy. The break with Leninism is not consummated: that the USSR is revisionist means nothing more than this: it is a socialist state with a Bernsteinian deviation! There is a failure to identify the class nature of the relations of production in Russia.

> *Irritation, exhaustion, and exasperation among the cops: poorly coordinated offensives always followed by withdrawals, that is, by routs. To make up for the lack of action, which is taking place on the side of the students, the sergeants make their men carry out small-group maneuvers. The strategy is irresolute: orders and counterorders manifest the disagreements between the brass hats and the men in suits. Blatant errors provide the students with the spectacle of the cops sprinting desperately after being abandoned at the bottom of building C, under an avalanche of diverse missiles. The cops' rage expressed itself, from the beginning, in their fighting methods: horizontal firing of lance grenades, the use of special weapons—gadgets, slingshots with steel balls, chair legs, stones, chlorine grenades, probably a few attack grenades—and toward evening damaging parked cars.*

This is to say that even those who introduce profoundly different attitudes and modes of action into the struggle are not free of "political" phraseology and ideology. All the same, the important element is this new attitude that appears here and there in the world: to critique the system practically, by obliging it to throw aside the mask of legality in which it envelops the relations of exploitation and alienation, and to show itself in its truth. You may say that a boycott of ticket punching in three Métro stations will not overthrow capitalism. But let's be understood: neither will the seizure of power by a large party of the Bolshevik kind. The results of experience are now conclusive. The latest generation of revolutionaries starts from these conclusions; it realized in May 1968 that an intervention on the spot and for the moment, one that the adversary could not predict, was more capable of unbalancing it than any passively applied slogan whatsoever. But something more is needed.

In truth, what is required is an apedagogy. For a century the Marxist workers' movement has only *reversed* the conduct of its class adversaries. Its leaders, hierarchy, troops, schools, discourse, directives, tactics, and strategy all offered the inverted image of their bourgeois models. For a long time spontaneism was the only alternative to this mimicry by reflection. But spontaneism does not even represent for bolshevism what primitive Christianity is for the church; there is no reason to believe that the workers will of their own accord go so far as the practical critique of the system, even if it may be possible to imagine that sinners have no need of pastors to save themselves. The "here and now" attitude breaks with spontaneism just as it does with bolshevism. It does not propose the seizure of power, but the destruction of powers. It knows that until a significant minority of workers have managed a de facto break with the institutions by which they are infiltrated, a new class power will form itself again. This attitude itself only serves as an example of a break with the initial repression, that which made us forget to invent, decide, organize, execute. I call it apedagogy because all pedagogy participates in this repression, including that which is implied in the internal and external relations of the "political" organizations.

11

March 23

(Unpublished introduction to an unfinished book on the movement of March 22)[1]

A historical phenomenon clearly and completely understood and reduced to an item of knowledge, is, in relation to the man who knows it, dead; for he has found out its madness, its injustice, its blind passion, and especially the earthly darkened horizon that was the source of its power for history. This power has now become, for him who has recognized it, powerless; not for him who is alive. The same youth . . . knows the magic herbs and simples for the malady of history. . . . It is no marvel that they bear the names of poisons: the antidotes to the historical are the "unhistorical" and the "superhistorical."

Nietzsche, *The Use and Abuse of History*

Weapon and Critique

The only way to excuse having written a history book on the March 22 movement is for it not to be a book of history, for it not to dissolve the delirium, the unjustifiability, and the passion into a simple phenomenon to be understood. Rather, such a book must in its turn be an *event*, an event like the displacement and reinforcement of critique of which the March 22 movement was the head and arm for a few weeks. Furthermore, the "author" may in this way be able to discharge his debt toward his "object," the debt he owes it for having got him out of the impasse between "militant" delirium and skepticism. Such an event would have critical momentum, and new weapons could be forged.

The explicit question of the March 22 movement is the critique of bureaucracy, not only of the state apparatus set against society, not only of the (revolutionary) party that confronts the masses, not only of the organization of productive labor that stands against free creativity, but also of alienated life as a whole in place of—what? That is where the search must be made, and it is to this question that the activity of reflection must be dedicated: what is this *other* of capitalist-bureaucratic reality that the movement sought and, so to speak, *announced* in its practice?

The latent problematic of the March 22 movement was, following and alongside that of situationism, the critique of *representation*, of the exteriorization of activity and the products of activity, of the *mise en spectacle*[2] that positions actors as passive role players and "public opinion" as a passive spectator. The practical extension of this critique to the *political* sphere is perhaps what best characterizes the March 22 movement. Of course, it was preceded by a long anarchist antiorganizational tradition. Above all, each time the critique of capitalism turned to action, in 1871, in 1905 and 1917, in 1936, in 1956, the practical formation of workers', soldiers', and peasants' councils had occurred, seizing the initiative from the existing parties. But the anarchists' critique itself remained within the political sphere and the importance of the councils was only generally acknowledged (except by the Workers' Council movements[3]) as a transitional moment in the process of the breakdown of previous power structures—as a formation destined to disappear once the new power structure was installed rather than as the very form by which power in general can be abolished.

Now if the May 1968 movement is going to have some repercussions, it is insofar as it managed to extend critique to many forms of representation, to the union, the party, to the cultural institution in the fullest sense, forms that "big politics," including those of Trotskyists and Maoists, had ignored or considered epiphenomenal. On the contrary, the March 22 movement perceived these forms of representation as immediate and lasting obstacles to the liberation of potential critical energy. The historical—or rather *superhistorical*—importance of this extension of critique ought to be recognized. This destruction of representation in the sociopolitical sphere should be placed in parallel with the structural autocritiques carried out over the past century in mathematics, physical science, painting, music, and literature in turn. And yet, this "setting in parallel" is still insufficient. If it is true that politics is not just one sphere among others but the sphere in which all the spheres are represented and in which social activity is distributed among them, then the critique of politics is not parallel but transversal to the critiques carried out in the various spheres in question. Modern mathematics, Dada, Cézanne and the cubists, Heisenberg: these are indeed the true contemporaries of the young rowdies of Nanterre, but those rowdies, by extending their critique of representation to society itself, marked not only the end of specific spheres, but also the end of *specific ends*—an end that will obviously have to be initiated many more times, but that is inescapable because it is, in a sense, already accomplished.

This is the question that this generalized critique has posed, and that is indeed the question of capitalism: What is its referential field, where is it coming from, whence does it speak and act? The question refers to an image (to a representation?) of nonrepresentational life, of spontaneity, of naturalness, of immediacy, of primitiveness, of the "nonreferential," of something that is in touch, self-managed, in opposition to what is mediated, referred, constituted, managed by others. And here is where the critical contribution of the "author" ought to occur. Simplifying, I would say this: the movement opposed the (equally dead) freshness of Rousseauism to the heavy Hegelian corpse that occupies the place of philosophy in capitalist-bureaucratic reality. Rousseauism is another fantasy, one that can, moreover, easily become one of the component parts of the old fantasy. Here again is something on which to reflect, something that was the problem that haunted the events of May: What is the other of the system of mediations, the other of all possible recuperation?

A naive question, which seems to have to give way to deadly Hegelian good sense: everything that is initially *other* ends up taking a place within a system of relations, of systematically opposed *identities*. Did not the March 22 movement, which sought an alterity to the political system, itself end up appearing as a fringe group (even if it was "anti-fringe-group"?), end up playing a role on the very stage that it wanted to destroy? Further away and closer to us: hadn't the union movement, which once took up arms against wage slavery, become an organization helping to govern the use of the labor force deep within the vast capitalist machine? It is easy to see how such considerations can lead one to renounce "transforming the world," to advocate reforming the working of a system that "has the merit of existing," to stick to the depressing "wisdom" of mediation and dialogue (which is in fact the whole political practice of the workers' organizations).

The movement of May provides a proof that ought to be opposed to this gloomy perspective, the proof that critique will not fail to erupt, even in a strongly integrated system, and that the dream (the nightmare) of social and cultural peace is thus a destitute ideology. This factual proof alone forbids any faith in the spontaneity of the masses, any belief that the workers want self-management, or the conviction that the social entity will ever be able to be reached without an intermediary and that society can become transparent to itself. However, just such a philosophy could be found underlying the practice of the March 22 movement, sometimes explained in certain reflections, notably those on exemplary action.

To understand the movement as the emergence of authentic freedom in an alienated society is to fail utterly to grasp its true force, its virtue as an event. Such an understanding merely opposes a metaphysics with another metaphysics, remains in the same sphere of thought and action. We have to get beyond the opposition between spontaneity and mediation, between the masses and the apparatus, between life and the institution. The importance of the March 22 movement also proceeds from the fact that it obliges one (at least if one does not begin by "liquidating" it by taking a politician's or a historian's point of view) to develop an understanding of the bureaucratic capitalist system and its disorder. This understanding must be one that breaks with the discourse of origins as well as with that of ends, with Rousseau as well as with Hegel, with spontaneism as well as with bolshevism. With Freud (but not with Marcuse or Reich), one can begin to perceive and roughly sketch out that "beyond" that Marx left undeveloped.

In what follows, the reader should not be surprised at not finding the *terminology* of the movement; referring to the documents will allow the measure of this distance to be gauged. Let me repeat that the *fact* of this separation from the terminology of the movement seems to me to attest to a fidelity to historical meaning and to the meaning of facts that the movement displayed, and also to afidelity to the movement as a fact. The movement never existed, because it was not an institution. Consequently, if many (the "author" among them) were able to recognize their own thoughts and at times their ancient hopes in the movement, no one is entitled to say "it enacted what I always thought"; the opposite is true. No one had thought about what the movement did. The movement *turned out* this way, caught everything established and all thought (including revolutionary thought) off guard, offering a figure of what this society represses or denies, a figure of its unconscious desire. Taking this mode of "truth" into consideration, the movement must not be made to *take its place* within a system of knowledge. Rather, one must try to show how it defeated the *distribution of places* imposed by the capitalist-bureaucratic system.

The System and the Event

1. One can imagine any society as an ensemble of persons ruled by a system whose function would be to regulate the entry, the distribution, and the elimination of the *energy* that this ensemble spends in order to exist. "Objects" (things, but also women and words, as Lévi-Strauss teaches) would only be specific concrete instances of this energy; institutions would be operators that make this energy usable by the ensemble, make it able to circulate within it. The institution, far from being only what presents itself as such to the observer, would in general be any stable formation, explicit or not, transforming related energy into bound energy[4] within a given field of the circulation of objects (the linguistic field, the matrimonial field, the economic field, etc.).

2. The accent would thus be placed on the energetic aspect ("economic," as Freud said of the psychic apparatus) of the institutional function rather than on its semantic or semiological function. A considerable difference: an approach guided by the model of structural linguistics alone does not allow one to understand the functioning of symbolic systems like those described by Mauss, nor even the appearance of ("revolutionary") events in a semantically "well-regulated" system like that of modern capitalism. In the former case as in the latter, there is a dimension of *force* that escapes the logic of the signifier: an excess of energy that symbolic exchange can never regulate, an excess that "primitive" culture thematizes as debt; a "disorder" that at times shakes the capitalist system and produces events in it that are initially *unexchangeable.*

3. In the division of scientific labor, the task of constructing the system of regulation falls to political economy, social anthropology, linguistics, and so on. If history were included, it would take the role of considering the event. One could call an event the impact, on the system, of floods of energy such that the system does not manage to bind and channel this energy; the event would be the traumatic encounter of energy with the regulating institution.

4. Capitalism is a system structured as a regulator of growth (to speak in cybernetic terms); in principle it allows the introduction, the circulation, and the elimination of ever greater quantities of energy. The general principle that governs the entrance of new quantities of energy is that of exchange value: energy being the labor force and labor time its unit of exchange in the system, any object can enter into the system provided that it is exchangeable for another object containing the same number of units of energy. It is immediately clear, from the element of absurdity in such a formulation, that it contains the enigma of increased accumulation or, simply, of surplus value. The ideology of "growth," of "development," of "enrichment" that Marx uncovers and criticizes consists in obscuring this *overabundance*, the surplus that a "primitive" society on the contrary knows how to recognize as its own disruption and that it seeks to harness in the symbolic. (By calling it labor force, Marx is perhaps only forcing bourgeois political economy to recognize that *there is, in capitalism too, a debt*, and that the creditor is the proletariat.)

5. The event in capitalist society, as we know, can arise from two situations: either the system of exchange value, in extending itself to precapitalist social regions, encounters institutions that are incompatible with its principle of functioning; or energy refuses to be harnessed, bound, and circulated in the "objects" of the system. In the latter case (the only one that counts if it is true that, here at the end of the twentieth century, bureaucratic capitalism seems likely to exhaust all the precapitalist institutions, such as religion, family, property, labor, decency), it would be necessary to distinguish be-

tween events of a quantitative order, so to speak, and a much more enigmatic, qualitative order of events. We can draw an idea of the former from what political economy calls a crisis of overproduction or technological unemployment: these are blockages (moments of stasis) in the circulation of energy, in the form of unexchangeable products or labor force. Such stases have gravely endangered the system (1929–52) though they have not destroyed it; indeed, in the final analysis these quantitative events provided the system with the chance to improve its capacity to bind energy (modern capitalism). However, the qualitative event occurs when the very forms through which energy is rendered circulable (the institutions, in the sense that I have given to the term) cease to be able to harness that energy—they become obsolete. The relationship between energy and its regulation undergoes a mutation. This enigma is thus the only event worthy of the name, when the regulator encounters energy that it cannot bind. There are models of this event in the pictorial crisis of the beginning of the quattrocento, and in the appearance of entrepreneurs in Flanders a century later. I insist on the fact that in both cases, the established institution (the Gothic international in art, the corporation in economies) *was running perfectly* at the time.

6. This "economic" description returns us to a theory of desire. The system, with its bindings, its repetitions, and its accidents, is analogous to a "libidinal system," which may be neurotic, psychotic, or perverse. The objects that appear within the system are set up so that desire (eros and the death drive)[5] is fulfilled in their production and in their destruction. A positioning of desire underlies all social systems, a positioning that of course differs between "primitive" society (cf. Mauss) and capitalist society (cf. Marx). The event, as a qualitative force, is an inexplicable mutation in the position of desire: for example, where desire was *repressed* in the object (in religious societies, where debt is acknowledged), it will appear *foreclosed* (in the scientific, economic, political, etc. "positivism" of post-Renaissance and capitalist society).

7. The March 22 movement is tuned into all three kinds of turmoil: it belongs to the crisis of the university and the social crisis, but it owes its proper dimension to the space that it has created, even though it is minimal and violated by ideologies, for a mutation in the relation between what is desired and what is given, between potential energy and the social machinery. The movement's participation in the first two orders of events and its attempt to respond to them, to provide a cure or solution, situates it like any other group within the order of *politics*, as an institution with the function of regulating the flow of energy in the system according to its specific fashion but just like other institutions. But insofar as the March 22 movement belongs to the third type of event, it has performed a work of unbinding, an

antipolitical work, that brings about the collapse rather than the reinforcement of the system.

A Book of Antihistory

It is clear why history seems to us to also be an institution contributing to the general work of the binding of energy. A historian of May and a disciple of Isaac Deutscher, who can hardly be suspected of conservatism, involuntarily confirms this in this statement: "A historical fact can be interpreted, studied, exploited, and acted upon—or it can be ignored. To a great extent the outcome of the next crisis depends on the seriousness and skill with which the contesting parties will profit from the lessons of previous experience."[6] "To profit" is to produce the theoretical and practical apparatuses that will allow free energy to be bound the next time that it attacks the system. Writing a history book always aims to produce a *historian's knowledge* as its content, that is, a discourse that is at once consistent and complete, in which the non-sense of the event will be rendered intelligible, fully signified, and thus in principle predictable. It is to seek to institutionalize something that appeared at the time as foundationless, anarchic. To do so is to contribute to *power* by destroying *force*.

Despite its "author," this book will assuredly accomplish, in its turn, this work of binding, of recuperation. However, it bears the traces of the potential incomprehensibility of the events of May and of the potential antipolitics of the March 22 movement.

In the first place, it seemed to me necessary to let the movement speak for itself by printing many unpublished documents. I do not claim that this book is the book of the movement (which would be impossible anyway), but it is desirable for readers to take on most of the responsibility for constructing an understanding of the facts for themselves.

Secondly, in the "economic" hypothesis that I advance, the value of discursive documents, written or spoken (that is, the value of documents as bearers of *signification*), must not be privileged. Rather, priority should be accorded to acts, gestures, situations, silences, or even intonations, to all the traces of a *sense* that is transmitted in spite of discourse rather than by it, a sense that for this reason is usually considered to be non-sense and is therefore not taken into consideration by the historian. The chapter on the "facts" is in reality an inventory of these *figures*[7] of the March 22 movement. Two things are clear from the comparison of these figures to the *discourses* of the movement: first, that the mainspring of the movement is provided by several events blocked together. Above all, however, the most important of these events, the mutation of desire in regard to the system, did not in most cases find its words in the movement, even as it projected its figures onto it.

Finally, readers should not expect a *narrative* of the deeds and gestures of the movement in this book. If there is no narrative here, it is because narrative is a figure of discourse that lends its form to myth and tale, and that has, like them, the function of distributing the "facts" in a necessarily instructive succession, the function of drawing a "moral," so that the story always fulfills a desire, above all the desire that temporality should make sense and history should be signifiable, a desire that it fulfills by its very form. It is time to get rid of the illusion that universal history provides the universal tribunal, that some last judgment is prepared and fulfilled in history. The events of the March 22 movement contributed energetically to the destruction of this religiopolitical ideology, in the manner in which I hope this entirely analytic account (in which the figures of the movement are arranged according to their value as events in relation to the system, rather than by virtue of their relevance to a teleology) will make its contribution. A list of the interventions of the March 22 movement, classified according to the institutional regions affected, is thus provided under the heading of *facts*. I would like to emphasize that the order of presentation of these regions has no particular significance.

12

Concerning the Vincennes Psychoanalysis Department

(1975) (with Gilles Deleuze)

What has happened recently at the faculty of Vincennes in the psychoanalysis department is apparently quite simple: the firing of a certain number of part-time teachers for reasons of administrative and pedagogical reorganization. In an article in *Le Monde*, Roger-Pol Droit nevertheless asks if it is not a matter of a Vichy-style purge. The process of termination of employment, the choice of those fired, the handling of opposition, and the immediate naming of replacements could indeed remind one, mutatis mutandis, of a Stalinist operation. Stalinism is not the monopoly of the communist parties; it has also occurred in leftist groups, and psychoanalytic associations have been no more immune to its influence. This would seem to be confirmed by the lack of resistance shown by those sacked and by their allies. They did not actively collaborate in their own trials, but one can imagine that a second wave of purges might bring things to this point.

The question is not one of doctrine but of the organization of power. Those in charge of the psychoanalysis department, who carried out these sackings, declare in official texts that they are acting on the instructions of Dr. Lacan. He is the one who inspires the new statutes, he is even the one to whom, if need be, candidacies will be submitted. He is the one who is calling for a *return to order*, in the name of a mysterious "matheme" of psychoanalysis. It is the first time that a private person, whatever his competence may be, has arrogated to himself the right to intervene in a university to carry out, or to have carried out, a unilateral reorganization entailing dismissals and appointments of teaching personnel. Even if the whole psychoanalysis department were in agreement, the affair and the threat it conceals would remain the same. The Freudian School of Paris is not only a group that has a leader, it is a very centralized association that has a clientele, in every sense of the word. It is difficult to imagine how a university department could subordinate itself to an organization of this kind.

That Christian charity and faithful worship should shape the dialogue among followers of Christ is indisputable.

Ongoing Questions and Concerns

As the conversation continues about evolution and the problem of evil, several key questions and concerns are at the forefront. First, doesn't evolution make the problem of evil worse? An evolutionary account is used by some Christians not just as a way of explaining the reality of natural evil but as a way of vindicating God. On this view, God chose to create not a mechanistic universe, compelled by the inner necessity of its own being to develop in utter conformity with God's purposes, but a world endowed with some operational independence, capable of developing into freedom and creativity. On this view, therefore, God is not directly responsible for the disease, predation, death, and destruction that are so much a part of the natural world. But doesn't this just push the problem back one step? Some traditional creationists avoid this problem by appealing to human free will as not only the source of human evils—holocausts, genocides, slavery—but, because of the fall and subsequent curse, the source of natural evil also.

Giberson and Collins respond to this appeal by remarking, "This intriguing point of view, unfortunately, cannot be reconciled with what we know about the history of life."[20] They go on to ask whether anyone is really willing to suppose that "almost every animal on the planet had its way of life dramatically transformed by the curse. Sharp teeth and poison glands—and the genetic code to produce them—had to pop into existence, since animals were now going to start killing each other for the first time. Thorns had to suddenly appear on bushes. Vast numbers of vegetarian animals became carnivorous. And all this had to happen without leaving any trace in the fossil record."[21] They answer their own question by appealing to evolution: "We need not consider these options, however, as they have been ruled out by careful measurements of the age of the earth, which show it to be billions of years old and occupied with countless life forms long before human beings appeared."[22] The use of evolutionary theory to dismiss the possibility of some sort of catastrophic change in the past as a result of the fall seems much too facile to traditional creationists. Furthermore, the confidence in what science purports to "know" and to "rule out" is breathtaking to those who believe that science is fallible and has frequently been wrong.

20. Giberson and Collins, *Language of Science and Faith*, 130.
21. Giberson and Collins, *Language of Science and Faith*, 130.
22. Giberson and Collins, *Language of Science and Faith*, 131.

A theistic evolutionary account must offer a convincing answer not only to the *why* and *when* of the origin of evil but also to the *why* and *when* of human moral culpability. We do not hold nonhuman animals morally accountable for their acts. When a lion stalks an aging wildebeest, we do not say "bad lion." On the contrary, despite the sometimes apparent savagery of nature, we accept predation as the cycle of life. Remarkably, despite their intelligence and genetic similarities to humans, we do not attribute moral delinquency to chimpanzees when they savage one of their own—or even when they attack a human.

But this again raises a host of questions: If humans descended from common nonhuman ancestors, how, why, and at what point in evolutionary history did the human species become morally praiseworthy and morally blameworthy? Were early hominids moral creatures? What about Neanderthals and Denisovans? Are humans exceptional because they are uniquely made in God's image or only because they are the most highly evolved creatures we know? These and other questions bring theological anthropology to the forefront and make the quest for the so-called historical Adam increasingly important. As a 2011 editorial in *Christianity Today* put it, "No Adam, No Eve, No Gospel."[23]

The Christological Constraint

However these questions and concerns are addressed, for Christians the central issue remains christological. As John Polkinghorne has said, "The depth of the problem posed by the demands of theodicy is only adequately met in Christian thinking by a Trinitarian understanding of the cross of Christ, seen as the event in which the incarnate God shares to the uttermost in the travail of creation."[24]

Whatever the source, the whole creation groans in the face of the horrendous evil in the world—much of it wrought by humans themselves. To paraphrase Pascal, humans are both the trash and treasure of the universe. Yet Christians believe that the incarnate God—Jesus Christ—is finally the answer to the most pressing questions we face. This is by no means to suggest that these questions about evolution and the problem of evil only represent

23. "No Adam, No Eve, No Gospel," *Christianity Today*, June 2011, 61. See also Richard N. Ostling, "The Search for the Historical Adam," *Christianity Today*, June 2011, 23; Matthew Barrett and Ardel B. Caneday, eds., *Four Views on the Historical Adam* (Grand Rapids: Zondervan, 2013); John H. Walton, *The Lost World of Adam and Eve: Genesis 2–3 and the Human Origins Debate* (Downers Grove, IL: IVP Academic, 2015).

24. John Polkinghorne, *Science and the Trinity: The Christian Encounter with Reality* (New Haven: Yale University Press, 2006), 72–73.

internecine debates between members of an academic cottage industry, "the faith/science dialogue." They are real problems made more real by palpable human and animal suffering. But it is to say that somehow either all of this relates to the suffering God in Christ—who groans with his suffering creation and, by taking its suffering into himself, defuses it of any power to frustrate his loving purposes for his world and enables it to share in his resurrection—or we are of all people most miserable indeed (1 Cor. 15:19).

15

Can Nature Be "Red in Tooth and Claw" in the Thought of Augustine?

Stanley P. Rosenberg

In debates surrounding biological evolution, one of the challenges for theologically minded discussions is accounting for the problem of evil and a good God. The gauntlet is thrown down: to accept evolution means that chaos and evil are original parts of creation, with violence, cataclysm, animal predation, and other forms of destruction being essential to the evolutionary process. But this raises a number of questions: How can a good God allow this? And how can a theologian believe in the goodness of a bloodstained creation before a fall? Is accepting the possibility of such destructive elements in the cosmos, predating a human fall, simply giving up on biblical and theological commitments to the divine nature? Much of the polemic surrounding discussions of theology and evolution is marked by fear that one undermines the goodness of God by accepting evolutionary positions.

Augustine of Hippo (354–430) is an authoritative source for some rejections of biological evolution. The manner of exegeting the problem of evil that theologians ascribe to Augustine has had immense influence on the Christian tradition. In its most basic form, his theological system is thought to propose that the world was created pure, free from evil, and that evil, chaos, decay, and corruption entered into the world as a result of the fall of the first couple. In the conventional teaching, Augustine argues that when the first couple ate of the fruit, the consequences were world shattering. The progenitors of the human race became alienated first from God, second within themselves, and third from each other. This view is a bedrock to Augustine's theology. So far, so good.

A fourth type of alienation ushered in by Adam and Eve's choice is also typically presented as Augustinian: the physical cosmos itself became alienated from God. This alienation is the point of this study, as it challenges any easy acceptance of evolutionary science. It was through the fall, it is supposed, that disease, physical cataclysms such as earthquakes and hurricanes, and animal predation all entered the natural world. Nature was not originally "red in tooth and claw" but was made so by the fall. The primal purity was degraded and ruined by the selfish act in the garden, and hence the world—spiritual, moral, psychological, social, *and* physical existence—was knocked off its axis.

Augustine held that evil is a lessening of an original perfect state. His account of evil as a *privatio boni*—a privation or lessening of original goodness—argues that all existence is a gift of the Creator and is, by definition, good.[1] The fall undermined the integrity of reality, and the world consequently suffers the effects of privation: while it still necessarily retains vestiges of its original goodness, it is now corrupted and afflicted. On the face of it, his system appears to reject a notion of original chaos in the world. Nature surely cannot be understood as being "red in tooth and claw" from the outset since Augustine asserts a primal purity and a fall that corroded the original state. Such a view is incompatible with an acceptance of evolutionary development in which so-called natural evil, or physical suffering, animal predation, and natural cataclysm are original, essential, and ongoing operations in the physical and biological world.[2]

No generally accepted interpretation of the empirical evidence accepts that the physical world somehow transformed and became violent only after a recent human fall or that it was only after such a moral cataclysm that physical cataclysms—such as lions eating lambs or two-cell creatures eating single-cell creatures—began. None of these so-called evils can be traced back to, or said

1. Augustine's privation theory will be explained below.

2. Arguably his approach to evil as privation leaves much unanswered and has been pushed aside by recent theologians. For broader discussions of evil and the natural world—though without reference to privation theory and with only brief discussion of the Augustinian theological tradition—see Christopher Southgate, *The Groaning of Creation* (Louisville: Westminster John Knox, 2008); Michael Murray, *Nature Red in Tooth and Claw: Theism and the Problem of Animal Suffering* (Oxford: Oxford University Press, 2008).

to be caused by, an act of will by a created being (unless one ascribes them to the work of the demonic or agrees with Origen on a precorporeal fall of the soul or with others asserting the fall of a world soul).[3] This evidence would seem difficult to square with Augustine's contention that pride is the origin of all sin and evil and distorts the original goodness established by the Creator. It would seem difficult for an Augustinian privation account of evil to support an understanding of nature as "red in tooth and claw" from the outset when it asserts a primal purity and a fall that corroded the original state.

This chapter investigates whether Augustine's privation theory has been appropriated and understood correctly, asking whether the fall and the subsequent privation of nature are the cause of chaos, decay, and violence in nature and whether Augustine's theology even accepts these as essential operations of the natural world from the outset.[4] In Augustine's extant works—93 books, some 950 sermons, and numerous letters—he established one of the most influential traditions of theological interpretation. As his approach to solving the problem of evil shaped his whole theological vision, to accept evolution appears, on the face of it, to reject his view of evil and thus force one to reject much of Augustinian theology. This results in rejecting vast swaths of both Roman Catholic and Protestant theological developments, presenting an insuperable problem for many. The stakes are high indeed. Fortunately, the problem is not quite what we have been taught to think it is.

This chapter thus has two purposes: first, it seeks to clarify Augustine's position, and, second, it offers a case study in how a tradition can adapt and even unwittingly revise a thinker—in the process reshaping the position into something new, which perhaps is unrecognizable and incorrect, even if it is plausible.

Projecting a Problem

The conventional teaching of Augustine's theology argues that Augustine believed the physical world to be alienated from God as a result of the fall of the first pair. Dislocated by the fall, it is itself disjointed and suffering, and humans suffer all the more for the alienation they inflicted on the world. Hence, any disruptive physical phenomena are a result of the fall. Had the pair

3. See Michael Lloyd's discussion of the demonic in chap. 17 below.

4. The point here is not to argue whether Augustine would have favored or rejected Darwinian evolution, as was suggested by various readers from 1871: modern evolutionary theories were of course unknown to him.

not eaten of the fruit, there would be no carnivores, no cataclysmic weather or geological activity resulting in pain. Such a view both creates a challenge to explain pain and violence in nature and leaves no room for evolutionary development: How does one account for larger animals eating smaller animals, disease from pathogen-infested water, or microbes killing complex, multicellular organisms? How does one interpret the role of canine teeth or the fangs of the modern wolf or the extinct saber-toothed tiger, except as having function outside the domain of what empirical data and reason indicate? This standard representation of Augustine, which has been conventional in most of the Western theological tradition until the last century, posits a reading of Scripture that contradicts scientific findings from paleobiology to zoology and geology.

A trained Augustine scholar, I shared this interpretation. I cannot think of a time, though, when one of my mentors suggested such a notion to me. Yet it has been part of my intellectual framework, and I taught it to my students for many years. A cursory look at three representative authors suggests the reason.

In his influential book *Evil and the Love of God*, noted philosopher John Hick presents Augustine as arguing that the privation and loss of order in nature is a breakdown of some imagined ideal ordering of the natural world: "In all such cases the evil state of affairs can plausibly be seen in the collapse of a good state of affairs, and as tending towards non-existence, at least in the relative sense of the dissolution of a previously established arrangement of life or matter."[5] Elsewhere he asserts "that the Augustinian type of theodicy, based on the fall from grace of free finite creatures—first angels and then human beings—*and a consequent going wrong of the physical world*, is not logically impossible."[6] In his reading of Augustine, all of nature is afflicted and disrupted by the fall of Adam and Eve, which imposed a penalty on all of the natural world, altering its course and structure. The physical world was perfect and without sources of pain and suffering before the pair broke the law. While Hick emphatically rejects this position as a nonsensical, idealized ordering of nature that offers an untenable position, he engages with it as a serious option held by many as the specific directive of Augustine and strives to dismantle it.

Meanwhile, certain core interpretations of a Reformed worldview were set out in a brief, influential work by Albert Wolters, *Creation Regained: Biblical*

5. John Hick, *Evil and the God of Love*, 3rd ed. (New York: Palgrave Macmillan, 2010; first published 1966), 55, 56. Hick dismisses this position as inadequate but believes it is part of the Augustinian system.

6. John Hick, "An Irenaean Theodicy," in *Encountering Evil: Live Options in Theodicy*, ed. Stephen T. Davis, new ed. (Louisville: Westminster John Knox, 2001), 39 (emphasis added).

Basics for a Reformational Worldview. In his representation of Augustine's thought, when humans used their free will and disobeyed the command, they alienated themselves from God, within their own selves and against each other, *and caused the alienation of the natural world*. They did not simply alienate themselves from creation, but they introduced a disjunction between God and nature and introduced natural violence, pain, and suffering into the world. "But the effects of sin range more widely than the arena of specifically human affairs, touching also the nonhuman world," writes Wolters, citing Genesis 3:17. "The very soil is affected by Adam's sin, making agriculture more difficult."[7] Not only did all suffer as a result of the primal disobedience; they introduced a new set of conditions, or epiphenomena, into the physical world. The nonhuman world was altered and estranged. At the moment sin was introduced into the world, all of creation's systems suffered a massive restructuring and were the worse for it. Such a view leaves little room for macro- or microevolution.

These interpretations are matched by the work of an able scholar of early Christianity, Joseph Kelly, whose *Problem of Evil in the Western Tradition* also presents this standard view:

> Augustine so emphasized the historical reality of the Garden of Eden that for generations people have accepted his notion that once the world had been perfect and that we had lived in harmony with all creation. We had nothing to fear from animals nor did they have anything to fear from us. The lion did indeed lie down with the lamb. Our first parents spoiled all that with original sin, and the world as we know it is a broken one, one distorted by sin and the evil that accompanied it. People brought up on evolutionary concepts, on the belief that all life forms struggle for survival, usually against other life forms, see Augustine's theory as something fantastic. But he meant it literally. At one time this physical world was free of strife, illness, suffering, and death.[8]

With this view of Augustine presented by philosophers, theologians, historians, and indeed the Augustinian tradition, we should not be surprised that it is the standard one. But we still must ask the question: Is it the position that Augustine held? In order to answer that, we must first study Augustine's search to solve the problem of evil and the formulation he arrived at in response to other solutions posed and rejected.

7. Albert Wolters, *Creation Regained: Biblical Basics for a Reformational Worldview* (Grand Rapids: Eerdmans, 1985), 46.

8. Joseph Kelly, *The Problem of Evil in the Western Tradition: From the Book of Job to Modern Genetics* (Collegeville, MN: Liturgical Press, 2002), 58–59.

Sorting Out Evil: Augustine's Privation Theory in Brief

The North African Christian context that shaped Augustine had a tendency toward literalism and rigorism, which set the terms of some key debates. As a young man, Augustine fled from his mother's Christianity, dismayed at its literalist handling of the problem of evil, and went to a gnostic sect, the Manichaeans, who taught that the divine was not all-powerful and that this world was created by an evil divine being at war with a good one; our suffering and pain come from the warfare between these forces.

His move into Manichaeism and later abandonment of it demonstrate Augustine asking the questions: Whence comes evil? How can a good God allow it? And what precisely is evil? He was convinced that God and all divine creative activity must be good by definition. He relates his search in the *Confessions*, and it forms a substantial backdrop to the biographical reflections as he moves from the pear tree that marked him as sinful in book 2, to the tree in the orchard under which he sat when he converted in book 8, to the glimpse of the eschaton while sitting with his mother overlooking the orchard in Ostia in book 9. Amid the story that unfolds in the first nine books, he describes his quest to solve the seemingly intractable problem of defending the goodness of God in the face of evil. The influence of a group of Christian Platonists led him to think about evil in a new way (related in *Confessions*, books 5–7). Adapting their views substantially, he devised a new solution that arguably undergirds his whole theological system. It is here set out briefly.

Beginning with the doctrine that God made all things out of nothing (*creatio ex nihilo*), Augustine's conviction and assumption was that all things must by definition have been made good and that anything that exists, in either its original state or a later state, retains some of that goodness to the extent it still exists. He writes, "By this Trinity, supremely, equally, and unchangeably good, all things have been created: they are not supremely, equally, or unchangeably good, but even when they are considered individually, each one of them is good; and at the same time all things are very good, since in all these things consists the wonderful beauty of the universe."[9] Existence thus implies goodness. Hence, "God created substance not vices; vices are not a substance."[10] Anything that is evil is not a created thing but reflects a degree of loss of its

9. Augustine, *Enchiridion* 3.10. Citations from the *Enchiridion on Faith, Hope and Charity* are based on the translation in *The Augustine Catechism: Enchiridion on Faith, Hope and Charity* in the *Works of St. Augustine for the Twenty-First Century*, trans. Bruce Harbert, ed. Boniface Ramsey (Hyde Park, NY: New City Press, 1999).

10. Augustine, *Enarration on Psalm 48.5*, in Augustine, *Expositions of the Psalms*, vols. 1–6, trans. Maria Boulding (Hyde Park, NY: New City Press, 2000–2004).

original substance or essence. Evil is the absence of good.[11] This affects how one looks at the world, as each created thing originally contained, and still retains, a degree of goodness. Two helpful comments are worth noting here. The first concerns the problem noted in the *Confessions*. Augustine writes,

> It was obvious to me that things which are liable to corruption are good. If they were the supreme goods, or if they were not good at all, they could not be corrupted. . . . If there were no good in them, there would be nothing capable of being corrupted. Corruption does harm and unless it diminishes the good, no harm would be done. . . . All things that are corrupted suffer privation of some good. If they were to be deprived of all good, they would not exist at all. . . . Hence I saw and it was made clear to me that you made all things good, and there are absolutely no substances which you did not make.[12]

This introduces a critical word in the Augustinian lexicon: "corruption." Evil is understood as a corruption of the original state. Corruption undermines the order and quality of the state, altering the being and lessening its power and strength. As with rust on a car, some of the vitality is sapped. But it is only *some* of the vitality. Corruption has disrupted the order and quality of things—it does not destroy it. Those things afflicted by evil, so long as they still exist, retain some portion of the original gift of life from the Creator and still have some good left in them. Evil, as a privation of the good, disrupts and harms and undermines but is not omnipotent. Were something utterly evil, it would become nothing. So nothing can be utterly evil. Evil is a quality describing a relative lack of existence, and were evil to exist absolutely—a logical incoherence, to be sure—it would cease to be. Hence, goodness is absolute; what is evil is only relatively so.

This idea takes on a further and critical component in the next quotation from Augustine. Here we see also the coherence of order and structure and the relationship that all things, even corrupted ones, pose in the overall ontological structuring offered by the divine gift of existence:

> In this universe even that which is called evil, well ordered and kept in its place, sets the good in higher relief, so that good things are more pleasing and praiseworthy than evil ones. Nor would Almighty God, "to whom," as even the pagans confess, "belongs supreme power," since he is supremely good, in any way allow anything evil to exist among his works were he not so omnipotent and good that he can bring good even out of evil. For what else is that which is called evil

11. Augustine, *Enchiridion* 3.10.

12. Augustine, *Confessions* 7.12.18, trans. Henry Chadwick (Oxford: Oxford University Press, 1991). All quotations from *Confessions* in this chapter are from this translation.

> but a removal of good? . . . A wound or a disease is not in itself a substance but a defect in the substance of flesh. The flesh itself is the substance, a good thing to which those evil things, those removals of the good, known as health, occur. In the same way all evils that affect the mind are removals of natural goods: when they are cured they are not moved to somewhere else, but, when they are no longer in the mind once it has been restored to health, they will be nowhere.[13]

Augustine's view presented in this quote presents an interesting solution to the problem of evil, as it attempts to protect the goodness of God and the validity of created things, and offers a winsome vision for the good to be found in the world, even those things (all those things) that are nonetheless undermined by corruption. Augustine understands the gift of salvation as offering a process of healing for the corruption humans suffer.[14] But this is not a complete answer as it still begs a question: If God created a good world, how did privation come to corrupt the physical and biological world?

For an answer to this, we must turn to Augustine's many works discussing free will and particularly *On the Free Choice of the Will*. In what has come to be described as a freewill defense,[15] Augustine argues that God, by definition, could create only contingent beings potentially subject to corruption. It is not possible to create beings who are not open to corruption, or God would be creating his equals. This does not indicate jealousy but logical impossibility. All other beings must be less than divine and so must undergo change and therefore have the possibility of decay. Add to this a relationship bounded by love; intelligent beings, in order to fully express love, must have a will and so must be free. To be able truly to love—an act of will—requires being able *not* to love.[16] Pride was the first sin, according to Augustine; it distorts the will and is the cause of all evil. A perverse will, perverted by pride, was the cause of evil.[17]

Privation of the soul, the corruption of the spiritual state, is substantially different from the decay endemic in any created state. While decay is an

13. Augustine, *Enchiridion* 3.11.

14. See my chapter "Not So Alien and Unnatural after All—the Role of Deification in Augustine's Sermons," in *Visions of God and Ideas on Deification in Patristic Thought*, ed. M. Edwards and Elena Ene D-Vasilescu (London: Routledge, 2016), 89–117.

15. See Alvin Plantinga's discussion in *God, Freedom, and Evil* (Grand Rapids: Eerdmans, 2002; first published 1974).

16. We must not confuse this discussion with his later debates with Pelagius about the possibility of those with free will, who are corrupted, still having sufficient freedom to love God without initial prompting and intervention. Freedom, for Augustine, describes an ontological state in which one is able to live and act fully toward the end for which one was designed. It is teleological and a description not of one's liberty to act but of the ability to fulfill one's purpose.

17. Augustine, *On the Free Choice of the Will* 3.17.47.

ontological alteration possible for any being aside from God, privation leads to alienation between God and the being so corrupted and results from an immoral choice.[18] It also has an ontological impact, leading to a particular type of decay. As a result of privation, humans lost their natural state of being. The freely chosen actions in the garden distorted human nature and undermined the original state, so the existence enjoyed is something other and less than it was created to be,[19] and this altered human nature was handed on to subsequent generations. This is the cornerstone of Augustine's doctrine of original sin.

One might interject that this synopsis demonstrates that authors such as Hick and Wolters got Augustine right. If privation came with the fall for Augustine, one who follows his system or systems influenced by him must believe that no state of brokenness existed before the fall and that one cannot genuinely hold to the theological tradition while accepting the discoveries of evolutionary scientists. The problem, however, comes from treating a foundational set of ideas only in synopsis and not in context. In chess, novices are admonished to play "the whole board" lest they miss the bishop waiting to pounce. This is good advice for treating the works of Augustine as well. And for that we must turn to his cosmology and look more deeply into the texts expressing notions of privation in order to determine if he predicates privation of the physical cosmos as well as the human soul.

Cosmology and the Discovery of Nature

Understanding Augustine's view of the *saeculum*—the secular state, existing as part of the created order, which is in itself neither holy nor profane—is critical to unraveling his political theology and contributes to a chapter in the history of science.[20] Augustine was keenly interested in Genesis 1–3; it was one of the most important scriptures in his formation. His studies of these chapters enabled him to solve some of his earlier tensions that had previously contributed to the abandonment of his mother's Christianity and offered an alternative to the Manichaean cosmology. His works on the first part of Genesis fill three commentaries and major sections of two other works.[21]

18. Augustine, *On the Free Choice of the Will* 3.24.72.

19. Augustine, *On the Free Choice of the Will* 3.17.51.

20. Those interested in Augustine's political theology should turn to the classic work by R. A. Markus, *Saeculum: History and Society in the Theology of St. Augustine*, rev. ed. (Cambridge: Cambridge University Press, 1988).

21. Augustine wrote five commentaries on the opening chapters of Genesis: *On Genesis against the Manichaeans*, an allegorical interpretation written in 391; the *Unfinished Literal*

Augustine marshals arguments from Genesis regularly, citing Genesis 1:1 at least seven hundred times and the first chapter of John's Gospel more than one thousand times.[22]

Augustine's explorations of Genesis map out the implications of the doctrine of *creatio ex nihilo* (or rather, *facio ex nihilo* and other variants he employed).[23] These demonstrate that his views of natural reason and the nature of the world changed substantially in the decade before he wrote the *City of God* (413–426). One must study these changes in order to understand Augustine's thought, allowing him to grow and develop (and not extract his views on reason and nature based only his earlier works). His development gave him a new intellectual tool—the desacralization of society and history—which enabled him to respond to the theological crisis spawned by the sack of Rome by the Gothic tribes in 410. It also offered him a substantially different reading of nature and the natural world and the ability of the human mind to understand it.[24]

Augustine did not think that the opening chapter of Genesis narrated natural history; few church fathers treated Genesis 1–2 as a historical narration, and there was some disagreement about Genesis 3. Rather, it indicated the metaphysical substructure and God's intent for the cosmos and was a revelation to the angelic hosts of God's purposes. Augustine believed that these chapters focus on cosmology (here defined as metaphysical speculations regarding the cosmos), and they form the basis of much of the mature Augustine's theology.

Augustine posits a cosmology with a threefold structure.[25] First, the pattern of creation existed first and foremost in the mind of the Maker. The eternal and unchangeable ideas in the Word of God are the blueprint for the work

Commentary on Genesis (392); *Confessions*, books 11–13 (late 390s or early 400s); *Literal Commentary on Genesis* (12 books, ca. 404–18); and *City of God*, books 11–14 (ca. 415–18). His use of the word "literal" refers to the meaning of the words *as intended by the author*; so if the author intended one to read the work as history, that is the literal reading, but if intended as poetry or allegory, or figuratively, then the reader should engage the form *intended* as the proper literal reading.

22. Henri I. Marrou, *St. Augustine and His Influence through the Ages*, trans. Patrick Hepburne-Scott (London: Longmans, Green, 1957), 83.

23. Cf. Augustine, *Literal Commentary on Genesis* (*De Genesi ad litteram*) 7.21; 10.4; 10.9. Augustine uses a variety of forms of the words. Translations of this commentary are based, with some emendations, on *The Literal Meaning of Genesis*, trans. John H. Taylor, SJ, Ancient Christian Writers 41 and 42 (New York: Paulist Press, 1982).

24. See Stanley P. Rosenberg, "Forming the *Saeculum*: The Desacralization of Nature and the Ability to Understand It in Augustine's *Literal Commentary on Genesis*," in *Studies in Church History*, vol. 46, ed. P. Clarke and T. Claydon (Woodbridge, UK: Ecclesiastical History Society, 2010), 1–14.

25. Augustine, *Literal Commentary on Genesis* 5.12.28.

of creation.[26] According to Augustine, Genesis 1 offers the second part of the structure of creation. It describes the creation of the underlying and enduring principles, which are spiritual and metaphysical realities and so precede the physical creation. These principles, which Augustine calls "reasons," inform the material creation. This creation was immediate: the reasons were created simultaneously.[27] The potential creation was not yet affected by decay or sin.[28]

The production of the physical world is the third stage of creation and is represented in the second creation story of Genesis 2. At this stage comes the creation of seminal reasons, which are implanted in the world. These have physical properties and guide the continuing structure and development of the cosmos.[29] They are rather like the DNA of physical objects (to adapt a modern analogy), which shapes both their actual development and their transmission across generations.

The *reasons* are not always evident, and some are employed only for a particular purpose in time.[30] By means of these, writes Augustine, "God moves His whole creation by a hidden power, and all creatures are subject to this movement . . . stars moving in their courses, the winds blow on earth . . . meadows come to life as their seeds put forth the grass, animals are born and live their lives according to their proper instincts." All are subject to God's providence exercised through such natural means. "It is thus that God unfolds the generations which He laid up in creation [*saecula*] when first He founded it."[31] The Creator's ongoing power and governance sustain the cosmos when it both progresses and decays. There is an order to the cosmos and a motion, not because of an animated substrate (as in most late antique cosmologies) but because it operates according to a structure imposed and maintained by an external Creator. Hence, the divinely ordered world has natural laws of its own and is rational, contingent, changeable, and describable.[32] He begins to present us with a notion of a world that is natural in a more modern sense but nonetheless deeply dependent on divine initiative.

26. Cf. Augustine, *Enarration on Psalm* 49.16.

27. Augustine, *Literal Commentary on Genesis* 6.6.10. The phrase he uses for these is *rationes incommutabile*.

28. Augustine, *Literal Commentary on Genesis* 2.8.17.

29. Augustine, *Literal Commentary on Genesis* 6.5.8. Augustine describes these as the *rationes seminales*, a phrase used as early as the second century that he adopts here.

30. This notion was adapted by some interpreters soon after Darwin's works were published and again after the Scopes trial to suggest that Augustine held a notion akin to evolution. This imposes an anachronistic reading. See, e.g., Kevin Guinagh, "Saint Augustine and Evolution," *Classical Weekly* 40, no. 4 (1946): 26–31.

31. Augustine, *Literal Commentary on Genesis* 5.20.41; cf. 4.12.22; 9.15.27. Note the positive use of *saeculum*—from which we derive the later word "secular"—as the cosmos God created.

32. Augustine, *Literal Commentary on Genesis* 3.6.8 and 9.17.32.

Decay and Change in Nature before an Adamic Fall: "Red in Tooth and Claw" but Not Evil

Violence, Decay, and Natural States

Augustine's cosmology provides him with the means for explaining the ongoing governance of activity in nature, which for him necessarily includes advancement and *decay*—that is, change is necessary for any created being. If a contingent being can advance, it necessarily can also regress and decay. While Augustine does not appear to argue specifically for violence before the fall, there are suggestive comments. In *Confessions* 7.17, he describes a poisonous viper and the worm that causes rot as being created good. He does *not* describe them as having once been good, only later altered into something less, but expresses their present state—poisonous—as consistent with their original state. Poisonous creatures were created that way; animals' ability to kill is part of their original created nature. Rot and decay were part of the world's design. There was not, for Augustine, a postlapsarian alteration of the physical and biological landscape.

After the fall, however, humans find the physical world to be a source of pain: "I learnt by experience that it is no cause for surprise when bread which is pleasant to a healthy palate is misery to an unhealthy one; and to sick eyes light which is desirable to the healthy is hateful. The wicked are displeased by your justice, even more by vipers and the work which you created good, being well fitted for the lower parts of your creation."[33] The viper, a poisonous snake, is described here as good; it is because of something wrong in humans that we find such creatures to be a problem. Vipers, in other words, did not change; they possessed poison and the ability to kill as part of their original form. Rather, what changed was humans' relationship to them. Augustine nowhere suggests that the animal world underwent a biological transformation after the fall.[34]

The same is true of the physical cosmos. Augustine recognizes the passing of seasons, both metaphorical and the real cycles of the year, as part of the original state of the earth by which comes change, including decay. He comments on "the very ordinary and accustomed course of nature, whereby the seasons are rapidly revolved, in all things after their kinds, however temporal and perishable."[35] Augustine recognizes that nature's operations include created

33. Augustine, *Confessions* 7.16.22.

34. One might find Augustine's answer unpersuasive and turn to options presented elsewhere, including in this volume. The point here, however, is not to argue it is the best answer but to show how his work has been misread and misused and hence has influenced others predicated on an improper reading.

35. Augustine, *Enarration on Psalm 118*, Sermon 27.1, in Augustine, *Expositions of the Psalms*, vols. 1–6, trans. Maria Boulding (Hyde Park, NY: New City Press, 2000–2004).

things that perish: "So because eternity means immobility, while time means change—in eternity everything stands fast, while in time things come and things go—you can find a son following his father in the changing course of time."[36] Augustine thus reads Romans 8:21 as indicating only that the *human* cosmos, not the entire created order, is suffering as a result of the fall. He interprets this passage as describing the human world—human society, individual humans, and all their intertwined relationships—but not the physical and biological world.[37]

Like Athanasius—who played such an important role in the development of trinitarian theology in the fourth century—Augustine treats decay as essentially a part of any contingent being.[38] Existence for creatures is not absolute, and so return toward nonbeing is a "natural" movement to be expected unless there is direct, divine intervention to sustain the creature's state. Hence, in Augustinian terms, the fall is characterized as a sort of tragic irony: in choosing to express their will in contravention of the divine will, humans turned away from the one Being who could sustain their existence.

The notion of defect plays a vital role in the argument of book 3 of *On the Free Choice of the Will*. Decay is so obviously a part of a temporal, creaturely state, Augustine suggests, that to think otherwise would be absurd. Such defects are not blameworthy, as they are not voluntary; nor does he describe them as coming later in time or as a secondary result of the fall (as they are often presented). Decay and destruction are necessarily to be expected from anything that does not have its own absolute being. Augustine does not qualify this in any of the key passages. He does not suggest that God sustained creatures so that they would not experience decay or that physical decay was loosed on the cosmos only after the fall, though the fall certainly altered the human pair's natural condition for the worse (and had they persisted faithfully, their condition would have been enhanced).[39]

This is explained even more clearly and directly in the *City of God* (indeed, it is central to it), which serves as one of his commentaries on Genesis 1–3:

> It would be ridiculous to regard the defects of beasts, trees and other mutable and moral things which lack intelligence, sense or life, as deserving condemnation. Such defects do cause their nature to decay, which is liable to dissolution; but

36. Augustine, Sermon 117.10. Sermons not belonging to a special category, such as the *Enarrations on the Psalms*, are usually referred to as *Sermons to the People*. For simplicity here they are simply cited as Sermon. Translations used here are from Augustine, *Sermons*, 11 vols., trans. Edmund Hill, Works of Saint Augustine III/1–III/11 (Hyde Park, NY: New City Press, 1990–97).

37. Augustine, *Propositions from the Epistle to the Romans* 53.

38. See Athanasius, *On the Incarnation* 4.

39. Augustine, *City of God* 13.23.

> these creatures have received their mode of being by the will of their Creator, whose purpose is that they should bring to perfection the beauty of the lower parts of the universe by their alternation and succession in the passages of the seasons; and this is the beauty in its own kind, finding its place among the constituent parts of this world. . . . Consequently, in those areas of the universe where such creatures have their proper being, we see a constant succession, as some things pass away and others arise, as the weaker succumb to the stronger, and those that are overwhelmed change into the qualities of their conquerors; and thus we have a pattern of a world of continual transience. We, for our part, can see no beauty in this pattern to give us delight; and the reason is that we are involved in a section of it, under our condition of mortality, and so we cannot observe the whole design, in which these small parts, which are to us so disagreeable, fit together to make a scheme of ordered beauty. . . . As for those defects, in things of this earth, which are neither voluntary nor punishable; if we observe them closely we shall find that, on the same principle as before, they attest the goodness of the natures themselves, every one of which has God as its sole author and creator.[40]

This telling passage draws together many of the comments made above. Noting that decay is necessarily a part of a created order, and of the order and coherence of the world, we find here a strong argument for allowing not only the possibility but the requirement that one understand the cosmos to have contained within itself the necessity for destruction before any sin was committed.

In a passage in *On the Free Choice of the Will* (a work started in the 390s but revised quite late in Augustine's life, making it uncertain whether it reflects his later as well as his early view), Augustine pushes this notion even further, indicating that no blame should be attached to any defect or fault in the cosmos, as it did not come about through a willful act but was structurally present from the first and that, further, without opportunity for decay, there can be no progress. Progress and development require change, and change, the unfolding development of any future state, requires a passing away of a prior state:

> The defect, however, would not deserve blame unless it were voluntary. . . . Consequently it would be most absurd to say that temporal things ought not to decay. They are placed in an order of things such that, unless they decay the future cannot follow the past, nor can the beauty of the ages unfold itself in its natural course. They act in accordance with what they have received, and

40. Augustine, *City of God* 12.4, trans. (with some emendations) Henry Bettenson (New York: Penguin, 1972).

> they pay their debt to Him to whom they owe their being, in accordance with the measure of their being. . . .
>
> Therefore no one rightly blames a failure in these things which thus decay. They have received no further being, in order that everything may occur at its proper time. No one can say: It ought to have lasted longer; for it could not pass the limits assigned to it.[41]

Deficiency of being will be found in any created thing, as it cannot be complete in itself and have the fullness of being. Only one Being can conceivably have no deficiency. So the problem is not deficiency or decay; the problem is encountered only when a being willfully chooses a deficient action. Fault is adjudged only of those creatures that will to do evil and suffer any decay related to that choice. Decay not related to a particular choice is not blameworthy and is to be expected.

Decay is not total, however, and the Creator is still involved, invested and holding all things together and maintaining the beings' existence through a constant and dynamic gift of life—the gift of being. Paul's comment in Colossians about all things being held together in Christ (Col. 1:17) appears regularly in Augustine's works—for instance, in his *Literal Commentary on Genesis*: "For the power and might of the Creator, who rules and embraces all, makes every creature abide; and if this power ever ceased to govern creatures, their essences would pass away and all nature would perish."[42]

The Universe as a Well-Ordered Whole: Teleology and the Ability of the Whole to Absorb the Part

It is critical to remember that, for Augustine, creation remains good, even when intellectual creatures have darkened themselves and their progeny by sin. He frequently compares the Creator to an artisan and artist, able to beautify even when there is a flaw. In Sermon 301 he comments: "The painter knows where to place the shades in order to beautify his paintings; and you think that God would not know where to place the sinner in order to establish order in His creation?"[43] In *Enarration on Psalm 144* (sec. 13), he describes the continuum of being, from the highest spiritual objects to the lowliest physical objects. The higher end of the spectrum offers a greater degree of being without mortality, but those are just the angels; mortality—decay in

41. Augustine, *On the Free Choice of the Will* 3.15.42–43, trans. Dom Mark Pontifex in *The Problem of Free Choice* (New York: Newman Press, 1955).

42. Augustine, *Literal Commentary on Genesis* 4.12.22. Cf. 5.20.41 and 9.15.27; Augustine, *Enarration on Psalm 118*, Sermon 18.3.

43. Augustine, Sermon 301.5.4.

its gory finality—is experienced by all lower creatures as part of their design. Together, these compose an ordered, rational design in the cosmos, expressing the Creator's will. Remember here that this includes objects subject to decay:

> God has ordered every thing, and made every thing: to some He has given sense and understanding and immortality, as to the angels; to some He has given sense and understanding with mortality, as to man; to some He has given bodily sense, yet gave them not understanding or immortality, as to cattle: to some He has given neither sense, nor understanding, nor immortality, as to herbs, trees, stones: yet even these cannot be wanting in their kind, and by certain degrees He has ordered His creation, from earth up to heaven, from visible to invisible, from, mortal to immortal. This framework of creation, this most perfectly ordered beauty, ascending from lowest to highest, descending from highest to lowest, never broken, but tempered together of things unlike, all praises God.[44]

This introduces a vital notion in Augustine: the whole contains and demonstrates a beauty that both gathers together and transcends its individual parts. The goodness of the whole includes the frailty of individual creatures. Due proportion, certainly, was critical to Augustine's religious aesthetics:

> At that time I did not know this. I loved beautiful things of a lower order, and I was going down to the depths. I used to say to my friends: "Do we love anything except that which is beautiful? What then is a beautiful object? What is beauty? What is it which charms and attracts us to the things we love? It must be grace and loveliness inherent in them, or they would in no way move us." I gave the subject careful attention, and saw that in bodies one should distinguish the beauty which is a kind of totality and for that reason beautiful, and another kind which is fitting because it is well adapted to some other thing.[45]

Each individual thing is good, but the sum is very good.[46] Further, part of a creature's goodness and propriety is defined by when it exists: "I saw that each thing is harmonious not only with its place but with its time."[47] Augustine argues that one needs perspective in order to define the good of a thing. One has to step back and look at the whole mosaic, so to speak, and not just at an individual tessera or bit of glass. Similarly, a particular frailty, a presentation of some type of decay, cannot be understood without reference to the whole structure. What appears blameworthy as a particular bit of decay may—when

44. Augustine, *Enarration on Psalm 144*.13.

45. Augustine, *Confessions* 4.13.20; cf. Augustine, *Enarration on Psalm* 47.19.31 and *Enarration on Psalm 135*.4–5.

46. Augustine, *Confessions* 7.12.18.

47. Augustine, *Confessions* 7.15.21.

understood as a part that contributes to the whole—shed new light on the phenomenon. And so, as should now be evident, decay and destruction are not themselves endemic as a result of the fall for Augustine.[48]

Conclusions

If the commonly presented view of Augustine's teaching on the impact of the fall on the cosmos is mistaken, then in Augustinian terms, it is wrong to describe violent physical and biological acts in nature as evil. Evil is a relation to corruption in souls. Hence, evil is to be found only in spiritual, reasoning creatures and is a corruption of the original states of moral goodness. The more recent scientific discovery of decay and change in the natural world before humans existed and became alienated from God would not surprise Augustine. Decay does not undermine the creation by suggesting it lacks goodness, nor does it subvert God's work; it is a simple acknowledgment that the creation is fundamentally contingent, limited, and different from God.

After the fall, humans are alienated from creation, but nowhere do I find Augustine saying that the corporeal world has metamorphosed into something else as a result of the fall and is alienated from God. Numerous comments and the implications of his exegesis of Genesis suggest the opposite. While some commentators infer or assume that Augustine believed that the creation is alienated from God and that decay has come into the world as a result of the fall, these authors and the tradition of interpretation have confused the nature of the alienation as used by Augustine. For Augustine, the core problem that humans face is *dislocation* resulting from the fall. This is fundamentally a relational problem: humans no longer relate properly to God, others, and their own selves. Physical phenomena, objects, and corporeal decay now torment humans and are a cause of pain, but such pain is not because these phenomena come unexpectedly into a once-pristine scene from which they were previously absent.

In other words, the fall did not produce hurricanes, earthquakes, plagues, and the like. As a result of the fall, however, humans relate to such things differently and so experience torment. Fear, anguish, and other such responses are moral reactions to physical phenomena, and Augustine blames the fall,

48. This raises the further question of how to account for the problem of pain. If decay is not a result of the fall, is pain? Things that can cause pain, such as animal predation or the sun burning brightly in one's eyes, are not evil and so are not a sign of a postlapsarian corruption. But our reaction, our manner of handling them, are affected by the fall. Pain comes with creatureliness, but mental suffering resulting from that pain is a consequence of evil. Cf. Augustine, *On the Free Choice of the Will* 3.14.40.

not the physical pain itself, for suddenly adding these to the human condition. Certainly, Augustine thought that if Adam and Eve had continued in purity, a greater grace would have been gained, which would have preserved them against decay. But this is a case of failure to receive and to perfect.

The physical world is not by nature evil for Augustine; this point undergirds much of Augustinian thought. Its implications, though, have not always been understood: neither animal violence nor physical cataclysms should be understood as forms of evil resulting from the fall. They are part of nature's operations, and decay is a necessary aspect of any created thing. Only spiritual beings can experience and cause evil; material and sentient beings cannot be said to do so.

This study serves as a salutary demonstration of how a tradition of interpretation, amounting to a substantial misinterpretation, can be read into a major author; it appears logically plausible if considered away from the broader context and so seems "natural," expressing what Augustine must have thought. Yet it is a creation of a later generation. In this signal issue of Augustinian theology, there is no contradiction in accepting the notion of a good creation and Creator while acknowledging the presence of decay and destruction from its initial state as advanced through evolutionary mechanisms.

16

Theodicy, Fall, and Adam

Michael Lloyd

The Problem Observed

You only have to look at the natural world (or look at documentary programs about the natural world) to see that it is riddled with pain, death, disease, and predation. And a moment's reflection will further reveal that these are not incidental to creation but appear to be built into its very fabric. For many animal species, survival involves the necessity of killing and ingesting other animals. The intrinsically violent competitiveness of the natural world and the endemic nature of what looks indistinguishable from suffering[1] raise serious questions for those Jewish and Christian traditions that present us with a prophetic vision of the future in which "the wolf shall live with the lamb" (Isa. 11:6; cf. 65:25)[2]—questions that constitute a challenge to belief in the

1. I put it no more strongly than that because some argue that attributing suffering to animals involves an unwarranted anthropomorphic projection, and some allow that animals do suffer but deny that there is any moral significance to that fact. I have discussed this issue briefly in Michael Lloyd, "Are Animals Fallen?," in *Animals on the Agenda*, ed. Andrew Linzey and Dorothy Yamamoto (London: SCM, 1998), 148–49.

2. This does raise the question of whether these verses should be interpreted as prophetic of a healed and harmonious natural order, free from violent competition and threat—or whether they are best interpreted as being symbolic, like Isa. 40:4, which presumably did not intend its readers to expect a literal flattening out of the geographical and geological landscape. However, it is reasonably clear what the language of Isa. 40:4 is symbolic *of*—the facilitation of Israel's return from exile. It is not clear what the language of Isa. 11:6–9 and 65:25 would be symbolic

goodness of the Creator.[3] I have argued elsewhere that these questions and this challenge are nontrivial and nondismissable, especially for a Christian theologian, for "the cross reveals God as the one who lays down His life that others might live," whereas "the natural world is one in which animals kill others that they themselves might live. The movement of the one in reckless self-giving is in a totally different direction from the movement of the other in ruthless self-preservation."[4]

On the face of it, therefore, the world we inhabit "is *certainly* not the sort of world which one would expect the God we meet in Christ to have created."[5] As it stands, the predatory nature of much of the animal world would tend to disconfirm the belief that this world has been created by the God we meet in Jesus. As Tennyson famously wrote, humans

> trusted God was love indeed
> And love Creation's final law
> Tho' Nature, red in tooth and claw
> With ravine, shriek'd against his creed.[6]

The Problem Intensified

We have always known the predatory nature of the animal world—because such knowledge only takes observation and reflection. Tennyson and his contemporaries also already knew, from geology, of the great antiquity of the earth and, from the fossil record, of the disappearance of whole species.[7] And nine years after the publication of Tennyson's poem, Darwin's *Origin of Species* confirmed the findings of geology and further revealed that our own emergence as humans depended on the same competitive processes that

---

of, if not of a healed and harmonious natural order. The commentaries I consulted take them as prophesying "peace among the animal world" (Claus Westermann, *Isaiah 40–66* [London: SCM, 1969], 410); "the radical transformation of nature" (R. N. Whybray, *Isaiah 40–66* [London: Oliphants, 1975], 278); the overcoming of "the most elemental hostilities in creation" (Walter Brueggemann, *Isaiah 40–66* [Louisville: Westminster John Knox, 1998], 250); and an "ideal scene of harmony in the animal world" (Joseph Blenkinsopp, *Isaiah 55–66* [New York: Doubleday, 2003], 290), etc.

3. Or, on the face of it, to God's omnipotence, for, if the sort of world God wanted is one in which nature is at peace, why could God not have created it that way in the first place?

4. Lloyd, "Are Animals Fallen?," 148.

5. Lloyd, "Are Animals Fallen?," 148.

6. From Lord Alfred Tennyson, *In Memoriam*, canto 56.

7. "'So careful of the type' [i.e., species]? But no. / From scarped cliff and quarried stone / She [Nature] cries, 'A thousand types are gone: / I care for nothing, all shall go'" (Tennyson, *In Memoriam*, canto 56).

led to the loss of a thousand other types. The discovery that some dinosaurs were carnivorous and some had cancerous tumors, for example, and that they were long extinct by the time that humans evolved, meant that pain and suffering and death and disease and predation occurred for eons before there were humans to fall. Therefore, the old theodical move of blaming all natural evil straightforwardly on the fall of Adam and Eve needs to be modified, supplemented, or replaced in the light of pre-Adamic natural evil (which will henceforth be known, appropriately if less than literately, as PANE).[8] This and the following chapter will therefore look at one whole family of such modifications and supplements—one that maintains a concept of nature as in some sense fallen.

The Problem (Mildly) Ameliorated

Before exploring that family of responses, it is worth noting that evolutionary theory is in some ways helpful (as well as in other ways problematic) for the project of theodicy. For the theory of evolution arguably puts moral distance between the Creator and the details of creation, rather as the prologue to the book of Job arguably puts moral distance between God and the acts of natural and moral evil that assail Job and his family. An example is provided by the different perspectives of Charles Darwin and his friend the American naturalist Asa Gray. Darwin pointed out the theodical problem at its sharpest: "I cannot persuade myself that a beneficent and omnipotent God would have designedly created the Ichneumonidae with the express intention of their feeding within the living bodies of caterpillars."[9] Gray, however, found Darwin's evolutionary theory helpful in this regard: "A process in which the laws were designed but the details left to chance might explain nature's more repulsive products without having to ascribe them directly to divine action."[10]

Other (human) examples are offered by Francisco Ayala: "If we claim that organisms and their parts have been specially designed by God, we have to account for the incompetent design of the human jaw, the narrowness of the

8. I say "straightforwardly" because, as I shall discuss below, William A. Dembski has attempted to modify the traditional doctrine of the fall of Adam and Eve in the service of a theodicy for pre-Adamic natural evil. See his *The End of Christianity: Finding a Good God in an Evil World* (Nashville: B&H Academic, 2009).

9. Charles Darwin to Asa Gray, "Letter No. 2814," May 22, 1860, Darwin Correspondence Project, http://www.darwinproject.ac.uk/DCP-LETT-2814.

10. See John Hedley Brooke, "Darwin and Victorian Christianity," in *The Cambridge Companion to Darwin*, ed. Jonathan Hodge and Gregory Radick (Cambridge: Cambridge University Press, 2003), 206.

birth canal, and our poorly designed backbone, less than fittingly suited for walking upright."[11] He therefore suggests that "a major burden was removed from the shoulders of believers when convincing evidence was advanced that the design of organisms need not be attributed to the immediate agency of the Creator, but rather is an outcome of natural processes," and that we should therefore "accept natural selection as the process that accounts for the design of organisms, as well as the dysfunctions, oddities, cruelties, and sadism that pervade the world of life. Attributing these to specific agency by the Creator amounts to blasphemy."[12]

This in no way compromises the ultimate createdness and creaturehood of all things, but it does prevent us from speaking as if the exact form of every creature is fully and unambiguously as it was originally intended to be by the Creator. Evolution acts as a kind of demythologized demiurge operating to some extent independently, under and within the ultimate providence of God. This does not by any means provide a complete answer to the problem, for evolution and the competitive and violent form it has taken (and the "laws" of which Gray writes) do not escape the need for explanation themselves within the creation of a loving God. As Michael Tooley writes of the idea that evolution, not God, is responsible for the design faults of creation: "If the theist who is not a creationist attempts to appeal to this idea, he or she needs to say why an omnipotent, omniscient, and morally perfect being would employ evolution as a way of designing different species. Why leave things at the mercy of a morally unguided process that has had, as one would have expected, a number of bad results?"[13] The theodicist still has a great deal of work to do.

Nevertheless, when Quentin Smith utilizes the predatory nature of the tiger as an argument against the existence of God,[14] or when David Attenborough similarly employs the example of the species of worm that tunnels through the eyeballs of children, leaving them blind by the age of five,[15] the theologian is entitled to respond by attributing such horrendous qualities to the evolutionary process without thereby attributing them to the direct causation of

11. For a list of other proposed "design faults," see Michael Tooley, "Does God Exist?," in *Knowledge of God*, ed. Alvin Plantinga and Michael Tooley (Oxford: Blackwell, 2008), 110–15.

12. Francisco J. Ayala, *Darwin's Gift to Science and Religion* (Washington, DC: Joseph Henry, 2007), 159–60. I do not agree that we should accept natural selection because of its (limited) theodical utility; I believe we should accept it because of the scientific evidence for it and because of its explanatory utility at a scientific level. Having accepted it on its scientific merits, we must then face the theological and theodical questions it raises.

13. Plantinga and Tooley, *Knowledge of God*, 110.

14. See Quentin Smith, "An Atheological Argument from Evil Natural Laws," *International Journal for Philosophy of Religion* 29, no. 3 (June 1991): 159–74.

15. See my *Café Theology* (London: Alpha International, 2005), 82.

God (unless that theologian believes the sovereignty of God to imply that all that occurs is in conformity with the will and purpose of God). The theistic evolutionist does not have to justify every phenomenological and physiological detail as being the direct product and will of the Creator—and, indeed, as I shall argue later, the Christian theologian has a set of christological criteria for disentangling the will of God from the unintended phenomena of creaturely occurrence. Prior to the discovery of the process and mechanism of evolution, there was more pressure on the Christian theologian to justify the world exactly as it was. So to that extent the theory of evolution relieves the theologian of the repugnant apologetic task that she might otherwise at least have perceived to be required of her.

The Problem Addressed

The problem of pre-Adamic natural evil (PANE) has been addressed in a variety of ways (and it is the aim of part 3 of this book to expound something of the breadth of the spectrum of possible theodicies). The different possible approaches could be grouped together under three headings: (1) PANE as instrumental to the purposes of God, (2) PANE as inevitable within the purposes of God, and (3) PANE as inimical to the purposes of God.

PANE as Instrumental to the Purposes of God

In instrumental accounts, God allows PANE or builds PANE into creation because it is instrumental to his purposes. He wants it to occur in his world, not for its own sake—that would make God "The Cosmic Sadist," as C. S. Lewis contemplated characterizing him in a dark moment[16]—but for the sake of some other purpose. What that purpose is differs from account to account. For Augustine and for Karl Barth, it is aesthetic richness—a painting needs dark paints as well as bright paints, a symphony needs discords as well as chords, and in the same way human life, for its richness, requires pain as well as pleasure.

For John Hick, God's purpose for PANE is freedom[17]—because if the world reflected the love, glory, and peacefulness of the immediate presence of God,

16. C. S. Lewis, *A Grief Observed* (1961; repr., London: Faber & Faber, 1966), 27.

17. It is also human growth or "soul-making." But, though that is an essential element of Hick's account of natural evil generally, it is hard to see how that would figure in an account of *pre*human evil in particular. Hick's whole theodicy has been criticized for displaying a similar anthropocentricity. See, e.g., Smith, *Atheological Argument from Evil Natural Laws*, 169. Even with the good of freedom, it is clear that Hick is primarily interested in *human* freedom.

it would not be possible to reject God. Only in a world that is ambiguous, a world that it is possible to see as the good creation of a good God but also possible to see as the godless product of time and chance—only in such a world are we free to choose or reject God. Natural evil contributes to the ambiguity that makes possible the great good of freedom.[18] Hick writes, "Emerging within the evolutionary process as part of the continuum of animal life, in a universe which functions in accordance with its own laws and whose workings can be investigated and described without reference to a creator, the human being . . . is free to acknowledge and worship God; and is free . . . to doubt the reality of God."[19]

For Richard Swinburne, God's purpose in allowing natural evil is to enable "higher-order goods."[20] If I am to show bravery, I need to experience threat. If I am to show compassion, there needs to be suffering that induces that compassion within me. If I am to investigate the natural world in order to fight disease, enable warning to be given of forthcoming earthquakes, and direct lava flows away from inhabited areas, then there needs to be disease, earthquakes, and volcanoes that threaten to cause intense suffering. And, argues Swinburne, it is good that we are able to develop these higher-order goods in ourselves—it deepens us and increases the number of significant actions in which we may engage, thus enriching our lives. He further posits that some of these second-order goods are also experienced enrichingly by animals, thus justifying PANE. Some sort of compassion is arguably demonstrated within the animal world. Some sort of self-sacrificial behavior is demonstrated in defense of offspring. And, though animals clearly do not investigate their world scientifically in the way that humans do, they do "have to work hard, overcoming pain and disease and rejection, to get food and drink for themselves, to avoid predators"—and "the suffering involved in their actions gives a value to their lives that they would not have if they were totally protected and fed by humans."[21]

These instrumental accounts of PANE are generically open to a number of challenges. First, the Christian theologian, who believes that the fullest revelation of God is to be found in the person of Jesus Christ, has to ask why disease and death are so assaulted in the ministry of Jesus, if they are so

18. I have briefly expounded and critiqued the instrumental views of natural evil in Lloyd, "Are Animals Fallen?," 150–55, and more extensively in my doctoral thesis, "The Cosmic Fall and the Free Will Defence" (DPhil thesis, Oxford University, 1997), chap. 2.

19. John Hick, "An Irenaean Theodicy," in *Encountering Evil: Live Options in Theodicy*, ed. Steven T. Davis (Edinburgh: T&T Clark, 1981), 43.

20. See chap. 18 below.

21. See chap. 18 below.

instrumentally necessary to the purposes of God. If courage and fortitude in the face of pain and disease are so highly esteemed by God as to warrant the permission of natural evil, aren't the healing miracles of Jesus depriving the sick person of the opportunity to develop and demonstrate courage and depriving others of the opportunity to demonstrate compassion? Doesn't the immediate healing militate against the need, and therefore diminish the motivation, to investigate the world scientifically in order to combat disease? If it be replied that Jesus is here benefiting from the opportunity to display compassion himself and setting an example for others to do the same, is it not fair to ask whether his acts of healing are done primarily with his own benefit and the benefit of the bystanders in mind—or the benefit of the sufferer? The more positive a view one takes of the instrumental good of suffering, the more this approach comes into tension with the apparent antipathy of Jesus toward suffering, whenever and wherever he saw it. I see no reason why this should not be as true of animal suffering as of human suffering.

Second, instrumental accounts of PANE tend to set up a gnostic-like split between creation and redemption. If it is God's will to create a natural order that is inherently predatory for the instrumental goods that that order will enable, then some account needs to be given of how that may be reconciled with the prophetic vision of a future in which predators and prey lie down together. If natural evil in general and PANE in particular are so necessary to the enrichment brought about by the higher-order goods, will a healed and harmonious new creation be thereby diminished and impoverished? Will there be a loss of richness and opportunity when all things are reconciled, pain and sorrow and the order of things that engendered them have passed away, and God is all in all? The challenge to instrumental accounts here is to demonstrate why that which is desirable in the beginning will not be desirable at the end.

Third, in the absence of such a demonstration, instrumental accounts are vulnerable to the charge that they diminish the praiseworthiness of God, for he who brings an end to pain, loss, and disharmony at the eschaton remains the one who established them in the first place. The victims of that pain, loss, and disharmony, therefore, may be more muted in their gratitude and praise than they would be if God rescued them from an evil that was none of his making and alien to his purposes.

PANE as Inevitable within the Purposes of God

Inevitable accounts take a less positive and fertile view of PANE. For them, God does not *want* it to occur in his world, and a world that was free of all natural evil would be better than the pain-riddled, threatening, and threatened world that we actually inhabit, but it is not possible for God unilaterally to create such a pain-free world. Different versions of the PANE-as-inevitable position give different accounts of the nature of that impossibility.

Process Theology

Process theologians have developed a metaphysic in which, even though God holds as much power as it is possible to hold, it is not possible for him to impose his will or purpose on any creature.[22] For Alfred North Whitehead, the father of process philosophy and theology, the basic building block of reality is not a unit of space, such as an atom or a quark, but a unit of space-time that Whitehead calls an "actual occasion."[23] These actual occasions occur at the rate of between four and ten per second and therefore give the impression of continuity, rather like an old-fashioned cine film whose separate frames are shown at such a rate that they create the illusion of continuous movement. Every moment of space-time, every "actual occasion," has freedom—and has it essentially, not by divine gift.[24] God's only power over any entity is therefore the power of persuasion. God seeks to lure every actual occasion into greater complexity and greater harmony, but he cannot compel any actual occasion to comply. He offers to every actual occasion the best possible option for it to instantiate—what Whitehead calls its "initial aim"—but it is free to accept or reject that recommendation, and there is nothing that God can do if it chooses to reject the initial aim that he offers except to keep offering it the best possible course of action, to keep wooing it. Thus God seeks a world that is harmonious and nonviolent, but he is unable to impose that purpose on an independently free world.

Such a metaphysic successfully defends the goodness of God. If God is unable unilaterally to bring about a world free from pain and predation, then

22. Strictly speaking, process theology does not see PANE as inevitable, as it is logically possible that every actual occasion throughout the history of the cosmos might have accepted God's initial aim on every single occasion. However, I have included process theology as an inevitable position because, as in Augustinian and only way arguments, God wishes a state of creational harmony but is unable unilaterally to instantiate it.

Process theologians treat God's inability here in different ways. On the one hand, in his book *God, Power and Evil: A Process Theodicy* (Philadelphia: Westminster, 1976), David Ray Griffin *redefines* omnipotence as "the power a being with the greatest conceivable amount of power could have over a *created* . . . world" (269); Charles Hartshorne, on the other hand, simply *denies* the doctrine of God's omnipotence—hence his book *Omnipotence and Other Theological Mistakes* (Albany, NY: SUNY Press, 1984).

23. Alfred North Whitehead, *Process and Reality* (Cambridge: Cambridge University Press, 1929), 101.

24. Consequently, process theologians tend to reject the doctrine of creation from nothing, as they fear that such a doctrine would allow for God completely to determine another entity, leaving it without essential freedom.

the facts of pain and predation cannot be used as an argument against either his goodness or his existence. Where such a metaphysic is vulnerable, however, is in failing to provide the basis of a substantial eschatological hope. If God is unable to impose his will on any entity, then he cannot be considered culpable for the current state of the world, but neither is it clear how any final putting right of all things might be confidently predicted. God simply does not have the ability to ensure ultimate reconciliation and restoration. Given the centrality of hope to the Christian gospel, this would seem to render process theology evangelically deficient.

Augustinian Nonbeing Approaches

Stanley Rosenberg has helpfully demonstrated that Augustine did not believe there was no pain or death prior to the fall of Adam and Eve.[25] Thus PANE, for Augustine, was to be explained not as the punitive consequence of human sin but as the natural consequence of finitude. That which comes from nonbeing has a natural tendency to return to nonbeing. That which once did not exist will—without the miraculous intervention of God—return to not existing. Decay is therefore the natural condition of that which has been created out of nothing. So it is an arguable development of Augustine's categories here to suggest that, while God does not intend or desire the decay or death of his creatures, there is an inevitable tendency for that which is finite to cease, and for that which is limited to compete—only God, who is infinite, has life in himself and competes with no other being for space or flourishing.[26]

The difficulty with this view as the basis for a theodicy, however, is the fraught phrase "without the miraculous intervention of God." If this is to be a credible theodicy for PANE, there would need to be some articulation of why that miraculous intervention was not given. If God does not want decay and death to occur to his *ex nihilo* creatures, one might ask, why did he not miraculously preserve them from their inherent tendency to decay? And if he cannot so preserve them, on what basis may we expect a creation set free from its bondage to decay? Christopher Southgate writes movingly of the divine love that is the only possible ground for hope in the face of our innate drive to dissolution:

> It is from the love of the Father for the world, and for the glory of the Son, that other selves gain their existence, beauty and meaning, that which prevents them

25. See chap. 15 above.
26. I am indebted for this idea to Rowan Williams, who often says that "God does not compete with us for space."

> from reverting to nothingness. It is from the self-sacrificial love of the Son for the Father and all his works that each created entity gains the distinctive pattern of its existence, that which prevents the creation from collapsing back into an undifferentiated unity. It is from the power of the Spirit, predictable only in its continual creativity and love . . . that each creature receives its particularity.[27]

But this raises the questions: What is more certain than the love of the Father for the world? What is more fundamental than the self-sacrificial love of the Son for the Father and all his works? What is more given and grounded than the creativity and love of the Spirit? Why then are the beloved creatures of the Triune God not constantly preserved from any internal propensity to perish? The second creation account in Genesis 2 presents us (pictorially) with precisely such a God-given provision for the permanent preservation of finite humanity: the tree of life (v. 9). Humans are finite and mortal—the tree of life is external to them, not an intrinsic part of them. But the tree is God's provision for them, whereby their innate propensity to decay and perish is countermanded. In Genesis 3, their self-separation from God separated them from that provision (vv. 22–23). But what account may we give of why no similar provision was made to preserve God's other beloved creatures? If such nonprovision, or withdrawal of provision, can similarly be traced back to creaturely self-separation from God, then Augustinian nonbeing approaches should be seen as particular examples of a fall argument. If God's nonhuman creatures are seen as lacking sufficient value to warrant such provision, then that would seem to raise existential questions regarding the purpose of their creation, theodical questions regarding what warrants or outweighs their suffering, and ethical questions regarding whether they should be the object of our environmental concern. And if God *cannot* counterbalance their innate tendency toward nonbeing, then this position faces questions concerning the potency of the Creator and the solidity of eschatological hope.[28]

Only Way Approaches

Only way approaches acknowledge that the redness of nature in tooth and claw, the suffering and frustration of individual creatures, and the extinction

27. Christopher Southgate, *The Groaning of Creation: God, Evolution, and the Problem of Evil* (Louisville: Westminster John Knox, 2008), 78. Southgate does not adopt the Augustinian nonbeing approach; he offers a version of the only way argument, which I discuss in the next section.

28. We note in passing that Augustine's theodicy did not depend on the resource of a nonbeing approach alone. He also believed in the fall of Adam and Eve and in the fall of the angels. We shall return to both of these in due course.

of whole species constitute a serious challenge to the goodness of the Creator (which will have to be in some way overcome eschatologically), but they posit, in the words of Christopher Southgate, that "this ambiguity of process was the *only* way in which God could have given rise to a biosphere containing all this value and beauty (including the eventual evolution of a species capable of bearing the image and likeness of God)."[29] They point out the inextricability of value and disvalue in the evolutionary process. It is the competitive, violent, destructive struggle for survival that brings about the admirable speed of the cheetah, the breathtakingly beautiful (but predatory) flight of the swift, and, indeed, the intellectual ability of the human. It was the extinction of the dinosaurs that created the space for the emergence of primates. So interwoven are the value and the disvalue that Holmes Rolston was led to comment that "the cougar's fang has carved the limbs of the fleet-footed deer, and vice versa."[30]

Such a view has to face two serious challenges. The first concerns precisely this apparent assertion of the unique creativity of violence. Surely a religion built on the cross of Christ would shrink from allowing violence such a monopolistic role in the creation of values. Does not the cross of Christ suggest that, contrary to all perception to the contrary, it is the *refusal* of violence that is most creative of value? Where the extinction of one species has led to the rise of another, should we not attribute that more to the extraordinary fertility of a God who brings good out of evil within a fallen creation than to the fertility of violence per se?

The second challenge that only way approaches have to face concerns eschatology. Southgate, one of the leading advocates of an only way theodicy, quotes with approval Keith Ward's assertion that "if there is any sentient creature which suffers pain, that being—whatever it is and however it is manifested—must find that pain transfigured by a greater joy."[31] However, a theodicy that relies on eschatology to the exclusion of any concept of a fall is particularly vulnerable to Ivan Karamazov's challenge to Alyosha: "Imagine that it is you yourself who are erecting the edifice of human destiny with the aim of making men happy in the end, of giving them peace and contentment at last, but that to do that it is absolutely necessary, and indeed, quite inevitable, to torture to death one tiny creature . . . and to found the edifice on her unavenged tears—would you consent to be the architect on those conditions?"[32] Only

29. See chap. 19 below by Christopher Southgate.

30. Holmes Rolston III, *Science and Religion: A Critical Survey* (1987; repr., Philadelphia: Templeton Foundation Press, 2006), 134.

31. See Southgate, *Groaning of Creation*, 78.

32. Fyodor Dostoyevsky, *The Brothers Karamazov*, trans. David Magarshack (Harmondsworth, Middlesex: Penguin, 1982), 287.

way approaches are particularly vulnerable to (a nonanthropocentric version of) this challenge, because they do see the predatory character of nature as being inevitable and thus see the eschatologically transfigured creation as being founded on the necessary suffering of creatures. Fall-based theodicies, by contrast, see predation and suffering as being contingent on the free choices of creatures rather than as being a necessary part of the architecture and a necessary tool of the Architect. We now turn to see whether such theodicies can form a less problematic response to the problem of PANE.

PANE as Inimical to the Purposes of God

Following the divine assault on suffering in the ministry of Jesus, a third family of responses to the problem of PANE refuses to pay it the respect of seeing it as in any way uniquely creative or intrinsic to the purposes of God. On the contrary, it sees PANE as being inimical to the purposes of God and traces it not to God's creational choices nor to his creative limitation but to the choices of free creatures, whose freedom is part of their God-given purpose. It sees PANE as part of the evidence that creation has fallen away from God's original harmonious purposes for it. If the wolf will lie down with the lamb (Isa. 11:6), that is because God's original purpose for them was nondestructive coexistence. If God will eventually reconcile all things (Col. 1:20), that is because it was his original purpose for all things to be in harmony with one another as they are in harmony with him. Destructive disharmony is contrary to and a falling away from his purpose. In the rest of this chapter and the next, we shall explore possible causes of that fallenness.

The story of Adam and Eve's disobedience has traditionally been at the forefront of Christian responses to the problem of evil, and not least to the problem of natural evil (i.e., the suffering that is not caused by human volition and sin). Genesis 3 was commonly read etiologically, as a story told to explain the various disharmonies within the good creation of a good God. The relationship between humans and their environment became disharmonious as a result of the fall (vv. 16–19), just as the relationship between the man and the woman became accusatory and oppressive (vv. 12 and 16), and in Genesis 4 the relationship between their children became violent and lethal. Thus natural evil and moral evil (the suffering that *is* caused by human volition and sin) were both seen to have their origins in the rebellion of the first human couple against the protective and life-giving command of God. Natural evil was unleashed into a formerly harmonious world, making it a place of conflict and threat. The taint of and momentum toward moral evil was passed on by the first couple to the entire subsequent human race—of whom they were believed to be the ancestors—via a punitively painful reproductive process.

Any attempt to use the fall of Adam and Eve for theodical purposes today faces three significant challenges from modern evolutionary theory and genetics: the challenge to inheritance, the challenge to historicity, and the challenge to chronology.

The Challenge to Inheritance

Modern genetic research has made it highly unlikely that the entire human race is descended from a single human pair. The current evidence seems to point to a reproductive community of a few thousand people—and at a date much earlier than the rise of agriculture or cities presupposed by Genesis as the cultural environment of Adam and Eve and their children (see Gen. 4:2, 17).

Though this is a difficulty for those who hold to Augustine's view that original sin is transmitted physically through reproduction,[33] it weighs little against the theodical use of the Adamic fall narrative, for four reasons. First, 1 Corinthians 15 speaks of Adam as "the first man" and of Christ as "the second man" or "the last Adam" (vv. 47, 45).[34] As John Walton points out, "Jesus was neither the second man in time and history, nor was he the last man in time and history,"[35] so clearly physical descent is not part of Paul's understanding of how we are in Adam or how we are in Christ. Second, being "in Christ" can have nothing to do with physical descent, as Jesus had no physical descendants, so there is no reason to believe that being "in Adam" should necessarily involve being physically descended from him either. Third, one of the points on which Paul is most insistent is that being part of Israel does not require one to be physically descended from Abraham, so it is hard to imagine that Paul would have thought being "in Adam" required being physically descended from Adam. And fourth, the Genesis text itself implies that there are other humans in existence at the same time as Adam and Eve: Who else could their children have married, and how else could Cain have founded a city (Gen. 4:17)? So a theodicy based on the fall of free humans is not vulnerable to this finding of modern genetics.

33. For more on this see chap. 15 above by Stanley Rosenberg.

34. For some reason, virtually every English version of the Bible, including those that generally seek to use inclusive language, translates *anthrōpos* as "man" on both occasions in this verse. However, *anthrōpos* is not gender specific, so it should really be translated as "human."

35. John H. Walton, *The Lost World of Adam and Eve: Genesis 2–3 and the Human Origins Debate* (Downers Grove, IL: IVP Academic, 2015), 94.

The Challenge to Historicity

It is commonly assumed that the evolutionary account of human origins in which were discovered the deep continuities of our relationship with other and earlier species and, further, the genetic uncovering of our huge continuities with other species today are in significant tension with the doctrine of the image of God (implying, as it does, a decisive discontinuity with other species, extinct or extant). It is further assumed that the fossil record (demonstrating, as it does, a relentless consistence of predatory patterns of interaction within the created order) is downright incompatible with any historical reading of the Genesis 3 narrative (implying, as it appears to do, a historical disruption of God's harmonious purposes for creation).[36]

It is not the case, however, that continuity need be entirely incompatible with discontinuity. To use the analogy employed in this context by the late Donald MacKay, if you turn a gas tap on very slowly, there will not be enough gas in the air for it to ignite; keep turning it, and still not enough gas in the air; keep turning it, still not; a little further, and suddenly it will ignite. So there can be a completely smooth progress, and yet a decisive difference can occur at a particular moment.[37] The picture of evolution that has been revealed by modern biology is by no means a smooth one, but, in the same way that the increasing gas/air ratio can enable something distinctly new and different to occur at a particular moment, so increasing mental capacity, tool-making ability, social cooperation, aesthetic sensibility, moral awareness, and consciousness of God can lead to the point at which something decisively new happens, and God decides to relate to these creatures in a new way, to give them a new vocation, and to hold them accountable for their actions in a way that would not have been appropriate before that point. An evolutionary account of human origins, with its emphasis on continuity, therefore, is not materially at variance with the doctrine of the image of God, with its implication of a certain discontinuity and difference.

Nor it is incompatible with a symbolic but in some sense historical reading of the human fall narrative. On the contrary, such a scenario logically requires a fundamentally historical account of human sin. If there is a particular moment at which moral awareness has evolved to the point at which it is now appropriate to hold these hominids to account for their actions, there must

36. See part 1 of the present volume for different accounts of the implications of evolutionary theory and modern genetics for the doctrine of the image of God.

37. Donald MacKay used this analogy in a lecture I attended. The nearest I can find to such a usage in his published writings occurs in Donald M. MacKay, *The Open Mind, and Other Essays: A Scientist in God's World*, ed. Melvin Tinker (Leicester, UK: Inter-Varsity, 1988), 73, where this analogy is used to different effect.

have been a first occasion on which a morally responsible hominid made a morally culpable decision. Or, to put it in terms arguably more reflective of the cultural context of Genesis 1–4, if there is a point at which humans have reached the stage of being aware of the divine calling on them, there must have been a first occasion on which they knowingly dissented and diverted from that calling. This second challenge to the theodical utility of the fall of Adam and Eve thus also fails to inflict any significant damage.

The Challenge to Chronology

We noted above that the story of Adam and Eve's disobedience has traditionally been at the forefront of Christian responses to the problem of natural evil. The discovery, therefore, that there has been disease, death, extinction, and predation for eons before humans evolved would seem to be fatal for the theodical use to which the story of the human fall has traditionally been put. How could humans be held responsible for that which predated them by millions of years? As John Polkinghorne puts it, "It is obvious that our knowledge of the long history of life, with the mass extinctions that have punctuated it, does not permit us today to believe that the origin of physical death and destruction is linked directly to human disobedience to God."[38] And therefore, as we noted earlier, the traditional theodicy based on the fall of free humans will need to be modified, supplemented, or replaced.

In his book *The End of Christianity: Finding a Good God in an Evil World*, William A. Dembski attempts just such a modification. Although an advocate of intelligent design, and therefore not persuaded by all the implications of modern evolutionary biology, he offers a theodicy that he claims is completely compatible with all those implications:

> Much of my past work has been on intelligent design and the controversy over evolution. Nothing in this book, however, takes sides in that debate. In arguing that the Fall marks the entry of all evil into the world (both personal [moral] and natural evil), I make no assumptions about the age of the Earth, the extent of evolution, or the prevalence of design. The theodicy I develop here looks not to science but to the metaphysics of divine action and purpose. At the heart of this theodicy is the idea that the effects of the Fall can be retroactive as well as proactive (much as the saving effects of the Cross stretch not only forward in time but also backward, saving, for instance, the Old Testament saints).[39]

38. John Polkinghorne, *Exploring Reality: The Intertwining of Science and Religion* (London: SPCK, 2005), 139.

39. William Dembski, *The End of Christianity: Finding a Good God in an Evil World* (Nashville: B&H Academic, 2009), 9–10. The idea that, though natural evil predates the human

Dembski suggests that God allows natural evil in order "to bring humanity to its senses." Others take a similarly educational, reformative view—notably Eleonore Stump, who writes:

> Natural evil—the pain of disease, the intermittent and unpredictable destruction of natural disasters, the decay of old age, the imminence of death—takes away a person's satisfaction with himself. It tends to humble him, show him his frailty, make him reflect on the transience of temporal goods, and turn his affections towards other-worldly things, away from the things of this world. No amount of moral or natural evil, of course, can *guarantee* that a man will seek God's help. If it could, the willing it produced would not be free. But evil of this sort is the best hope, I think, and maybe the only effective means, for bringing men to such a state.[40]

What is new—and, in my view, self-defeating—about Dembski's position is his suggestion that *prehuman* natural evil was intended to have this reformative effect:

> To make us realise the full extent of human sin, God does not merely allow personal evils (i.e., the disordering of our souls and the sins we commit as a result) to run their course *subsequent* to the Fall. In addition, God allows natural evil (e.g., death, predation, parasitism, disease, drought, floods, famine, earthquakes and hurricanes) to run their course *prior to* the Fall. Thus, God himself wills the disordering of creation, *making it defective on purpose*. God wills the disordering of creation not merely as a matter of justice (to bring judgment against human sin as required by God's holiness) but, even more significantly, as a matter of redemption (to bring humanity to its senses by making us realize the gravity of sin).[41]

It is hard to see the coherence of this position. In any case, in order to be viable as a credible theodicy, it would have to answer four questions that Dembski does not address. The first two questions challenge the analogy that Dembski makes between the retrospective effects of the cross and the (alleged) retrospective effects of the fall. The cross is, in Christian understanding, an act

---

fall, it is nevertheless caused by it, is not a new one. It had nineteenth- and twentieth-century exponents. See Edward Hitchcock's *The Religion of Geology and Its Connected Sciences* (Boston: Phillips, Sampson, 1851); J. Jay Dana, "On the Relations between Religion and Geology," *Biblical Repository and Classical Review* 26 (1846): 296–320. In the twentieth century, see Jock Stein and Howard Taylor, *In Christ All Things Hold Together* (Edinburgh: Fount, 1984), 63, where this view is (briefly) expounded rather than advocated.

40. Eleonore Stump, "The Problem of Evil," *Faith and Philosophy* 2, no. 4 (October 1985): 392–424.

41. Dembski, *End of Christianity*, 145 (emphasis original).

of God (as well as of humans), whereas the fall is precisely *not* to be understood as an act of God. Indeed, the fall is more accurately to be understood as an act *against* God. God is often portrayed in Christian theology as being outside time, and even those Christian theologians who do not see him as being outside time see him as being less limited by the time frames of creation than any of his creatures. So the fact that the effects of the cross may be operative before the historical event of the crucifixion is not, perhaps, impossible.[42] But the first question that Dembski's theodicy would have to answer is this: Why might the choices of time-bound creatures have similarly time-defying effects?

The cross is, in Christian understanding, an act of grace, whereas the fall is precisely to be understood as an act of ungrace, of antigrace, or of disgrace. It is understandable why God might reverse the normal direction of the arrow of time to make the undeservedly good effects of the cross available to those who lived before the crucifixion, precisely because he is gracious. But the second question that Dembski's theodicy would have to answer is this: Why might God reverse the normal direction of the arrow of time in order to inflict the bad effects of the fall on prelapsarian creatures who did nothing to deserve it? Such a move would simply increase the amount of suffering in cosmic history—and utterly innocent suffering at that.

Dembski states that there are two reasons why God has made creation defective on purpose, but both need much more justification than he gives them. The first reason he gives is punitive: as "a matter of justice (to bring judgment against human sin as required by God's holiness)." So the third question his theodicy would have to answer is this: How is it just to make innocent prelapsarian nonhuman creatures suffer for human sin? How does the infliction of suffering on nonhuman creatures "bring judgment against human sin"?

The second reason Dembski gives for why God has willed the disordering of creation in advance of the human fall is redemptive, "to bring humanity to its senses by making us realize the gravity of sin." But punishment must not only fit the crime; it must be as closely associated with it as possible. When you are training a dog not to foul the carpet, you traditionally rub the dog's nose in the mess so as to associate the crime with the punishment in the dog's mind. It would be pedagogically perverse to punish the dog *before* it fouled the carpet. It would be even more pedagogically perverse to punish

42. It is also possible to see the effects of the cross operating before the historical event of the crucifixion on the analogy of a bank giving a loan to a customer on the basis that they are the legitimate heir of a very rich, elderly relative. The bank is thus treating the customer leniently now on the basis that they *will* inherit vast riches in the future. Such a conception of the effects of the cross requires no reversal of the arrow of time.

the *cat* in the foreknowledge that the dog was going to foul the carpet. So the fourth question that this theodicy would have to answer before it could be regarded as a credible theodicy is this: How is it redemptively coherent for the punishment to precede the crime and to be meted out on other creatures than the criminals?

So this attempt to modify the traditional fall of free humans hypothesis, at least in its current form, fails to meet the challenge to chronology.

Conclusion

This chapter has argued, first, that all the families of theodical response to pre-Adamic natural evil (PANE) that do not include some sort of fall account face real challenges. It has argued, second, that the divine assault on the effects of natural evil in the ministry of Jesus suggests that natural evil should be seen as inimical to the purposes of God. Third, it has maintained that a doctrine of the human fall is compatible with the discovery of modern genetics that it is not possible to trace the lineage of all humans back to a single ancestral pair. It has argued, fourth, that a historical human fall is compatible with an evolutionary account of human emergence and, indeed, that it is logically required by such a schema. But, fifth, it has concluded that humans cannot be held accountable for that natural evil that the discovery of evolution has shown to be pre-Adamic. And therefore, sixth, it has suggested that theodical use of the human fall narrative will need to be supplemented in the light of PANE. The next chapter will examine various attempts to supplement the human fall narrative with other fall accounts.

17

The Fallenness of Nature

Three Nonhuman Suspects

MICHAEL LLOYD

I argued in the last chapter that views of suffering as *inevitable* struggle eschatologically and therefore evangelically (i.e., as gospel) and, further, that views of suffering as *instrumental* to the purposes of God fail both individually and generically[1]—that is, they fail to meet the christological criterion of reflecting and grounding the divine hostility to suffering revealed in the healing miracles and the resurrection of Jesus. This left us with the conclusion that only the belief that suffering is *inimical* to the purposes of God is fully compatible with that divine hostility.

This conclusion entails that we must locate the cause of such suffering in some other will than the divine will—in the will of a creature rather than that of the Creator. If God is hostile to suffering and yet suffering occurs,

1. For clarity, the defining characteristic of an instrumental account of suffering, in my usage, is the belief that some element of suffering is necessary to the purposes of God. That is the belief that I am keen to combat. I do not deny (indeed, I rejoice) that God can and does use suffering for good—the crucifixion is *the* case in point. What I deny is that the suffering is necessary to the good. My contention is that, while suffering is harnessable to the purposes of God, it is not harmonizable with those purposes. And that is why God assaults suffering in the healing miracles, nature miracles, death, and resurrection of Jesus—and through the compassionate actions and prayers of his people.

then it is to creaturely agency that we must trace the roots of suffering. If we are not "to regard evil and disorder in the universe as in any way intended or as given a direct function by God in the development of his creation,"[2] then we have to find a plausible way of suggesting how the universe came to have a character that is so at variance with the intentions of its Creator. We must, in other words, articulate a doctrine of the fall. And, as evolutionary biology has demonstrated the occurrence of pre-Adamic natural evil (henceforth PANE), and, as attempts to reclaim the fall of Adam as the retrospective cause of PANE have failed to establish their philosophical or ethical coherence, then a doctrine of the fall must look beyond the human realm in order to explain that occurrence.

There are three nondivine and nonhuman agents or agencies that have been argued to have occasioned the disruption of God's harmonious purposes for creation. Each has been the focus for an account of the fall: the fall of the world-soul, the fall of a free process, and the fall of the angels.[3] In this chapter, we examine each in turn.

The Fall of the World-Soul

Like all the thinkers whose work is outlined in this chapter, and, indeed, all who seek to give an account of evil that traces it to some sort of fall narrative, N. P. Williams refuses to allow any legitimacy, positivity, or divine intentionality to the "ruthless egotism which asserts the right on the part of the individual or the species to live at the expense of others."[4] Instead, writes Williams,

> If we face the facts candidly, we must admit that no one of us, if he had been in the position of Demiurge, would have created a universe which was compelled by the inner necessity of its being to evolve the cobra, the tarantula, and the bacillus of diphtheria. How, then, shall that God, the infinite ardours and pulsations of Whose love bear the same relations to our weak emotions of sympathy

2. T. F. Torrance, *Divine and Contingent Order* (Edinburgh: T&T Clark, 1998), 139.

3. I have elsewhere considered a fourth possibility: a nonprocess view of the fall of nature, as adumbrated by Paul Fiddes. I am not addressing it here, as I believe that it collapses back into an instrumental view of suffering (or a freewill supplement, as I call it). See Michael Lloyd, "The Cosmic Fall and the Free Will Defence" (DPhil thesis, Oxford University, 1997), 214–23.

4. Norman P. Williams in *The Ideas of the Fall and of Original Sin: A Historical and Critical Study* (London: Longmans, Green, 1927), 520. For my similar critique of Austin Farrer's positive attitude toward "that enormous vitality of force" that causes "every physical creature to absolutize itself, so far as in it lies, and to be the whole world," see Michael Lloyd, "Are Animals Fallen?," in *Animals on the Agenda*, ed. Andrew Linzey and Dorothy Yamamoto (London: SCM, 1997), 149.

> and fellow-feeling as the infinity of His wisdom does to our dim and limited knowledge, have done so? The answer can only be that He did not do so; that He did not create such a universe; that, in the words of the most ancient scriptures of our monotheistic faith, in the beginning "God saw everything that he had made, and, behold, it was very good." To explain evil in Nature, no less than in man, we are compelled to assume a Fall—a revolt against the will of the Creator, a declension from the beauty and glory which God stamped upon His work at the beginning.[5]

This raises the questions: Who fell? Who revolted? Who declined from that beauty and glory? Williams draws on Plato's conception of a world-soul to posit the existence of a corporate being, comprising in a unity all the personal and impersonal created agents of cosmic history.[6] It is this metapersonal life force, this inclusively conscious world-soul, that is the agent of rebellion and the cause of cosmic fallenness. And it is to this declension of the world-soul from the beautiful and glorious purposes of God that the created world owes its inglorious conflict and its ugly violence—not to the indifference, impotence, or ulterior motives of God. Williams writes,

> If we can assume that there was a pre-cosmic vitiation of the whole Life-Force, when it was still one and simple, at a point of time prior to its bifurcation and ramification into a manifold of distinct individuals . . . , we shall be in possession of a conception which should explain, so far as explanation is possible, the continuity and homogeneity of evil throughout all ranks of organised life, from the bacillus up to Man. This remote and mysterious event, and not the comparatively recent failure of primitive man to escape from already existing evil, would then be the true and ultimate "Fall." Such a view of the primeval catastrophe and its effects is vaster, more solemn and more awe-inspiring than that which regards the Fall merely as the affair of our species, and it proportionately increases the scope, the amplitude, and the magnificence of redemption.[7]

Williams is aware, however, that he needs to adapt Plato's world-soul if it is to be serviceable for his theodical purposes. Williams's world-soul needs to

5. Williams, *Ideas of the Fall*, 522–23.

6. This view is also advocated by Peter Green, *The Problem of Evil* (London: Longmans, Green, 1920); C. W. Formby, *The Unveiling of the Fall* (London: Williams and Norgate, 1923). Dan Mullaney, in his unpublished article "Creation and Evolution: The Problem of Evil in the Writings and Lectures of Alexander Men," shows that the idea of a fall of the world-soul had already been expounded in the writings of Vladimir Solovyov and Alexander Men. I have expounded the fall of the world-soul hypothesis in more detail in Lloyd, "Cosmic Fall," chap. 3.

7. Williams, *Ideas of the Fall*, 523–24.

be "free, personal, and self-conscious."[8] This attribution of freedom, personhood, and self-consciousness is required if it is the world-soul, rather than the Creator, who is to be held responsible for the vitiation of the creative process. Without freedom, there could be no other "decision" than the one that was made; without personhood, there would be no "other" to make a decision; and without self-consciousness, a decision would be no more than a quasi-neurological impulse. But with freedom, personhood, and self-consciousness, the world-soul becomes a creature that is capable of a loving relationship with its Maker and of significant moral choice—a creature that is therefore arguably so existentially meaningful as to warrant the risks of exactly that rebellion, declension, and vitiation of the whole creative process that is posited as having occurred.

The fall-of-the-world-soul hypothesis might seem implausible today. With Jung's collective unconscious and Bergson's life force very much in the air in the 1910s and 1920s, Williams's position of a corporative being might have felt more plausible. But despite its implausibility to many today, it nevertheless constitutes a genuine fall account, in that it attributes the apparently necessary unchristlikeness of the natural order not to the will of the Creator but to the will of a creature. And it is a genuine attempt to wrestle with the tensions between the character of the natural world as revealed by evolutionary science and the character of God as revealed in Jesus Christ. It is a self-consistent hypothesis, involved in no internal contradiction. And it fits the facts, in that it does not find itself in opposition to any finding of modern science or to any doctrine of the church or any deliberation of Scripture. It does rely on speculation, but it is probably fair to say that that is true of all serious theodical ventures in this area.

The weakness of this position derives from its provenance. Though Williams has sought to extract Plato's world-soul and insert it into an otherwise unchanged Christian theology, it is arguable that in doing so he has in fact brought a Greek philosophical horse into the Trojan city of Christian theology. His world-soul requires not just the separability of body and soul in straightforwardly Platonic fashion but also the existence of the world-soul prior to the physical creation of the world.[9] This was a move that the church

8. Williams, *Ideas of the Fall*, 525.

9. It might be possible to develop a fall-of-the-world-soul hypothesis in which the fall takes place not, as Williams suggests, prior to but after the physical creation of the world. Such a restatement would have to face two challenges. First, it would have to posit such a fall prior to the occurrence of any morally significant conflict. One of the pressures that pushed Williams into positing a *premundane* fall is the need for that fall to predate (if it is to explain) the apparent unharmoniousness of the constituent parts of creation—manifested in the incompatible interests of those constituent parts at the inanimate level, predation at the animate level, pain

was not prepared to make with regard to individual human souls, and it is difficult not to see this move as indicative of a Platonic preference for the soul over the body. The fact that the fall of the world-soul was simultaneous with its fragmentation into "a manifold of distinct individuals" and their embodiment into material existence makes it vulnerable to the criticism that Williams has unintentionally bought into a Platonic unease with both diversity and physicality—an unease that seems in tension with a fully Christian doctrine of both creation and resurrection.[10] I have argued elsewhere that "with God seen as omnipotent . . . , there seems no reason why, if diversity and physicality are to be seen as positively (and not just relatively) good, they were not a feature of the original creation of God."[11] The fact that this hypothesis makes them not original but subsequent to and dependent on sin gives grounds for concern regarding whether this is a graft that the body of Christian theology can accept or the transplant of such different genetic material that it leads to the doctrinal equivalent of graft-versus-host disease. The dependence of this position on speculation is not in itself a weakness—as mentioned above, any serious hypothesis in this area, including my own, is likely to make use of a degree of speculation. However, it will need to be speculation that is compatible with the Christian faith it is attempting to defend, and it is here that the fall of the world-soul hypothesis might be seen to be vulnerable.

The Fall of a Free Process

John Polkinghorne believes that "God no more expressly wills the growth of a cancer than he expressly wills the act of a murderer, but he allows both

at the sentient level, and suffering at the conscious level. Second, the later the fall is posited to have occurred, the more vulnerable the account would be to the charge that such a fall becomes decreasingly plausible. For the longer a moral agent persists in a particular moral direction, the less likely it is for a different direction to be taken, as a particular moral direction forges a particular moral character. Moral agents are thus more vulnerable to declension from the divine will when they are newly created. (Was it an implicit acknowledgment of this fact that led the Jewish tradition to date the fall of the angels to either the second or the fourth day of creation?) However, some such revised account of the fall-of-the-world-soul hypothesis might be possible.

10. First Corinthians 15 insists on the continuing importance and glory of the physical aspects of human existence in their renewed form as opposed to the Platonic and gnostic hope to be redeemed *from* the body. First Corinthians 15:35–49 also insists on the continuing importance and glory of the whole diversity of God's creation in a way that would be inconceivable within a Platonic frame of reference. See N. T. Wright, *The Resurrection of the Son of God* (London: SPCK, 2003), 312–61.

11. Lloyd, "Cosmic Fall," 152. I have drawn on my unpublished doctoral thesis extensively in this section.

to happen. He is not the puppetmaster of either men or matter."[12] This puts Polkinghorne in the category of those who see PANE as inimical to the purposes of God. In the same way that N. P. Williams refuses to see the cobra, the tarantula, and the bacillus of diphtheria, in their current destructive forms, as direct instantiations of the will of God, so Polkinghorne refuses to see the growth of a cancer as the express will of the Creator for any of his creatures. If, as I have written elsewhere, fallenness refers to "the perceived gap between the universe as it is now and the universe as it was intended to be in the creation purposes of God,"[13] then Polkinghorne would appear to believe in the fallenness of the created order. Natural evil is not willed by God for the goods that come in its wake; indeed, it is not directly willed by God at all. But this raises the question: How then does it occur within God's world?

It is here that Polkinghorne introduces the theodicy for which he is known: "the free-process defence."[14] Just as the freewill defense seeks to defend God against the charge of being responsible for moral evil by attributing it to the free will of individual creatures, so Polkinghorne's free-process defense seeks to defend God against the charge of being responsible for natural evil by attributing it to the freedom that he has given to the created order as a whole. As Polkinghorne writes,

> Rather than this world being a ready-made divine puppet theatre, we have seen that its character of being the home of an evolving process can be understood theologically as showing it to be a creation in which creatures are allowed "to make themselves." This seems indeed to be a great good, but it also has a necessary cost. . . . All of created nature is allowed to be itself according to its kind, just as human beings are allowed to be according to our kind. As a part of such a world, viruses will be able to evolve and cause new diseases; genes will mutate and cause cancer and malformation through a process that is also the source of new forms of life; tectonic plates will slip and cause earthquakes. Things will often just *happen*, as a matter of fact, rather than for an individually identifiable purpose.[15]

In other words, it is good for the interactions of creaturely entities to be undetermined. It is good for the system of creaturely systems to be free and able to

12. John C. Polkinghorne, *Science and Providence: God's Interaction with the World* (Philadelphia: Templeton Foundation Press, 2005), 78.

13. Michael Lloyd, "Fall," in *Dictionary of Ethics, Theology and Society*, ed. Paul Barry Clarke and Andrew Linzey (New York: Routledge, 1996), 368.

14. See, e.g., Polkinghorne, *Science and Providence*, 77.

15. John Polkinghorne, *Exploring Reality: The Intertwining of Science and Religion* (London: SPCK, 2005), 143 (emphasis original).

bring about new possibilities, for creation in some manner to be free to create itself—and not merely to unfold passively according to the predetermined blueprint of its Creator. Polkinghorne is suggesting that this gives creation a dynamic, creative potentiality that is a good great enough to warrant the negative consequences of such a freedom—especially when combined with an eschatology that will eventually restore what is lost, repair what is fractured, and resurrect what has died.

However, the free-process defense is open to two significant challenges. The first concerns the eschatology that is so important to Polkinghorne and his free-process defense[16] but that is open to a serious criticism. Polkinghorne believes that God will usher in a new age in which "death will be no more; mourning and crying and pain will be no more, for the first things have passed away" (Rev. 21:4).[17] Indeed, he believes it to be coherent to think that the laws of the redeemed universe "will be perfectly adapted to the everlasting life of that world." But, as he frankly acknowledges, "if this is so, there is a problem that we have to face squarely: If God can do that eventually, why was it not done straight away? To put it bluntly, if the new creation is going to be so wonderful, why did God bother with the old, so seemingly less than wonderful in its change and decay?"[18] To answer this "very serious question," Polkinghorne makes use of two concepts: Jürgen Moltmann's reworking of the Kabbalistic notion of *zimzum* and John Hick's notion of epistemic distance.[19] What these concepts have in common is the assumption that the overt presence of God would render creaturely freedom impossible and that, therefore, the creation of a free, self-creating universe requires that God, in some sense and to some extent, absents himself from his handiwork.[20] As

16. It is revealing that Polkinghorne has coedited one book and authored two others on eschatology. See John C. Polkinghorne and Michael Welker, eds., *The End of the World and the Ends of God: Science and Theology on Eschatology* (Harrisburg, PA: Trinity Press International, 2000); John C. Polkinghorne, *The God of Hope and the End of the World* (London: SPCK, 2002); and the popular-level *Living with Hope: A Scientist Looks at Advent, Christmas, and Epiphany* (Louisville: Westminster John Knox, 2003).

17. See Polkinghorne, *God of Hope*, 115.

18. Polkinghorne, *Living with Hope*, 46–47.

19. For a criticism of Hick's concept of epistemic distance, see Keith Ward, "Freedom and the Irenaean Theodicy," *Journal of Theological Studies* 20 (1969): 249–54. For my assessment of the points at issue between them, see Lloyd, "Cosmic Fall," 66–68.

20. Polkinghorne, *Living with Hope*, 47. Polkinghorne does not address the question of whether the universe will still be free and self-creating after its eschatological transformation. If he were to answer in the affirmative, he would have to face this question: How do we know that the suffering will not continue? If he were to answer in the negative, then creation's eschatological transformation would seem to involve a loss of value. In a personal communication, Vince Vitale points out that there might be certain valuable states of affairs in the old creation that could not be present in the new "and certain (even more) valuable states of affairs in the

Polkinghorne writes, "The present creation exists at some distance from its creator. Of course, God is present to this world, but in a way that is veiled, so that creatures are not overwhelmed by the sheer power and majesty of divine reality."[21] But this raises the questions: Is the power and majesty of God overwhelming? Is the absence of God more creative, fertile, and liberating than his presence? Is it not a (pagan) misconception of God to see his presence as a threat to creaturely freedom? Where can creatures be more fully themselves and more free than in the direct presence of God? When Moltmann writes of God's withdrawal into himself as "a movement which allows creation the space for its own being,"[22] do we not have to ask whether space can ever rightly be conceived as a zero-sum game between God and creation? Would that not make God himself a spatial being? A part of his own creation? As Rowan Williams likes to say, "God does not compete with us for space." God's presence does not cramp, warp, or misshape—it is his presence, surely, rather than his withdrawal, that lets be.

The second challenge that the free-process defense needs to face is that it is not clear that the freedom of the evolutionary process—or of the cosmic processes more generally—is a good that is sufficiently valuable to warrant the frustration, waste, damage, pain, tragedy, and grief that it occasions. The free-process defense needs to argue that the freedom of the process is a good that is valuable enough to justify the evil that it enables. But it is difficult to see how the freedom of a nonpersonal being (or of a nonpersonal nexus of nonpersonal beings) might constitute such a good. Indeed, it is difficult to see what the freedom of a nonpersonal being might mean or how it differs from randomness or, if it doesn't differ from randomness, what the good of randomness might be.

---

new that could not be present in the old, and perhaps God values all of these states of affairs, recognizes that they cannot all be actualized at the same time, and so allows for different ages such that at different times a diversity of the valuable states of affairs He values will be realised." Thus there would not need to be a loss of value *overall*. Indeed, Vitale offers support for the view that some valuable states of affairs will not be possible in the new creation: "We will not, for example, be able to carry the burden of another's suffering, something which is of great value." Thus the sketch that Polkinghorne gives of a free-process defense could be turned into a full canvas in which this challenge is met. The analogy of surgery, however, suggests that such a restated free-process defense might face continuing challenge. It would widely be granted that carrying out a surgical procedure to remove a malignant tumor is a valuable act. It might not be so widely granted that inducing a malignant tumor in a patient so as to make possible the valuable act of surgery would be in any way defensible. Some valuable acts are only justifiable in an already-messed-up context. Similarly, I would argue that, however good the "higher-order" goods that suffering makes possible, we still need a robust doctrine of the fall.

21. Polkinghorne, *Living with Hope*, 47.

22. Jürgen Moltmann, *God in Creation: A New Theology of Creation and the Spirit of God* (Minneapolis: Fortress, 1993), 87.

The freedom of a *personal* being makes relationship possible and love meaningful. The freedom of an intelligent being makes them a potential agent and a real person rather than a robot. The freedom of an intelligent being makes them capable of actions that may be said to be theirs and to make those actions significant. In contrast, it is difficult to imagine what the good of the freedom of an impersonal being might be or what such freedom makes possible that would not have been possible otherwise. Polkinghorne argues that it seems to be "a great good" that creation should have the capacity to create itself, but it seems invalid to use the word "create" of a nonpersonal entity. Does not the word "create" imply an element of intentionality? It is unclear what exactly is the good here for which God would be warranted in allowing the possibility—or probability or well-nigh certainty—of such terror and torment.

The freedom of a personal being, however, makes that being capable of relationship, of love, of significant action, of creativity—in short, of what might be expected to reflect and delight the Triune Creator God. It is therefore to a theodicy based on the freedom of a personal being that I now turn.

The Fall of the Angels

As in the other two fall accounts examined in this chapter, exponents of the fall-of-the-angels hypothesis adhere to a view of suffering as inimical to the purposes of God. Eric Mascall writes that "it is difficult to feel, when we consider the course that evolution has taken on this earth, that, even before man appeared, everything was going precisely as God ideally intended it to go."[23] In other words, he accepts the reality of PANE:

> It is therefore interesting to recall that before the creation of man, sin had already occurred in the angelic realm, and that a firmly based tradition ascribes to the angels, among other occupations, that of tending the material world. If there is any truth in such ideas, if the world in God's intention was to be one in which the realms of matter and of spirit were to be linked together in intimate union . . . , and if the lower levels of this cosmos were to be under the surveillance and loving care of the higher, it seems reasonable to suppose that defection and rebellion in the angelic realm will drastically disorder the material world, and that, while its development in accordance with God's purpose will not be entirely frustrated, it will be grievously hampered and distorted.[24]

23. Eric L. Mascall, *Christian Theology and Natural Science* (London: Longmans, Green, 1956), 36.

24. Mascall, *Christian Theology and Natural Science*, 36.

Mascall not only accepts the reality—and, implied within that, the wrongness—of PANE; he also has a narrative account to give of how such wrongness could happen within the good creation of a loving and omnipotent God. It is necessarily a narrative account, for any attempt to attribute the pain and suffering of the world to any other source than the Creator—and that, if one takes the inimical view of the relationship between suffering and the purposes of God, is simply what is required of a theodicy—must attribute it to a creature. And a creature, being finite and not eternal, necessarily exists in some relation to time and space. Narrative is thus the form that a doctrine of the fall must inevitably take.[25] Building on Mascall's narrative, therefore, we may offer the following narratival outline of how the fall-of-the-angels hypothesis accounts for the declension of the universe from its intended harmoniousness in the creation purposes of God to its current unintended dividedness, disintegration, and disorder, which are so contrary to the purposes of God as revealed in the healing, reconciling, and ordering work of Jesus Christ.

The Creation of Angelic Beings

We have already seen how, when N. P. Williams adapted the Platonic concept of the world-soul for theodical purposes, he recognized the need to attribute freedom, personhood, and self-consciousness to it. The same qualities are needed of angelic beings if they are to be theodically serviceable—and that is how they have historically been conceived of in Jewish and Christian tradition. The hypothesis is that they were created with that genuine otherness without which relationship is impossible, freedom is illusory, moral subjecthood is meaningless, and God is necessarily to be held directly accountable for their every action.

The Interrelatedness of the Human, Cosmic, and Angelic Dimensions of Creation[26]

Posited interaction between the angelic and human worlds goes back to early biblical tradition, as the story of Jacob's ladder reveals (Gen. 28:10–22). Toward the end of the Old Testament period, a belief developed that each nation was represented, defended, and protected by a guardian angel (Dan. 10). During the intertestamental period, this interaction between the angelic and the human was taken further. The Book of the Watchers, for example, has the angels playing an intercessory role on behalf of humanity: the fallen watchers

25. This is the implication, too, of Augustine's privation argument. If evil is not substantial, it must be historical. If it does not exist, then it must occur. There is, therefore, a narrative to be told of its occurrence.

26. This section is an abbreviation of Lloyd, "Cosmic Fall," 245–49.

who ask Enoch to intercede on their behalf are told, "It is you who should be petitioning on behalf of men, and not men on your behalf" (1 Enoch 15:2). In the book of Jubilees, the watchers are given the roles of watching over the children of men, instructing them in moral behavior and scientific progress (Jubilees 4:15–22). In the New Testament, these traditions seem to have developed into belief in both churches and individuals having guardian angels (see, respectively, Rev. 2–3; Matt. 18:10).

In addition to the interaction between the angelic and human realms, Jewish and Christian traditions also posit interaction between the angelic and the physical dimensions of reality. As we saw above, Mascall claims "that a firmly based tradition ascribes to the angels, among other occupations, that of tending the material world."[27] In support of this assertion, we might point to "the angels of the spirit of fire and the angels of the spirit of the winds, and the angels of the spirit of the clouds and darkness and snow and hail and frost, and the angels of the resounding and thunder and lightning, and the angels of cold and heat and winter and springtime and harvest and summer, and all of the spirits of His creatures which are in heaven and on earth" in the book of Jubilees (2:2). This same ascription is visible in the Similitudes, where we are told that "the spirit of the hoar-frost is its own angel, and the spirit of the hail is a good angel" (1 Enoch 60:17).[28] Again, this persists, more sparsely and with more restraint, in the New Testament (see Rev. 7:1; 16:5).[29] Mascall's claim thus seems justified.

Add to these traditions the assumption, in both the Old Testament and the New, that the prayers of physical humans make a difference in the heavenly realms (see Dan. 10:12; Eph. 6:10–20; Rev. 5:8), and the assumption that the angelic is involved with therapeutic, liberating, and resurrection purpose within the physical world (see, respectively, John 5:4; Acts 12:7; Matt. 28:2), and it is not implausible within this narrative to suggest that so interrelated are the different dimensions of creation that a rupture within the relationships of the spiritual dimension might rupture relationships within the physical dimension.

The Fall of the Angels

The freedom of any creature (vis-à-vis its Creator and its fellow creatures) not only makes its moral choices and its loving relationships meaningful; it also

27. Mascall, *Christian Theology*, 36.

28. H. F. D. Sparks, ed., *The Apocryphal Old Testament*, trans. M. A. Knibb (Oxford: Clarendon, 1984). The "Similitudes" is the name commonly given to chapters 37–71 of 1 Enoch.

29. I do not intend any authoritative equivalence between noncanonical texts (such as Jubilees and 1 Enoch) and canonical texts (such as Revelation). Nor do I think that Mascall intended such an equivalence. He is merely insisting that he is making use of an already existing tradition—not indulging in ad hoc innovation.

makes its fall possible. The story of the angelic fall is not directly narrated in the biblical traditions. However, the predominantly Lukan expression of "evil spirit(s)" (see Luke 7:21; 8:2; Acts 19:12–16) implies an event or process by which they became evil. Without some such fall narrative, it is difficult to see how God would not be responsible for creating them evil and therefore how he would not be culpable for their deleterious and destructive acts. Similarly, Jesus's reference to Satan falling like lightning from heaven (Luke 10:18), and John the Divine's vision of Satan being thrown out of heaven (Rev. 12:7–12), though they do not directly relate a fall narrative,[30] do imply knowledge of some such expulsion-from-heaven tradition as is embodied in (the notoriously difficult to date) 2 Enoch 29:4–5. The statements do not make sense without the assumption of such a background tradition. Nor, I suggest, is the original and essential goodness of creation possible to maintain (given the arguments of the previous chapter) without some such narrative, in which the intended harmony of creation in the purposes of the Creator is lost due to the free choice of free creatures.

The Consequent Distortion of Creation

Here is the innovative element in Mascall's hypothesis:

> If the world in God's intention was to be one in which the realms of matter and of spirit were to be linked together in intimate union . . . , and if the lower levels of this cosmos were to be under the surveillance and loving care of the higher, it seems reasonable to suppose that defection and rebellion in the angelic realm will drastically disorder the material world, and that, while its development in accordance with God's purpose will not be entirely frustrated, it will be grievously hampered and distorted.[31]

Given the interrelatedness of the different dimensions of creation, a division between elements of the angelic realm and their Creator occasioned divisions within the other dimensions also. Competitiveness within the relationship between the fallen angels and God led to competitiveness creeping into the network of relationships that constituted the natural order. This disharmony in the heavenly realms was reflected within the earthly realm, and creation

30. Luke 10:18 cannot directly and primarily refer to the traditional fall-of-the-angels narrative, as it relates to the mission of the seventy (or seventy-two). Revelation 12:7–12 cannot directly and primarily refer to the traditional fall-of-the-angels narrative, as the events related there are ascribed to "the blood of the Lamb and the word of [the Christian martyrs'] testimony" (v. 11) and are therefore to be located within church history. Thus it cannot directly and primarily refer to the event or process by which spirits created by a good God became "evil."

31. Mascall, *Christian Theology*, 36.

began to develop away from the *shalom* that was God's purpose for all he had made. Just as George Caird argued that "the solidarity of man with the rest of creation is so close that in some way or other nature must bear the consequences of man's sin,"[32] so those who advocate the fall-of-the-angels hypothesis suggest that the solidarity of the angels with the rest of creation is so close that sin in the angelic realm must also issue in a fallen and disrupted natural order.

The distortedness of creation prior to the human fall is often believed to be at odds with a plain reading of the early chapters of Genesis, which are thought of as assuming the harmony of creation and humanity prior to the rebellion of Genesis 3. The division between our first parents and their Creator is then perceived as having "brought death into the world and all our woe."[33] A closer reading of the text, however, does not suggest that prior to the human fall "everything was going precisely as God ideally intended it to go."[34] First, there is the serpent. However the serpent is interpreted, there is already within creation that which is deliberately working against the purposes of God.[35] Second, Adam and Eve are commanded to "fill the earth *and subdue it*" (Gen. 1:28)—the implication being that there is something there that requires to be subdued. Third, the narrative sets the action within a garden, and there is no suggestion that the garden was coextensive with the whole of creation. On the contrary, the location of the garden "in the east" (Gen. 2:8) and the expulsion of Adam and Eve from the garden (Gen. 3:23) show that it was not. Thus, even if the impression is given that prelapsarian humanity

32. George B. Caird, *Principalities and Powers: A Study in Pauline Theology* (Oxford: Clarendon, 1956), 55–56.

33. John Milton, *Paradise Lost* 1.3. I use the phrase "first parents" because of its association with Milton (see *Paradise Lost* 3.65). I recognize that modern geneticists do not believe all human beings to be descended from a single breeding pair. For my assessment of the theological significance of this conclusion, see chap. 16 above.

34. Mascall, *Christian Theology*, 36.

35. The objection is sometimes raised against the fall-of-the-angels hypothesis that Rom. 5:12 assumes that death came into the world "through one human being"—not through angels. However, Paul also assumes that *sin* came into the world "through one human being," but he is clearly aware of the Gen. 3 narrative in which Adam and Eve are tempted to rebel by the serpent (see 2 Cor. 11:3). However he interpreted the serpent, therefore, Paul was aware of a creature that was actively working against the purposes of God before Adam and Eve rebelled. He must therefore be restricting himself to the human dimension of the narrative when he writes of sin entering the world through one human being, and death through sin. If Paul had gone on to write of death spreading to all *creatures* from its initial entrée in human disobedience, that would indeed count against the narrative I am here building. But he doesn't. He writes of death spreading to all human beings, thus demonstrating that it is purely the human dimension of the narrative with which he is dealing at this point. So, as it stands, there is nothing in Rom. 5:12 that contradicts the fall-of-the-angels hypothesis.

lived in perfect harmony with its environment, it cannot be concluded that the whole of creation existed in such perfect harmony; the clear implication of the narrative as it stands is that it did not. There is therefore no discrepancy between the Genesis narrative and the belief that death and predation predated the emergence of humans.

But, if we accept—as modern science and the fall-of-the-angels hypothesis do—that disease and death and predation and pain predated the human fall, then God's evaluation of his handiwork as "very good" (Gen. 1:31) would seem to commit us to one of two beliefs: either (1) there is a discrepancy between the Genesis narrative and the findings of modern science or (2) disease and death and predation and pain are deemed good by God—in which case we need to go cap in hand to either the inevitable or the instrumental views of suffering, with all their inherent difficulties that we explored in the previous chapter. In response, however, we need to note the cultural context in which the Genesis narratives emerged. The Babylonian creation account Enuma Elish sees the creation of the physical world as the accidental by-product of the cosmic battle between Marduk (who assumes command of the gods) and Tiamat (the chaotic ocean from which the gods emerged). Marduk slays Tiamat, and her carcass becomes the raw material of the sky and the earth. In polemical contradistinction to the pagan assumption that the physical world was an accidental by-product of cosmic violence, the Hebrew creation account insists that creation was intended, willed, and valued by its Creator. The "very good" of Genesis 1:31 should therefore be seen as an insistence on the *ontological* goodness of the created order. The cosmos was not an accidental by-product. The creation of humans was not an afterthought. God created them deliberately and delights in his creation. This fundamental assertion of the ontological goodness of creation is not contradicted by the position that creation was already fallen, prior to the human rebellion. Creation is not now *as* God intended, but it is still *what* he intended. The substance of creation remains divinely intended, even though its injurious interactions are not. Even a fallen world remains ontologically good in the estimation of its Creator.[36] Seen in this way, Genesis 1:31 does not contradict either the findings of modern evolutionary science or the fall-of-the-angels hypothesis.[37]

36. This distinction between moral goodness and ontological goodness enables, at a personal level, the humble acknowledgment of our sinfulness alongside the simultaneous maintenance of a robust and psychologically healthy sense of self-worth.

37. I note with interest, but do not know how to evaluate, John H. Walton's intriguing argument that "the technicalities of the Masoretic assignment of accents patiently worked out according to their rankings indicate that in day five [of creation] the great sea creatures (*tannînim*) are not included in the statement that 'it was good.'. . . If the *tannînim* are chaos creatures, they are . . . not functioning in the ordered system as they were designed to do—they

The Evolution of Humanity

Though the angelic fall has "grievously hampered and distorted" the development of the material world, Mascall insists that God's purposes within it have not been "entirely frustrated." God's purposes for his creation have been sufficiently *non*frustrated for creatures to have evolved who reflect enough of the characteristics of their Creator to be realistically described as being "in his image."

I gave a conjectural account of the nature of this process in the previous chapter, so here I shall only note that one of the strengths of the fall-of-the-angels hypothesis is that it is fully able to accommodate an evolutionary account of human emergence without having to accept all the means and consequences of the evolutionary process as being directly the work or the will of God. The position of an angelic fall vitiating the development of creation enables us to accept the goodness of the project of creation—what, in the last section, we referred to as its ontological goodness—without thereby having to accept any and every method and product of the evolutionary process as being, in a direct and undifferentiated way, exactly in accordance with the creational intentionality of God. Mascall's ambivalence between the distortion of and the purposiveness within the development of the material world is exactly the ambivalence that theodicy requires and that the fall-of-the-angels hypothesis supports and sustains.

The Human Calling

Once humanity had emerged from the tangle of violent interactions and competitive struggles that make up the battle for survival, and once it became appropriate to speak of that emergent species as being in the image and likeness of God, then that species was given the task of ruling over the rest of creation (Gen. 1:26–28). Rule was not to mean exploitation but was to reflect the rule of God and therefore to be characterized by care (Gen. 2:15). And care, within the context of a world that was divided and distorted, necessarily entailed healing. Thus, in addition to filling the earth, humanity was called on to subdue it—to restore it, under God, to that harmony and *shalom* that was always God's intention for all that he had made. If we wish to know what would have constituted the nature of such a therapeutic vocation, we need look no further than the ministry of Jesus.

---

are in the ordered system but not of the ordered system" (*Lost World*, 55–56). If *tannînim* may be read as referring to fallen angels, then the latter may not be included within the "very good" of Gen. 1:31. However, I think I prefer the argument given above, that the "very good" is best understood as referring to ontological goodness.

The Human Calling Forsaken

As we noted above, the freedom of any creature (vis-à-vis its Creator and its fellow creatures) not only makes its moral choices and its loving relationships meaningful; it also makes its fall possible. This necessarily narratival hypothesis continues by suggesting that humans, far from being the solution to the problem, became part of the problem. Far from fulfilling their therapeutic vocation to restore creation from the deleterious effects of the angelic rebellion, they joined in that rebellion. Far from being instrumental in bringing creation back to that harmony that was the Creator's intention for it, they compounded its disharmony and became exploiters rather than healers. Thus the continued distortedness of creation is the consequence of the human failure to respond to the call and mission of God, though its original distortion was not of human making.

The Human Calling Fulfilled

There was one, however, who confronted those more sinister powers, who did not join in their rebellion,[38] who did not give those parasitic powers his divinely ordained authority,[39] and who therefore exercised that dominion over creation that humanity had always been intended to exercise: life-threatening storms were stilled, demons were exorcised, the sick were healed, the dead were raised. In other words, the fallenness of creation was subdued, the restoration of creation was inaugurated, and—as humans were intended to be the instantiaters and mediators of God's caring rule—the kingdom of God was seen and proclaimed.

The Cosmic Atonement

One solitary exception to the forsaking of the human vocation is, however, hardly a fulfillment of the plans and purposes of God. So, while the living out of the human vocation to heal creation is indeed seen in the ministry

38. See especially the accounts of Jesus in the wilderness in Matt. 4 and Luke 4, which seem to present Jesus's refusal of the temptations as him succeeding where Adam failed. Interestingly, it is this episode that Milton recounts in *Paradise Regained*.

39. In the Lukan wilderness narrative, Satan claims that the kingdoms of the earth and their splendor and authority have "been given over to" him (Luke 4:6). It is usually assumed that they have been given to him by God. I suggest that this verse is better understood as implying that human beings, by their worship of the creaturely rather than the Creator and by their consequent wrong decisions, have given Satan a de facto authority that he does not have de jure and an operational scope that he would not otherwise have. Hence demonic power is to some extent parasitic on human sin.

of Jesus, it is in the cross and resurrection that the soteriological vision of the New Testament is primarily focused. In New Testament perspective, the atonement is more than the reconciliation of humanity with God, Jew with gentile, slave with free, male with female, humanity with nature, people with themselves, and nature with itself. It is also the driving out of "the ruler of this world" (John 12:31) and the disarming, defeat, and reconciliation of the principalities and powers (Col. 1:20; 2:15). This reconciliatory aspect may help to explain why God allows evil and malevolent beings to continue to exist after their fall, despite the damaging and destructive effect of that continued existence—"not wanting any to perish, but all to come to repentance" (2 Pet. 3:9).[40] It is on the cross that the fundamental divisions of creation are ultimately healed, and it is in the resurrection that we see the firstfruits of the renewed and restored creation.

The Restoration of Creation

This eschatological vision of creation freed, healed, and glorified—grounded in the reconciling work of the cross and inaugurated in the resurrection of Christ—is expressed in the New Testament in terms of the fall being (at least) undone—Satan defeated (Rom. 16:20; cf. Gen. 3:15); the curse revoked (Rev. 22:3; cf. Gen. 3:14, 17); access to the tree of life opened (Rev. 22:2; cf. Gen. 3:22–24); heaven and earth remade (Rev. 21:1–4); death, sorrow, crying, and pain eradicated (Rev. 21:4); and human vice-regent rule over creation restored (Rom. 5:17; Rev. 22:5).

Conclusion

In this chapter, I have attempted to put flesh on the bones of Eric Mascall's sketched fall-of-the-angels hypothesis. It is my contention that this narrative—mythological though it clearly is[41]—provides a basis for the eschatological hope that inevitable views of suffering find difficult to ground and a basis for the divine hostility to suffering that instrumental views find difficult to ground. Indeed, I suggest that the constant attempt to relieve suffering and its causes manifested in the healing miracles of Jesus, the constant attempt to defuse the

40. Note, too, the call on the angels of the churches to repent in Rev. 2–3. The word ἄγγελος (*angelos*) can, of course, mean "messenger," but it would be odd for John to call on the ones carrying his letters to the churches to repent.

41. I use the word "mythological" here in its technical sense of offering an explanatory account of the human condition with reference to supernatural beings or events—not in the popular sense of "false or fictitious." The popular sense would, of course, invalidate my theodicy.

natural order of its threat and disorder in the nature miracles of Jesus, and the normative attack on death in the resurrection of Jesus together provide the Christian theologian with a much-needed set of christological criteria for disentangling the will of God from the unintended phenomena of creaturely occurrence. Thus this hypothesis has the significant pastoral advantage of not making God the enemy of the sufferer and the inflictor of their pain. On the contrary, when taken together with the cross and a high Christology, the fall-of-the-angels hypothesis makes God One who suffers with them rather than One who is the cause of their suffering and their pain.[42]

There is a host of possible objections that this hypothesis needs to meet, which we have not had space in this chapter to attempt to answer. All that I have tried to do is to present a coherent narrative, compatible with both the scriptural tradition and the findings of evolutionary biology and recent genetics, that attributes the violence, threat, and mortality endemic within the natural world to the actions of creatures rather than to the intentionality of the Creator. If we are to avoid problematizing hope and taking too positive (and pastorally damaging) a view of suffering, that is simply what is required of a theodicy.

42. These are, of course, not mutually exclusive. It is perfectly possible to believe that God causes our suffering (for a good and loving reason) and that he suffers with us. However, as I argued in the previous chapter, that would set up a gnostic-like split between the God who inflicts suffering on us and the God who suffers with us and (ultimately) takes it away. I suggest that it would also diminish our impulse to praise God for fighting and (ultimately) eradicating suffering, if we knew that it was he who had inflicted it in the first place.

18

An Irenaean Approach to Evil

RICHARD SWINBURNE

I suggest that it would be good for an agent P to allow (or to cause) a bad state of affairs E (an evil) to occur, if and only if (1) allowing E (or an evil equally bad) to occur is the only way in which P can bring about some good state G, (2) P does all he can to bring about G, (3) P has the right to allow E to occur, and (4) G is a sufficiently good state, such that the good of allowing it to occur probably outweighs the badness of E. Thus suppose P is the parent of a child suffering dental pain in an era before dentists could use anesthetics. It is not a bad act for P to take the child to the dentist and allow him to suffer the pain of a dental filling (E), for the sake of the child's subsequent pain-free dental health (G), so long as (1) that is the only way in which he can bring about that good state (G), (2) P takes the child to a competent dentist, and (3) as a parent, P has the right to take the child to the dentist. (This third clause is important. No complete stranger has the right to take a child to the dentist to have his tooth filled without the permission of the child's parents, even if that stranger thereby promotes a good state.) And (4) the good of subsequent dental health probably outweighs the evil of the suffering.

The theodicy presented in this paper is called "Irenaean" since Irenaeus (ca. AD 130–202), bishop of Lyons, taught that God made a world containing both good and evil in order that people might have the opportunity to freely choose the good. See especially Irenaeus, *Against Heresies* 4.37–39, and the summary of Irenaeus's views in John Hick, *Evil and the God of Love*, 3rd ed. (New York: Palgrave Macmillan, 2010; first published 1966), 211–15.

Now we humans could not always give a child dental health without the child having to suffer, but God, who is by definition omnipotent and perfectly good, could do so. It is only the logically impossible that an omnipotent God is unable to do. So extrapolating from the case of suffering to the case of evils generally, and from the case of humans to the case of God who can do anything logically possible, I suggest that God could allow an evil E to occur so long as the following four conditions are satisfied:

1. It must be logically impossible for God to bring about some good G in any other morally permissible way than by allowing E (or an evil equally bad) to occur. For example, it is logically impossible for God to give us libertarian free will to choose between good and bad (i.e., free will to choose between these despite all the causal influences to which we are subject) and yet also to cause us to choose the good. It is logically impossible for God to bring about the good of us having such a free choice without allowing the evil of a bad choice to occur (if that is what we choose).
2. God must do everything logically possible to bring about G. Thus if he brings about suffering in order to give us the opportunity of freely choosing whether to bear it courageously or not, he has also to have given us free will.
3. God must have the right to allow E to occur (i.e., it must be morally permissible for him to allow E to occur).
4. Some sort of comparative condition must be satisfied. It cannot be as strong as the condition that G be a good greater than E is an evil, for we are often justified, in order to ensure the occurrence of a substantial good, in risking the occurrence of a greater evil. A plausible formal way of capturing this condition is to say that the expected value of allowing E to occur—given that God does bring about G—must be positive.

I shall summarize the claim that with respect to some evil E, if there is a God, he could—compatibly with his perfect goodness—allow it to occur in order to promote a good G as the claim that *E serves a greater good*. I hold that these four conditions are satisfied with respect to all known kinds of evil. Clearly I cannot show that in detail in a short paper,[1] but I can give reason to believe that these conditions are satisfied for the main kinds of evil from which humans (and animals) suffer and so give reason to believe that they hold universally.

1. I argue this case at book length for many different kinds of evil in Richard Swinburne, *Providence and the Problem of Evil* (Oxford: Clarendon, 1998).

I begin by pointing out ways in which condition (1) is satisfied for various kinds of evil, starting with moral evil (i.e., the evil that either deliberately or through negligence humans cause to each other). I have already alluded to the traditional freewill defense, which points out that an agent having a free choice between good and evil can (logically) only be brought about by allowing the agent to bring about evil. It is good that the free choices of humans should include *genuine* responsibility for *other* humans, and that involves the opportunity to benefit or harm them. God has the power to benefit or harm humans. If other agents are to be given a share in his creative work, it is good that they have that power too (although to a lesser degree). A world in which agents can benefit each other but cannot do each other harm is one where they have only very limited responsibility for each other. If my responsibility for you is limited to whether or not to give you a wide-screen TV set, but I cannot cause you pain, stunt your growth, or limit your education, then I do not have a great deal of responsibility for you. A God who gave agents only such limited responsibilities for their fellows would not have given much. God would have reserved for himself the all-important choice of the kind of world it was to be, while simply allowing humans the minor choice of filling in the details. He would be like a father asking his elder son to look after the younger son and adding that he would be watching the elder son's every move and would intervene the moment the elder son did a thing wrong. The elder son might justly retort that, while he would be happy to share his father's work, he could only really do so if he were left to make his own judgments regarding what to do within a significant range of the options available to the father. A good God, like a good father, will delegate responsibility. But in order to allow creatures a share in creation, God has to allow them the choice of hurting (rather than benefiting) others and thus frustrating the divine plan. So by allowing such hurting God makes possible the greater good of humans freely choosing to benefit (rather than harm) each other and thus cooperating in God's plan.

But humans' good free choices are not merely good in themselves and in virtue of their immediate consequences. All human choices are character forming—each good choice makes it easier for the agent to make his next choice a good one—as agents can form their own characters. Aristotle famously remarked that we become just by doing just acts, prudent by doing prudent acts, brave by doing brave acts.[2] That is, by doing a just act when it is difficult—when it goes against our natural inclinations (which is what I understand by "desires")—we make it easier to do a just act the next time.

2. See Aristotle, *Nicomachean Ethics* 1103b.

Thus we can gradually change our desires so that—for example—doing just acts becomes natural. Thereby we can free ourselves from the power of the bad desires to which we are subject. But again the great good of us having the free choice of character formation (choosing the sort of people we are to be) can (logically) only be had if there is the danger that we will allow ourselves to corrupt our characters (and so become bad people).

I turn now to natural evil—that is, evil of a kind unpreventable by humans, such as the evil of suffering caused by disease of a kind currently unpreventable. What is known as the "higher-order goods" defense points out that certain kinds of especially valuable free choice are possible only as responses to evil. I can (logically) only show courage in bearing my suffering if I am suffering (an evil state). My suffering from disease when I have the strong temptation to self-pity gives me the opportunity to show courage. It is good that we should have the opportunity (occasionally) to do such actions as involve resisting great temptations because thereby we manifest our total commitment to the good. (A commitment that we do not make when the temptation to do otherwise is not strong is not a total commitment.)

It is good too that among the good actions that we should have the opportunity to do is to help others who are suffering and deprived by showing sympathy to them and helping them to cope. Help is most significant when it is most needed, and it is most needed when its recipient is suffering and deprived. But I can (logically) only help others who are suffering if there is the evil of their suffering. In these cases, if there is a God, he makes possible the good of free choices of particular kinds, between good and evil, which (logically) he could not give us without allowing the evils (or evils equally bad) to occur. If God is to give us a real free choice between helping and not helping others, he must make a world where others really do suffer. And merely allowing the suffering caused by moral evil would not give very much opportunity for such choices; for this we need disease, accident, and the weakness of old age.

It is good too that among the choices available to humans should be the choice not merely of helping others to cope with natural evils such as disease but also of whether to reduce the number of such natural evils in future (e.g., prevent diseases). But to have this choice we need to know what causes these evils. The normal way in which we (the scientists among us, supported by money from the rest of us) try to discover such things is the inductive way. We seek to discover the natural processes (bacteria, viruses, etc.) that bring about diseases and then construct and test theories of the mechanisms involved. But scientists can only do that if there are regular processes producing the diseases, and they can only learn what these are by studying many populations and studying under which circumstances some disease is transmitted and under which it is not. So for the great good of this choice of investigating (or alternatively—not bothering to investigate), there is required the necessary evil of the actual disease. If humans are to have the great opportunity of devoting their lives to scientific research for human benefit or not bothering to do so, there have to be sufferers from disease to make this possible. Many of the early church fathers saw rationality (of which the ability to pursue such scientific inquiry is a paradigmatic example) and free will as the two things that humans have that constitute their being made "in the image" of God.[3]

All the same, an objector may ask, would it not be better if God planted in us strong true beliefs about the causes of all diseases and other natural evils and then just left us with the choice of whether or not to cure them? Is the opportunity to exercise rationality in this way worth the price? But if God abolished the need for rational inquiry and gave us strong true beliefs about the causes of things, that would greatly reduce the difficulty of making moral decisions and so would make it much less easy for us to show total commitment to the good and to form heroic characters. As things are in the actual world, most moral decisions are decisions taken in uncertainty about the consequences of our actions. I do not know for certain that if I smoke, I will get cancer, or that if I do not give money to some charity, people will starve. So we have to make our moral decisions on the basis of how probable it is that our actions will have various outcomes—how probable it is that I will get cancer if I continue to smoke (when I would not otherwise get cancer) or that someone will starve if I do not give money (when they would not starve otherwise). These decisions in a situation of uncertainty about their consequences are not merely the normal moral decisions; they are also the hard ones. Since probabilities are so hard to assess, it is all too easy to persuade yourself that it is worth taking the chance that no harm will result from the less demanding decision (i.e., the decision that you have a strong desire to make). And even if you face up to a correct assessment of the probabilities, true dedication to the good is shown by doing the act that, although probably the best action, may have no good consequences at all.

So both in order to give us the opportunity to deal with all-important matters by exercising our rationality and in order to give us the opportunity

3. Thus ninth-century theologian John of Damascus wrote that God "creates with His own hands man of a visible nature and an invisible, after His own image and likeness: on the one hand man's body He formed of earth, and on the other his reasoning and thinking soul. . . . The phrase 'after his image' clearly refers to the side of his nature which consists of mind and free will, whereas 'after His likeness' means likeness in virtue so far as that is possible." *On the Orthodox Faith* 2.12, in *Hilary of Poitiers, John of Damascus*, ed. Philip Schaff and Henry Wace, trans. S. D. F. Salmond, *The Nicene and Post-Nicene Fathers of the Christian Church*, series 2, vol. 9 (Oxford: James Parker, 1899), 30–31.

to manifest our commitment to the good most strongly (and thereby make ourselves very good people) by making choices in a situation of uncertainty, it is good that God should not cause us to be born with strong true beliefs about the consequences of our actions but instead should give us the opportunity to choose whether to seek more certain knowledge of the consequences of our actions. Getting this knowledge will involve getting more data about the consequences of events—for example, data from the past about what has happened to people who have smoked in ignorance of the possibility that smoking causes cancer. Seeking more certain knowledge, in other words, involves once again relying on normal induction, and that requires the existence of natural evils.

What next about criterion (2)? Because this is a short paper, I shall assume that in these cases when free will—especially free will of certain kinds—is the great good for which God allowing evil to occur is a necessary condition, we do have the necessary free will by which we choose which action to do, and that that free will is libertarian free will (i.e., freedom to choose between alternatives despite all the influences to which we are subject).[4] Given that we do have libertarian free will, it is certainly responsible free will—our actions make the great differences to ourselves and each other that I have illustrated, and thereby we have serious responsibility for ourselves and each other. So suppose there are goods and evils for which conditions (1) and (2) are justified, what about condition (3)? Does God have the right to cause or allow evil to occur to humans for the sake of some greater good? The trouble may seem more acute in that in many cases, including some mentioned above, good for one human is promoted by evil endured by a different human. Does God have the right to make you suffer for my benefit?

To cause (or sometimes even to allow) someone to suffer for his own good or the good of someone else, one has to stand in some kind of parental relationship toward him. I do not have the right to let some stranger, Joe Bloggs, suffer for his own good or that of Bill Snoggs, but I do have *some* right of this kind in respect of my own children. I may let my son suffer somewhat for his own good or for the good of his elder brother—as when I entrust the younger to the temporary care of the elder with the risk that the elder may hurt the younger. Or I may make my infant daughter undergo the painful experience of a bone marrow transplant in order to save the life of my son. I have such a right in respect of a child of mine because in small part I am

4. For full-length defense of the claim that humans have libertarian free will, see Richard Swinburne, *Mind, Brain, and Free Will* (Oxford: Oxford University Press, 2013), esp. chaps. 4, 5, 7, and 8.

responsible for that life and for many of the good things that it involves. It is because the parent is the source of much good for the child that the parent is entitled to take some of it (or its equivalent) back if necessary (e.g., in the form of the life having bad aspects). If the child could understand, he would understand that the parent gives life, nourishment, and education, subject to the condition that the child's life might include periods of suffering, although remaining overall a good life. If this is correct, then a God who is so much more the source of our being than are our parents has so many more rights in this respect; for we depend on him totally from moment to moment, and the ability of parents and others to benefit us depends on him. But it must remain the case that God's rights are limited by the condition that he must not over time take back more than he gives. He must be on balance a benefactor.

But there do so often look to be lives in which bad outweighs good. I urge, however, that this is a wrong assessment of many lives because it does not take into account a good that I have so far not mentioned—the good of being of use to others. It is an enormous good for anyone to be of use—whether by what they do by free choice or by what they do involuntarily or by what happens to them—including what they suffer. Helping someone freely is clearly a great good for the helper. We often help prisoners, not by giving them more comfortable quarters but by letting them help the handicapped; and we pity rather than envy the "poor little rich child" who has everything and does nothing for anyone else. And one phenomenon prevalent in contemporary Western Europe in recent years draws this good especially to our attention—the evil of unemployment. Because of our systems of social security, the unemployed on the whole have enough money to live without too much discomfort; certainly they are a lot better off than are many employed in Africa or Asia. What is evil about unemployment is not just any resulting poverty but the uselessness of the unemployed. They often report feeling unvalued by society, of no use, "on the scrap heap." They rightly think it would be a good for them to contribute, but they can't.

It is not only intentional actions freely chosen but also ones performed involuntarily, which have good consequences for others, that constitute a good for those who do them. If the unemployed were compelled to work for some useful purpose, they would surely be right to regard that as a good for them in comparison with being useless. And it is not only intentional actions but experiences *undergone* involuntarily (or involuntary curtailment of good experiences, as by death) that have good consequences that constitute a good for her who has them (even if a lesser good than that of a free intentional action causing those consequences). Consider the conscript killed in a just and ultimately successful war in defense of his country against a tyrannous aggressor. Almost all peoples, apart from those of the Western world in our generation, have recognized that dying for one's country is a great good for the one who dies, even if he was conscripted. Consider, too, someone hurt or killed in an accident, where the accident leads to some reform that prevents the occurrence of similar accidents in the future (e.g., someone killed in a rail crash that leads to the installation of a new system of railway signaling that prevents similar accidents in the future). The victim and his relatives often comment in such a situation that at any rate he did not suffer or die in vain. Although they still normally regard the suffering or death as on balance an evil, they would have regarded it as a greater misfortune for the victim (quite apart from the consequences for others) if his suffering or death served no useful purpose. It is a good for us if our experiences are not wasted but are used for the good of others, if they are the means of a benefit, which would not have come to others without them.

Someone may object that the good for the victim is not, for example, dying in a railway crash when that leads to improved safety measures but dying in a railway crash when you know that improved safety measures will result; and, more generally, that the good is the experience (the "feel good") of being of use, not merely being of use. But that cannot be right, for what one is glad about when one learns that one's suffering (or whatever) has had a good effect is not that one learns it but that it has in fact had a good effect. If one did not think that—whether one knows about it or not—it would be good that the suffering should have some effect, one would not be glad about it when one learned that it did. To take an analogy: it is only because I think it a good thing that you pass your exams—even if I don't know about it—that I am glad when I come to know about it. And so generally. It is a further good that one has a true belief that one's suffering has had a good effect, but that can only be because it's a good in itself that it has had that effect. And if one thing that is good when one learns about it is not merely that others have benefited in some way but that by one's own suffering one has been of use in causing that effect, then that is good even if one does not learn about it.

It follows from being of use being a great good that whenever God allows some evil to occur to B (e.g., causes B to suffer) in order to provide some good for A (e.g., the free choice of how to react to this suffering) that B is benefited as well. His life is not wasted; he is of use (either by enduring some evil or by his availability to do so). He is of use to A but also of use to God; he plays a role in God's plan for A. And to be of use to the good source of being in the redemption of his creation is an enormous good. The starving are of use to the wealthy on whose doorstep they appear because—but for them—the wealthy would have no opportunity to be of use. They are the vehicle whereby alone the wealthy can be saved from self-indulgence and learn generosity. And thereby they are of use to God.

When one takes into account that those whose evil state is the means of great good to others (and also often to themselves) thereby also receive this enormous benefit, it becomes plausible to suppose that God has the right to cause the evil. However you weigh the one against the other, the evil carries with it the great good of being of use, which contributes toward making the lives of the victims on balance good lives and so ones in which God has the right to include some evil. But, I must add, if any life on earth is still on balance bad, God has an obligation to compensate for that bad in the afterlife so that the total life of such an individual will be on balance good. That, in his omnipotence, he can do. Christianity teaches that humans live again in a new world after their death, and clearly God can compensate any persons whose lives on earth are on balance bad with a good afterlife.

Before I turn to condition (4), I must say something about nonhuman animals. Animals do not—I reasonably assume—have libertarian free will to choose between good and evil and so do not do wrong. But all animals react to nociceptive stimuli (stimuli caused by bodily damage), and higher animals react to them in much the same way as do humans, which suggests that they suffer just as much as we do. Their reactions include not merely aversive behavior (e.g., quick withdrawal of a hand that touches a hot surface) but changes of blood pressure and heart rate and galvanic skin response. However, appearances may be misleading, and here is my *very* brief summary of the present stage of scientific research about this.[5] It is generally agreed that there are two neural pathways to the brain by which bodily damage affects human brains and thereby human conscious life: the discriminative path, by which we learn where and of what kind is the damage, and the affective path, which causes the suffering in the sense of the intensely disliked feeling. The aversive behavior is produced by brain events caused by events in the discriminatory path. The affective path may be blocked (e.g., by morphine) while the discriminatory path functions normally. Suffering is correlated with activity in an area of the brain called the anterior cingulate cortex (ACC). So whether animals suffer depends on whether they have an affective path. Invertebrates have entirely different nervous systems from ourselves, and so we do not have any evidence about whether they have an affective path. Only mammals have an ACC, and so we do not know whether any path to the brains

5. For scientific details see Colin Allen, Perry N. Fuchs, Adam Shriver, and Hilary D. Wilson, "Deciphering Animal Pain," in *New Essays on the Nature of Pain*, ed. Murat Ayede (Cambridge, MA: MIT Press, 2005), 351–66.

of nonmammalian vertebrates is an affective path. Although mammals have a neural path anatomically similar to the affective path in humans, it is only in humans and some humanoid primates that the path terminates in the prefrontal cortex (a brain area that only humans and some humanoid primates have). A human prefrontal cortex differs significantly from a humanoid primate one, notably in being three times larger. It is not implausible to suppose that in consequence humans suffer more than other primates, but no one knows just how much difference the nature of the prefrontal cortex makes. Further scientific research (including more research into the causes of reactions other than aversive behavior) may improve our knowledge in this area a little, but since animals cannot tell us about their feelings, and since all animal brains are somewhat different from ours, we will never be in a position to know with any very great confidence how much most animals suffer. The only reasonable assumption is that many animals do suffer, but that the further we go down the evolutionary ladder, the less they suffer.

Given that animals do suffer, clearly they often suffer when their suffering is not caused by humans and does not in any way benefit humans and so cannot be justified by the animals having the good of being of use to humans. This is most obviously the case with respect to the suffering of animals from disease or the actions of other animals in the many millennia before the evolution of humans.[6] Now, it can be a good thing freely to choose to do some action A only if doing A is a good thing in itself even if not freely chosen. Many of the good actions that we perform freely, and that necessarily involve responses to bad states, are ones that the higher animals also perform—I am assuming—unfreely. Animals have to work hard, overcoming pain and disease and rejection, to get food and drink for themselves, to avoid predators, and to save the lives of their offspring. When animals suffer through drowning or fire or predators, what happens to them often provides useful information to other animals of their group about how to avoid these things, and—evidence indicates[7]—makes other animals feel compassion for the sufferers (and for A to feel compassion for B is a good for both A and B). The suffering involved in their actions gives a value to their lives that they would not have if they were totally protected and fed by humans. Like ourselves, they cannot overcome suffering unless they have suffering to overcome, or learn from the suffering of others or feel compassion for them unless those others suffer, or sacrifice their own lives to save their offspring unless they are

6. Genesis 3:16–19 regards the fall as the cause of two kinds of suffering characteristic of humans—more intense birth pangs and the suffering involved in agricultural labor—but not of suffering in general.

7. See Jonathan Balcombe, *Second Nature: The Inner Lives of Animals* (New York: Palgrave Macmillan, 2010), 131–32.

killed, and so on. So in respect of much animal suffering also, it would seem that conditions (1) and (2) are satisfied; and so, for the same reason as with humans, is condition (3).[8] But since the goods that animal suffering makes possible for themselves and other animals are less than those that human suffering makes possible (since animals do not have the good of a free choice between good and evil and so the possibility of choice of character formation), it must surely be the case that, if condition (4) is to be satisfied, animal suffering must be less than that of humans. If there is any animal suffering (e.g., that of the great apes) not caused by humans and that does not in any way benefit humans, which is as bad as human suffering, my theodicy would be inadequate and would need to be supplemented by some other theodicy.

I come finally to the crucial issue of whether even human suffering satisfies the comparative condition (4). Someone may agree with me that one does need a substantial amount of various kinds of evil in order to provide the opportunities for various goods, but she may feel that there is just too much evil in the world for the good it produces. There is just not enough good made possible by Hiroshima, the Holocaust, the Lisbon earthquake, or the Black Death, claims the objector. With this objection—that, if there is a God, he has overdone it—I feel *considerable initial* sympathy. And when I now proceed to justify God allowing these things, I hope that the reader will not think me callous. These are horrible things, and when they happen to people, we must weep. But in cooler moments we must analyze the logical issues in as rigorous and dispassionate a way as we can and take very seriously the goods that the evils make possible. And the first thing to note when we reflect dispassionately is that each evil state or possible evil state eliminated eliminates at least one actual good. And each small addition to the number of sufferers makes a small addition to the number of those who can make serious good choices. Suppose that one less person had been burned by the Hiroshima atomic bomb. Then there would have been one less person able to show courage and several less relatives of those burned with stronger reasons than the rest of us to show sympathy for those burned and to campaign to avoid a similar disaster in future; and that means a few less very serious choices for several people. Of course, removal of one evil state or the possibility of one evil state will not

8. If, as Christians normally suppose, animals do not have a life after death, there will not be the possibility of compensation for any animals whose life is, on balance, not worth living. Trent Dougherty, *The Problem of Animal Pain: A Theodicy for All Creatures Great and Small* (New York: Palgrave Macmillan, 2014), chaps. 6–8, has urged that God's goodness requires him to provide a life after death for sentient animals and that some Christians have supposed that God provides such a life. Dougherty supposes that sentient animals are resurrected and develop into rational beings with the kind of moral choices that humans have (and indeed that both humans and sentient animals develop into much more godlike beings).

remove much good, any more than the removal of one grain of sand will make much difference to the fact that you still have a heap of sand. But the removal of one grain of sand will make a bit of difference, and so will the removal of one evil state. And each diminution in the seriousness of the evil caused diminishes the seriousness of the moral choices open to us.

Sometimes the problem with great evils is not the number of sufferers but the degree of the suffering. So, the objector might ask, if there is a God, is not the suffering that he imposes or allows others to impose sometimes too intense for the good that it makes possible? But evils wouldn't matter so much if only the lesser evils occurred, and so it wouldn't matter so much if we ignored them. By allowing the more serious evils to occur, God forces on people who have allowed themselves to live easy lives (and so become insensitive to more ordinary moral demands) the hard choices that alone (given those persons' moral torpor) will allow them to begin to become holy people rather than sink into subhuman selfishness. So many ordinary selfish people who see evils of serious torture or very painful disease are moved to make those life-changing choices (which no ordinary evils would move them to make), choices by which they eventually become saints.

What the objector is asking for is that even if there should be diseases, they not be ones that maim or kill; that accidents incapacitate people for a year or two but not for life; that we should be able to cause each other pain or not help each other to acquire knowledge but not to damage our own or each other's characters; that our influence should be limited to those with whom we come into contact, but that there should be no possibility of influencing distant generations for good or ill; and that most of our beliefs about how to cause effects, good or evil, should be beliefs with which we would be born. Such a world would be a toy world: a world where things matter but not very much; where we can choose, and our choices can make a small difference, but the real choices remain God's. The objector is asking that God should not be willing to be generous and trust us with his world and not give us occasional opportunities to show ourselves at our heroic best.

But surely, says the objector, there is a limit to the suffering that a God would be justified in causing for the sake of the good that it makes possible. Yes, of course, there is such a limit. And there is also a limit to the actual amount of suffering that any human suffers (except perhaps as a result of one's own choice). There is a limit of time—these days, it is roughly the eighty years of a human life—and there is clearly also a limit of intensity. What the objector must be claiming is that the actual limit is too wide—if there is a God, he asks too much of us. But the objector must take into account the great benefits for the sufferer, which I discussed earlier, of having a free choice of how to cope with his suffering and form a holy character and being privileged by his suffering to give others the opportunity to help him. When these things are taken into account, there begins, I believe, to be considerable plausibility in the claim that the expected benefit of God allowing that quantity and degree of suffering to occur that actually occurs outweighs the evil of the suffering.

Consider this small thought experiment. Suppose that you exist in another world before your birth in this one and are given a choice of the sort of life you are to have in this one. You are told that you are to have only a short life, maybe of a few minutes, although it will be an adult life in the sense that you will have the richness of sensation and belief characteristic of adults. You have a choice of the sort of life you will have. *Either* you can have a few minutes of very considerable pleasure, of the kind produced by some drug such as heroin, which you will experience by yourself and which will have no effects at all in the world (e.g., no one else will know about it); *or* you can have a few minutes of considerable pain, such as the pain of childbirth, which will have (unknown to you at the time of the pain) considerable good effects over several years on others yet to be born. You are told that, if you do not make the second choice, those others will never exist—and so you are under no moral obligation to make the second choice. (Moral obligations are obligations to someone, and you can only have moral obligations to those who exist at some time, past, present, or future.) But you seek to make the choice, which will make *your* own life the best life for *you* to have led. How will you choose? The choice is, I hope, obvious: you should choose the second alternative.

The great value for us of being of use (by our actions or suffering) to others is, I believe, something very near the surface of the New Testament. A relevant text is the words of Christ as cited by Paul in his farewell sermon to the church at Ephesus when he urged the importance of "remembering the words of the Lord Jesus, for he himself said, 'It is more blessed to give than to receive'" (Acts 20:35). Or, again, recall these words of Jesus: "You know that among the Gentiles those whom they recognize as their rulers lord it over them, and their great ones are tyrants over them. But it is not so among you; but whoever wishes to become great among you must be your servant, and whoever wishes to be first among you must be slave of all. For the Son of Man came not to be served but to serve, and to give his life a ransom for many" (Mark 10:42–45). Greatness, Jesus seems to be saying, consists in service and is not a reward for service. God would be mad to allow endless suffering to give endless such opportunities for painful service, but God does not give any of us (except perhaps as a result of our own choice) endless suffering. He makes us suffer at most for the short period of our earthly life in order that in that life we may help others and form ourselves—and we would be poorer without those opportunities.

19

"Free-Process" and "Only Way" Arguments

CHRISTOPHER SOUTHGATE

In this chapter I shall consider the problem of evil in evolution through approaches that acknowledge the ambiguity of the natural processes concerned.[1] The same processes that have given rise to this remarkable natural world—with its extraordinary creaturely diversity, intricacy, complexity, and beauty—also involve vast amounts of suffering among creatures,[2] many of which are denied, by predators or parasites, any possibility of flourishing.

I identify the theological problem associated with evil in evolution as being this: there seems to be so much disvalue, so much suffering, alongside the values that have arisen within the creation. The specific disvalues that concern me are not pain in and of itself, or death, or yet "waste," but the suffering engendered by predation and parasitism and the extinction of species, driven by natural selection.[3] How could an all-loving God have created a set of processes that

1. In this essay the term "evil" is used in its common sense in the literature of theodicy, to mean harms to creatures and the suffering those harms cause (in creatures capable of experiencing suffering). It does not necessarily connote moral wickedness.

2. For a justification of the term "suffering" as applied to creatures possessed of sophisticated sentience, see Christopher Southgate, *The Groaning of Creation: God, Evolution and the Problem of Evil* (Louisville: Westminster John Knox, 2008), 4–5, 136–37.

3. Southgate, *Groaning of Creation*, 7–10.

gave rise to "Nature, red in tooth and claw"? Worse, might there be a sense that God has used the suffering of creatures and the wholesale extinction of species as a means to an end?

I will consider two main types of arguments that seek to address this problem:

1. Types of argument that suppose that the freedom within the processes behind evolution is a good that can be a counterweight to the disvalues that arise from the processes. I group these under the heading "free-process arguments," even where the author concerned has not used that precise term.
2. Types of argument that suppose that this ambiguity of process was the *only* way in which God could have given rise to a biosphere containing all this value and beauty (including the eventual evolution of a species capable of bearing the image and likeness of God). I call these "only way arguments," as that term is increasingly being adopted in the literature.

Two starting presumptions need to be acknowledged. First, that the scientific consensus arrived at in the hundred years after the publication of Darwin's theory of evolution by natural selection represents, in broad terms, the truth about how species have arisen, evolved, and gone extinct. Evolutionary theory is a much-contested area of science that has seen some exciting expansions in recent years.[4] However, these disputes are all conducted within an overall neo-Darwinian frame. Note that the recent interest in cooperation in evolution does not dissolve the problem that successful creaturely characteristics are refined by the (often very painful) defeat of the unsuccessful.[5] Cooperation only changes the pattern of winners and losers—natural selection works because there are always losers.[6]

Second, and crucially, free-process and only way arguments all take as their starting point that *God* created these ambiguous processes and that the disvalues in creation cannot be attributed either to the first human sin or yet to some primordial event in which some force antithetical to God prevented creation from being free of these disvalues.

4. See, e.g., Eva Jablonka and Marion J. Lamb, *Evolution in Four Dimensions: Genetic, Epigenetic, Behavioral, and Symbolic Variation in the History of Life* (Cambridge, MA: MIT Press, 2005).

5. Cooperation in evolution is elegantly analyzed by Sarah Coakley, "Sacrifice Regained: Evolution, Cooperation and God" (lecture given at The Gifford Lectures, University of Aberdeen, Aberdeen, Scotland, 2012), http://www.giffordlectures.org/lectures/sacrifice-regained-evolution-cooperation-and-god.

6. See Christopher Southgate, "God's Creation Wild and Violent, and Our Care for Other Animals," *Perspectives on Science and Christian Faith* 67 (2015): 245–53.

This is a point that I have discussed extensively in a series of articles. It is vital to grasp as a basis for approaching the more difficult notion that God must bear responsibility for the disvalues within creation.[7] The problem under consideration would be much easier if another force could be blamed for these disvalues. I give my reasons for rejecting other-force arguments briefly here, with all due respect to their proponents writing in this volume and elsewhere.

The key problems with human-sin arguments are chronological and theological. The fossil record makes clear that animals were tearing each other apart and suffering from chronic diseases such as arthritis long before humans evolved. To blame these phenomena on human sin means either rejecting this very well-established chronology and resorting to a young-earth creationism for which there is no support within the peer-reviewed scientific literature, or invoking some contorted account of cause and effect in time or space. For example, William Dembski's God inflicts vast amounts of proleptic suffering on creatures because humans will one day sin, while Stephen Webb's God has seemingly abandoned the sphere of creation outside the "dome" of Eden to the pervasive influence of Satan.[8] Not only are these accounts problematic in themselves, but they do not seem to me to succeed at all in preserving the goodness of God in the face of creaturely suffering.

The key problems with primordial-fall arguments, based on another force operating against God before the time of this universe, are again theological and also scientific. Such views are deeply difficult theologically not only because of the lack of biblical evidence that the world is so corrupted but also because they assign to spiritual entities opposed to God more power than Christian theology has been willing to concede. God's sovereignty is severely compromised in schemes in which God set out to create straw-eating lions and was prevented from doing so. Furthermore, it is deeply difficult for theology in conversation with science to dissect out some elements of the physical world and assign those to malefic influences, while attributing all beauty, order, and

7. See Christopher Southgate, "Re-reading Genesis, John, and Job: A Christian's Response to Darwinism," *Zygon* 46, no. 2 (2011): 370–90; Southgate, "Does God's Care Make Any Difference? Theological Reflection on the Suffering of God's Creatures," in *Christian Faith and the Earth: Current Paths and Emerging Horizons in Ecotheology*, ed. Ernst M. Conradie, Sigurd Bergmann, Celia Deane-Drummond, and Denis Edwards (London: Bloomsbury, 2014), 97–114; Southgate, "Cosmic Evolution and Evil," in *The Cambridge Companion to the Problem of Evil*, ed. Chad Meister and Paul Moser (Cambridge: Cambridge University Press, 2017), 147–64.

8. See William Dembski, *The End of Christianity: Finding a Good God in an Evil World* (Nashville: B&H Academic, 2009); Stephen Webb, *The Dome of Eden: A New Solution to the Problem of Creation and Evolution* (Eugene, OR: Wipf & Stock, 2010). For a yet more complex trans-temporal account aimed at securing a literal reading of Gen. 3, see Hud Hudson, *The Fall and Hypertime* (Oxford: Oxford University Press, 2014).

creativity to God. The whole essence of the scientific picture as it has emerged since the nineteenth century is that the same processes—tectonics, creaturely decay, mutation, natural selection, to name only a few—generate both the suffering and the beauty, ingenuity, and diversity of the world of creatures.

It is very important to grasp that free-process and only way theodicies become necessary because a scientifically informed theology has to part company with these various versions of the "ancient Christian answer" that what we find ugly or disturbing about nature can be assigned to the activity of a force other than God.[9] Incidentally, it is worth reflecting that the diverse witness of the Hebrew Bible also tends to reject fall-based accounts of disvalue in nature.[10]

I do not aspire to have a neat or complete solution to an unfathomable problem. All theoretical theodicies have some sort of way of balancing goods and harms. Andrew Robinson and I have divided approaches into three kinds:[11]

1. *Property-consequence good-harm analyses*, in which the presence of a property that may be deemed good has a likely consequence of a range of harms. The classic example is the freewill defense against moral evil. The possibility of self-conscious, freely chosen action informed by an understanding of other creatures, in a creature such as a human, is taken to be so great a good as to balance the very many harms that may arise from the use of that freedom.
2. *Developmental good-harm analyses*, in which a process through which various types of value develop may also lead to disvalues. These may arise as a by-product of the value-generating process, or they may be instrumental in furthering the generation of value. An example of a harm as a by-product would be the exhaustion of a runner on a training program toward a marathon run for charity. The exhaustion is not an instrument of stamina development but a likely by-product. An example of an instrumental system would be a student assessment scheme with

9. John Polkinghorne, "Pelican Heaven," *Times Literary Supplement*, April 3, 2009.

10. On the range of accounts of creation in the Hebrew Bible, see William P. Brown, *The Seven Pillars of Creation: The Bible, Science, and the Ecology of Wonder* (New York: Oxford University Press, 2010). On the cursing of the ground in Gen. 3 (and its reversal in Gen. 8), see Bethany Noël Sollereder, "Animal Suffering in an Unfallen World: A Theodicy of Non-Human Evolution" (PhD diss., University of Exeter, 2014).

11. Christopher Southgate and Andrew Robinson, "Varieties of Theodicy: An Exploration of Responses to the Problem of Evil Based on a Typology of Good-Harm Analyses," in *Physics and Cosmology: Scientific Perspectives on the Problem of Evil*, ed. Nancey Murphy, Robert J. Russell, and William R. Stoeger, SJ (Berkeley: Vatican Observatory and Center for Theology and the Natural Sciences, 2007), 67–90.

severe penalties for plagiarism or excessive word count. The harms, or possibility of harms, are instrumental to the development of the habits of a good scholar.

3. *Constitutive good-harm analyses*, in which the good is inseparable from the harm. This most elusive and enigmatic possibility can be glimpsed in the experience of some human sufferers that only in and through their suffering did a certain closeness to God become possible. I have explored a possible application of this to the nonhuman creation[12] but will not pursue this further here.

Free-Process Arguments

It is important to be clear that proponents of free-process arguments are not the same as process theologians. Process thought in most of its variants regards processes, at their most fundamental, as coeternal with God. (This gives rise to an alternative type of theodicy.)[13] Free-process arguments, in contrast, regard God as having created natural processes and endowed them with freedom. These arguments regard freedom of process in nature as a good, which might balance the harms to which that freedom gives rise. They begin with the early theological responses to Darwinism, in which it was said—by, for example, Charles Kingsley—that it was a good that God had made creation make itself.[14] The realization that adaptation of creatures to their environment was a natural process, rather than a series of individual divine designs, enabled theologians to distance God from the detail of the unfolding of the process. God might then be distanced from direct responsibility for those adaptations (for instance, saber teeth) that gave rise to creaturely suffering.

A contemporary example of this type of argument is that of Ruth Page in *God and the Web of Creation*, where Page writes: "I cannot imagine it possible to worship a God responsible for natural evil any more than one responsible for moral evil. . . . To those who wish to affirm full-blooded . . . [divine] making and doing, [my] version will appear anaemic. But the consequences of belief in a more virile God, who has to be responsible for the removal of around 98% of all species ever, but who fails to do anything in millions of cases of acute suffering

12. Southgate, "Does God's Care," 112.

13. Described and evaluated in Kenneth Surin, *Theology and the Problem of Evil* (Oxford: Blackwell, 1986); see also Southgate, *Groaning of Creation*, 22–25.

14. John Hedley Brooke, *Science and Religion: Some Historical Perspectives* (Cambridge: Cambridge University Press, 1991), 293–94.

in nature and humanity, are scarcely to be borne."[15] Rather, Page wants to think of God as creating possibilities and then letting them be—a very open form of making creation make itself. I am not clear that this altogether relieves God of responsibility in respect of natural evil. After all, in this model God created and continues to companion particular possibilities, and therefore still bears responsibility for their existence and for the suffering to which they give rise.

But that very phrase about making creation make itself reveals an ambiguity within free-process arguments that needs further investigation. The question can be asked: Is the freedom of natural processes the good in itself, against which the harms that it causes may be balanced? This would be a property-consequence analysis in the terms given above. The alternative is that the freedom of process within the creation is a good because it allows values to develop and hence furthers God's purposes in creation, making it possible for entities and systems to arise in a way more conducive to flourishing than if God had created them directly. The freedom would then be a developmental good.

Given Page's rigorous rejection of long-term divine ends and her focus on "teleology now,"[16] I conclude that her model must be placed in the first category, a property-consequence free-process argument. As I implied above, there must be some question as to whether this is effective as a strategy in theodicy, for at least two reasons. First, it does not get God "off the hook" because God remains responsible for the existence of the processes. Second, it is not clear to me that freedom of natural processes *is* a good, in the absence of divine goals—certainly not a good that might balance myriad instances of creaturely suffering. Remember that the free-process argument is that natural processes are free, not simply that the living creatures that result from the operation of the processes have a degree of autonomy. The latter does seem to be an evident good.[17] This autonomy of living creatures is enabled to *develop* through (1) God having given the creation laws that make the universe fruitful for life, laws to which God remains faithful,[18] and (2) God allowing

15. Ruth Page, *God and the Web of Creation* (London: SCM, 1996), 104.

16. Page, *God and the Web of Creation*, 63–73.

17. I am, however, not at all convinced by efforts such as those of Joshua Moritz to propose that the choices made by creatures are themselves an explanation for evil in creation. See Joshua Moritz, "Animal Suffering, Evolution, and the Origins of Evil," *Zygon* 49, no. 2 (2014): 348–80. There may be isolated instances in which a creaturely choice directed a particular evolutionary trait down a particular path, but predation and parasitism are far too general phenomena and (in the case of predation) far too generative of value. See Holmes Rolston III, "Disvalues in Nature," *Monist* 75 (1992): 250–75, who considers whether this type of explanation is satisfactory. Is it meaningful to think of the tiger "sinning" as it stalks the buck?

18. Michael Murray calls this "nomic regularity." See Michael J. Murray, *Nature Red in Tooth and Claw: Theism and the Problem of Animal Suffering* (Oxford: Oxford University Press, 2008).

some processes to which chance is intrinsic (such as mutation) to further the processes of evolution. But those seem to me developmental values rather than goods in themselves. The freedom of natural processes, viewed instrumentally in free-process defenses, turns out not to be as closely analogous to the good of the freedom of freely choosing rational agents to make those choices in freewill defenses as is sometimes supposed.

I now turn to the author of the phrase "free-process defence," scientist-theologian John Polkinghorne. In his 1989 book *Science and Providence*, Polkinghorne writes, "In his great act of creation I believe that God allows the physical world to be itself, not in Manichaean opposition to him, but in that independence which is Love's gift of freedom to the one beloved. The world is endowed in its fundamental constitution with an anthropic potentiality which makes it capable of fruitful evolution."[19] In his 1998 book *Belief in God in an Age of Science*, Polkinghorne explicitly admits that the free-process defense is a restatement of the nineteenth-century image of God making the world make itself.[20] And in his 2005 book *Exploring Reality*, he takes this further: "Creatures are allowed 'to make themselves.' This seems indeed to be a great good, but it also has a necessary cost. . . . Things will often just *happen*, as a matter of fact, rather than for an individually identifiable purpose."[21]

This last phrase might seem to suggest that Polkinghorne is adhering to freedom of creation as a noninstrumental, nonteleological good. In other words, it may seem that he regards the "freedom" of entities—other than freely choosing conscious creatures such as humans—as still a good in itself. But I have always read him as adhering to a more teleological view, albeit in respect of a generalized rather than an "individually identifiable" purpose. This is confirmed by a 2012 essay in which he writes:

> The more science helps us to understand the world, the more clearly we see its inextricable entanglement of fertility and wastefulness. I have suggested that

19. John Polkinghorne, *Science and Providence: God's Interaction with the World* (London: SPCK, 1989), 66. Notably, Polkinghorne also allows for a very extensive divine providential interaction with the world. Such a position always intensifies the problem of theodicy. The more God involves Godself, the more agonizing the issue of instances when God seems to do nothing. An extensive account of providence such as Polkinghorne's also complicates the assertion of freedom within natural processes. His God does not merely companion possibilities, as Page's does, but in particular instances selects possibilities that lead to the furtherance of divine purposes (not necessarily violating laws of nature to do so).

20. John Polkinghorne, *Belief in God in an Age of Science: The Terry Lectures* (New Haven: Yale University Press, 1998), 14.

21. John Polkinghorne, *Exploring Reality: The Intertwining of Science and Religion* (London: SPCK, 2005), 143 (emphasis original).

> there is a free-process defence in relation to natural evil, parallel to the familiar free-will defence in relation to moral evil. Natural evil is not gratuitous, something that a Creator who was a bit more competent or a bit less callous could easily have eliminated. Created nature is a package deal, with the emergence of new forms of life and the shadow side of malformation and extinction necessarily intertwined.[22]

As we saw above, Polkinghorne is not quite right about the parallel between the freewill and free-process defenses since his understanding of the latter is really developmental, having to do with processes that lead to beneficial outcomes such as the emergence of new species rather than the freedom of nonconscious entities being the absolute good in itself.

It remains to consider one further articulation of the free-process defense, Ryan McLaughlin's 2014 work *Preservation and Protest*. McLaughlin is very aware of the problem of theodicy in evolution, but he wants to find a way to draw back from assigning blame to God for the processes that give rise to suffering. He does this by an extraordinary move, claiming that God "sets the world free *prior to the formation of its laws*."[23] This is, in effect, a further way of articulating the proposal of Ruth Page. There were primordial possibilities, and the creation "chose" its own laws from within them. This is tricky in relation both to the shape of current cosmology and to evolutionary theodicy. In the face of cosmological proposals that subvert the notion of an initial singularity and suggest that the initial emergence of this universe might have been a random event, theologians are inclined to propose the reverse of McLaughlin—namely, that it is through the underlying laws and parameters of the primordial state that God ensures the fruitfulness of the universe. This would indeed be a far more familiar understanding of the theology of creation.

But McLaughlin's proposal also faces the theological difficulty that I noted in my introduction. It is the *same processes* that lead to disvalues in evolution that also give rise to all the values that we see. The laws that—for him—arose spontaneously within creation and give rise to the disvalues we see in creation *are the very ones* that make this creation the amazing phenomenon it is, and we have no evidence that a different set of laws would give rise to a more favorable balance between value and disvalue.

22. John Polkinghorne, "Reflections of a Bottom-Up Thinker," in *God and the Scientist: Exploring the Work of John Polkinghorne*, ed. Fraser Watts and Christopher Knight (Aldershot, UK: Ashgate, 2012), 8–9.

23. Ryan McLaughlin, *Preservation and Protest: Theological Foundations for an Eco-Eschatological Ethics* (Minneapolis: Fortress, 2014), 331 (emphasis original).

Only Way Arguments

That last consideration brings me to only way arguments, which might also be termed "package deal arguments." We have already encountered the term "package deal" in Polkinghorne's 2012 essay, and it can also be found in an important article by Niels Gregersen and in Denis Alexander's work.[24] The basic proposition is that the disvalues in creation *necessarily arise* alongside the values. Whether the disvalues are instrumental to the evolution of values or a by-product,[25] the two form a package deal. This indeed tends to be the reaction of biologists when questioned about the presence of predation and parasitism in nature.

The position is given philosophical attention by Robin Attfield. He concludes on rational grounds, without reference to Scripture or the doctrines of the church, that there might not be any "better" created world that could be formulated for the realization of creaturely value and that this argument in itself constitutes a theodicy, even without recourse to other components such as an appeal to eschatology.[26] Another, more explicitly theological way to put this can be found in an essay by Arthur Peacocke, who writes,

> If the Creator intended the arrival in the cosmos of complex, reproducing structures that could think and be free—that is, self-conscious, free persons—was there not some other, less costly and painful way of bringing this about? Was that the only possible way? This is one of those unanswerable metaphysical questions in theodicy to which our only response has to be based on our understanding of the biological parameters . . . discerned by science to be operating in evolution. These indicate that there are inherent constraints on how even an omnipotent Creator could bring about the existence of a law-like creation that is to be a cosmos not a chaos, and thus an arena for the free action of self-conscious, reproducing complex entities and for the coming

24. Niels H. Gregersen, "The Cross of Christ in an Evolutionary World," *Dialog: A Journal of Theology* 40, no. 3 (2001): 192–207; Denis R. Alexander, *Creation or Evolution: Do We Have to Choose?*, 2nd ed. (Oxford: Monarch, 2014).

25. In *Science and Religion: A Critical Survey* (1987; repr., Philadelphia: Templeton Foundation Press, 2006), Holmes Rolston III stresses the instrumentality of the evolution process: "The cougar's fang has carved the limbs of the fleet-footed deer, and vice versa" (134). Nancey Murphy prefers to think of the suffering as a by-product; see her essay "Science and the Problem of Evil: Suffering as a By-Product of a Finely-Tuned Cosmos," in Murphy, Russell, and Stoeger, *Physics and Cosmology: Scientific Perspectives on the Problem of Evil*, 131–51.

26. Robin Attfield, *Creation, Evolution and Meaning* (Burlington, VT: Ashgate, 2006), 109–50. This only way argument is essentially the approach defended in Michael Ruse, *Can a Darwinian Be a Christian? The Relationship between Science and Religion* (Cambridge: Cambridge University Press, 2001), 130–38; Richard L. Fern, *Nature, God and Humanity: Envisioning an Ethics of Nature* (Cambridge: Cambridge University Press, 2002), 152–53, 222.

to be of the fecund variety of living organisms whose existence the Creator delights in.[27]

So although we are not in a position to be at all definite about this, it is a reasonable, scientifically informed theological guess that a natural world containing creatures evolving by natural selection is the only way—or perhaps the best type of way—in which God could have given rise to the biological values we see within our own world. Indeed the only way argument receives support from a surprising quarter—from Richard Dawkins, arch-antagonist of theologians of evolution. Dawkins has written: "If there is no other generalization that can be made about life all around the Universe, I am betting that it will always be recognizable as Darwinian life." "In short . . . if God was to create through law, then it had to be through Darwinian law. There was no other choice."[28]

I have indicated that this is a type of argument favored by a number of scholars coming from different approaches and traditions. I turn now to the objections that can be raised to it and finally to what I consider to be its limitations. The first objection might be posed by any student of the philosophy of religion. It is that the argument supposes a constraint on the omnipotent, omniscient Creator of the universe out of absolutely nothing. The objector is entitled to ask what the nature is of this constraint and wherein it derives. To this the only way theorist can only answer that the existence of the constraint is a plausible guess and then advance a further guess that the constraint is a logical one—in other words, that it is a logical impossibility that a different mode of creation would have led to a world with a better balance of values to disvalues. We do not have access to this logic, but logical constraints are agreed to limit even an omnipotent God.

Two extensions to the argument are pertinent at this point. The first is the inference that it must have been impossible for God simply to create directly the eschatological state that Christians believe will follow from the ultimate redemption of the cosmos. God could not simply create heaven (otherwise why did God not do so?).[29] The second is that God may have been constrained as to the creation of worlds by God's loving desire that the world be redeemable through the incarnation of the divine Logos.[30] We have no means of knowing whether this further constrained the type of world that could have been created.

27. Arthur Peacocke, "The Cost of New Life," in *The Work of Love: Kenosis as Creation*, ed. John Polkinghorne (Grand Rapids: Eerdmans, 2001), 36–37.

28. Richard Dawkins, "Universal Darwinism," in *Evolution from Molecules to Men*, ed. D. S. Bendall (Cambridge: Cambridge University Press, 1983), 423.

29. Southgate, *Groaning of Creation*, 90.

30. Southgate, "Does God's Care."

The second objection, eloquently raised by Neil Messer,[31] is that the only way argument involves God being the Creator of processes to which violence is intrinsic. For Messer this cannot be what is referred to in Genesis 1:31, when God calls creation "very good." This is an important point, and only way theorists must give an account of how their constrained creation is still "very good." That account could be based on the interpretation of that Hebrew word for "good" as meaning "fit for purpose" rather than "perfect" or yet "beautiful."[32]

Messer is convinced of the need to disentangle God's very good intention from the world as it has actually always been. Messer is therefore drawn back to a sophisticated type of fall-based argument involving Karl Barth's concept of "nothingness" (*das Nichtige*). I am happy to admit that the only way argument constrains our sense not only of divine omnipotence but also of omnibenevolence. In my published responses to Messer, I note that both of us in our different ways find ourselves constraining the sovereignty of God. Messer's constraint is that God cannot prevent the influence of nothingness on the created order. Also, crucially, Messer separates out on theological grounds what he concedes is scientifically inseparable—since the same processes give rise to value and disvalue.[33]

There are two further recent objections to only way thinking. The first is by Nathan O'Halloran, SJ, who shrinks, very understandably, from making God "overly complicit" in the contingency of the world. (I sympathize wholeheartedly with this reluctance—only way arguments should only be taken seriously because they are the least-worst option.) O'Halloran's own advocacy of a primordial spiritual rebellion, "a higher organizing principle of disorder and evil within the cosmos," is vulnerable to the same concerns indicated in my introduction.[34]

The second objection, by Mats Wahlberg, warrants a more careful analysis. Wahlberg's key point is that God, presumably knowing the precise molecular composition of the biosphere at any given moment, could create that molecular system *de novo*. So the result that God is presumed to desire could be obtained without the millennia of suffering necessitated

31. Neil Messer, "Natural Evil after Darwin," in *Theology after Darwin*, ed. Michael S. Northcott and R. J. Berry (Milton Keynes, UK: Paternoster, 2009), 139–54.

32. "In general usage 'good' [*tōv*] indicates a state or function appropriate to genre, purpose, or situation." Willem A. VanGemeren, ed., *New International Dictionary of Old Testament Theology and Exegesis* (Carlisle, UK: Paternoster, 1996), 2:353.

33. Southgate, "Re-reading Genesis, John, and Job"; Southgate, "God's Creation Wild and Violent."

34. Nathan W. O'Halloran, SJ, "Cosmic Alienation and the Origin of Evil: Rejecting the 'Only Way' Option," *Theology and Science* 13, no. 1 (2015): 43–63.

by evolution.[35] Two points may be made in response. The first is that such a world would still be one full of predation and parasitism and driven by natural selection. So the problem of suffering in the nonhuman world would not be solved but merely mitigated. But the second point is more subtle. It is that living things, creaturely "selves," are not merely a snapshot in time that could be photocopied by God. (The reader may consider whether God could reproduce an exact copy of the person that reader is at this instant of reading this section.) Creaturely selves have individual and also ancestral history. They have inherited experience that, as Jablonka and Lamb show,[36] is far more than molecular composition. So I am not persuaded of the reality of Wahlberg's thought experiment.[37]

One of the major thinkers in the science-theology conversation in recent years has been Robert J. Russell, and an essay of his on evolutionary theodicy is of particular importance. Russell recognizes the force of a version of the only way argument, but he concludes that this cannot be an adequate theodicy. The burden of creaturely suffering is too great, and so a theodicy of evolutionary evil requires for Russell an additional eschatological component.[38] This type of argument is also persuasive for the Australian ecotheologian Denis Edwards, for whom God's love even for the sparrow that falls likewise requires that there be a possibility of redemption for creatures.[39]

These considerations will raise for some the questions: Why should God have to redeem, or heal, what God has created? And, how does the dynamic of redemption operate without a fall event affecting the whole of creation? This is a very important and often misunderstood element in this type of argument. To be wholly consistent, the narrative must run like this: Only a Darwinian process full of ambiguity could give rise to a world in which myriad types of creature could flourish and in which the Logos could be incarnate and atone for the (inevitable) sins of an evolutionary world. That atonement—however understood—makes possible the eschatological phase of God's work, the "new creation" (Isa. 65:17; 2 Cor. 5:17). That phase leads ultimately to a dimension of existence in which there is no more suffering. But we are forced to conclude, if thinking this way, both that the initial ambiguous phase was a necessary

35. Mats Wahlberg, "Was Evolution the Only Possible Way for God to Make Autonomous Creatures? Examination of an Argument in Evolutionary Theodicy," *International Journal of Philosophy and Religion* 77 (2015): 37–51.

36. Jablonka and Lamb, *Evolution in Four Dimensions*.

37. I thank Bethany Sollereder for discussions on this point.

38. Robert John Russell, *Cosmology: From Alpha to Omega* (Minneapolis: Fortress, 2008), 249–72.

39. Denis Edwards, "Every Sparrow That Falls to the Ground: The Cost of Evolution and the Christ-Event," *Ecotheology* 11, no. 1 (2006): 103–23.

preliminary and that the post-cross eschatological phase is at a very early stage. The "not yet" of Christian eschatology remains both an agony and a source of longing for the believer. Perhaps that enigmatic text in Romans 8:19–22 offers some insight into this—suggesting as it does that human redemption into authentic freedom is a necessary preliminary to final consummation.[40]

I turn finally to my own conclusion in regard to evil and evolution—namely, that what I have called a "compound theodicy" is the best rational guess we can make about what is ultimately mysterious.[41] The only way argument (in turn one method of understanding the free-process defense) is a necessary but insufficient foundation. It is an argument about systems, and suffering happens to *individual creatures* in particular circumstances. God, the tradition leads us to believe, loves and cares for individual creatures, not merely systems. A consequentialist calculator of the least-worst system to create does not amount to a loving God. So an only way or package deal argument is an essential starting point, given the failure of fall-based arguments, but it needs to be combined with other elements. I agree with Russell, Edwards, and also Jay McDaniel that an eschatological component is required.[42] But I am also persuaded by a key move of Arthur Peacocke's, proposing that the cosuffering of God with the suffering of all creatures is a vital element in an evolutionary theodicy.[43] Last, I suggest that the elements must be combined in an overall narrative scheme that is consonant with the classic Christian confessions on creation, redemption, and eschatological consummation.[44]

This essay situates free-process and only way arguments within the range of possibilities in evolutionary theodicy. Both types of argument presuppose the failure of fall-based arguments and the need to understand the involvement of God, confessed as profoundly benevolent, the God of Jesus crucified and risen, in a world full of beauty and wonder but full too of ugliness and suffering. I have shown that the less problematic version of a free-process defense coheres with an only way approach and that such an approach survives some of its sharpest critics but is nevertheless inadequate unless incorporated into a compound theodicy.

40. Southgate, *Groaning of Creation*, chaps. 6–7.

41. Southgate, *Groaning of Creation*, 15–16.

42. Jay B. McDaniel, *Of God and Pelicans: A Theology of Reverence for Life* (Louisville: Westminster John Knox, 1989).

43. Arthur Peacocke, "Biological Evolution—A Positive Theological Appraisal," in *Evolutionary and Molecular Biology: Scientific Perspectives on Divine Action*, ed. Robert J. Russell, William R. Stoeger, SJ, and Francisco J. Ayala (Berkeley: Vatican Observatory and Center for Theology and the Natural Sciences, 1998), 357–76; Peacocke, "Cost of New Life"; see also Southgate, *Groaning of Creation*, 50–53, 56–57.

44. Note that Michael J. Murray's effort to analyze these matters philosophically in *Nature Red in Tooth and Claw* also leads him in the direction of a compound theodicy.

20

Non-Identity Theodicy

Vince Vitale

Starting Nonassumptions

Many people assume that current evolutionary science obliges the rational person to give up her belief that there was in history a literal Adam and Eve who fell into sin. I am suspicious of this assumption for at least two reasons. First, most scientific theories once judged by the majority to be true are now taken to be false. Science is constantly finding new evidence that requires its theories to be revised. That does not mean that currently accepted theories do not contain important elements of truth, but it does mean that a conflict between current science and a theological claim is not always strong evidence against that theological claim. This is especially the case if you take the theological claim to be endorsed by the Bible, and you take the Bible to be an authoritative communication from God.

Second, I agree with Alvin Plantinga (considered by many to be the foremost living philosopher of religion) that, contrary to popular opinion, "it

I am thankful to the editor of *Philosophia Christi* for granting permission to use material for this chapter in whole or in part from Vince Vitale, "Non-Identity Theodicy," *Philosophia Christi* 19, no. 2 (2017): 269–90. More information about *Philosophia Christi* can be found at www.epsociety.org.

certainly seems that there is no conflict between current science and a literal Adam and Eve who fell into sin."[1] As Plantinga writes,

> Some scientists speak of a bottleneck (perhaps 160,000 to 200,000 years ago) in the line leading to current humans, when the relevant population dwindled to 10,000 to 12,000 individuals. Here's a possible scenario. At that time God selected a pair of these individuals, bestowing on them a property in virtue of which they are rightly said to be made in the image of God. This pair was wholly innocent, with properly directed affections. Nevertheless, they fell into sin, which in some way altered their natures (original sin). Furthermore, both the image of God and original sin were heritable, and also dominant in the sense that if either parent has either of these properties, their offspring will also have those properties. In this way both properties spread through the whole population, so that at present all human beings are descendants of this original pair, and all human being possess both the image of God and original sin.[2]

I am not saying you should accept this specific account of humanity's origin, nor am I saying that I do, but it is both consistent with current mainstream views in evolutionary science and within the capability of an omnipotent God. The same could be said of a scenario that differs from Plantinga's in that, rather than being selected from already existing beings, Adam and Eve were made directly by God in a special act of creation.

Therefore, a starting point for considering the relations between evolution and the problem of evil should be to dismiss two widely held assumptions: first, that current majority positions in science are definitive and, second, that there is an obvious conflict between current majority positions in science and there being a fall of two literal people as described in the biblical book of Genesis.

Non-Identity Theodicy

Regardless of one's views about the methods used by God to originate and develop humans as a species, it will be an advantage to the Christian if she can show that God can be considered good, despite the existence of evil and suffering. What I therefore want to do in this chapter is present a *theodicy*—proposed reasons why an all-loving and all-powerful God might allow evil

1. Alvin Plantinga, "Historical Adam: One Possible Scenario," *Think Christian* (blog), February 14, 2013, http://thinkchristian.reframemedia.com/historical-adam-one-possible-scenario.

2. Plantinga, "Historical Adam."

and suffering[3]—that can be accepted regardless of one's views about human evolution. I call this theodicy "non-identity theodicy" because it takes as its primary claim the position that our existence as the individuals that we are depends on the evil and suffering that preceded our coming to be.[4] Robert Adams developed some elements of this theodicy, especially in articles in the 1970s,[5] but he says that his work in this area does not constitute a theodicy.[6] Here I aim to organize and add to Adams's ideas in order to construct a full theodicy. As I present the theodicy, it will become apparent why this theodicy can accommodate a variety of views about how humanity originated.

Once I have presented the theodicy, I argue for the moral sufficiency of the divine reasons it proposes by making an analogy between divine creation and human procreation. Reflection on the morality of human procreation implies, I suggest, that it is not always wrong to create people into an environment in which you know they will suffer seriously. I argue further that if you think voluntary human procreation is in general morally permissible, you have even more reason to think that divine creation and sustenance is morally permissible; conversely, if you think it would be immoral for God to create and sustain our universe, then you have even more reason to think voluntary human procreation is in general immoral.

For a theodicy to be successful, it must meet two primary conditions: first, it should show that God has not wronged anyone by allowing evil and

3. "Theodicy" has been used to mean a number of things. As I use it, the theodicist does not need to claim to *know* that the reasons proposed by his theodicy are in fact among God's reasons. He only needs to claim that *for all we know* they are among God's reasons and that, if they are among God's reasons, they plausibly depict God as loving and morally perfect despite allowing the evil and suffering he allows.

4. The idea for this name comes from Derek Parfit, *Reasons and Persons* (Oxford: Oxford University Press, 1984), where Parfit reflects on the following question: Does it matter morally whether the people harmed or benefited by an action would have existed had that action not been performed? Parfit calls cases where the affected people are not identical with anyone who would have existed otherwise cases of *non-identity*.

5. Adams considers the relevance of non-identity considerations to theodicy in Robert M. Adams, "Must God Create the Best?," *Philosophical Review* 81 (1972): 317–32; Adams, "Existence, Self-Interest, and the Problem of Evil," *Noûs*, 1979, repr. with corrections in Robert Merrihew Adams, *The Virtue of Faith, and Other Essays in Philosophical Theology* (Oxford: Oxford University Press, 1987), 65–76; and Adams, "Love and the Problem of Evil," *Philosophia* 34, no. 3 (2006): 243–51. Tim Mawson also considers the relevance of non-identity considerations to theodicy, in particular to the prospects for theodicy on the assumption that determinism is true. See Tim Mawson, "The Problem of Evil and Moral Indifference," *Religious Studies* 35, no. 3 (1999): 323–45.

6. Likewise, when discussing Adams's work in this area, William Hasker says that "the argument cannot bear the weight of 'positive theodicy'—that is, of the task of explaining *why* evil exists or why it is appropriate that God should allow it to exist." See William Hasker, *Providence, Evil and the Openness of God* (New York: Routledge, 2004), 19.

suffering, and, second, it should show that God's allowance of evil and suffering is motivated by virtue rather than by some flaw in character. Non-identity theodicy suggests that these two conditions can be met if three other conditions are fulfilled:

1. Those who come to exist could not have come to exist without God's policy of evil and suffering allowance.
2. God offers all who come to exist a great life overall.[7]
3. God is motivated in creating and sustaining the universe by a desire to love those who come to exist.

I will discuss (2) most briefly. While some may not accept the offer, I assume that God offers to every person an eternal life that would be a great good to them overall. There are interesting questions about how God can make it the case that a person in the afterlife will be the same person as me. Perhaps it is just that a person who exists in the afterlife needs to remember being me and share core aspects of my personality and interests. Perhaps, in addition to this, God needs to bring together enough of the physical matter that constituted me at some point in my life in a similar enough arrangement. Perhaps I am an immaterial soul, and God only needs to ensure that this immaterial soul exists in the afterlife or that it is connected to some physical body in the afterlife. For the purposes of this chapter, I assume (along with the vast majority of theodicies) that divine omnipotence is capable of meeting the challenge of allowing people who have died on earth to exist eternally, either continuously or through being brought back to life. I also assume that the goods present in the afterlife can be great enough and exist for long enough to outweigh even the greatest evils of the present age.

Condition (1) is the distinctive claim of non-identity theodicy.[8] Drawing on Kripkean identity theory,[9] Adams proposes that the evil preceding our existence—more or less—is a metaphysically necessary condition of our existence. Adams writes,

7. Among Christians, and theists more generally, there are a variety of views about how and when God makes this offer. The reader can fill in these details concerning condition (2) in a manner that she takes to be consonant with the actions of a perfect being.

8. Historically, a number of celebrated Christian theologians—among them Duns Scotus, Karl Barth, and Gottfried Leibniz—have attempted to make sense of the biblical idea (cf. Ps. 139:16; Jer. 1:4–5; Eph. 1:4–5) that God has chosen human persons individually prior to their conception.

9. Adams references Saul A. Kripke, "Naming and Necessity," in *Semantics of Natural Language*, ed. Donald Davidson and Gilbert Harman (Dordrecht, Netherlands: Reidel, 1972), 312–14.

> I do not think it would have been possible, in the metaphysical or broadly logical sense that is relevant here, for me to exist in a world that differed much from the actual world in the evils occurring in the parts of history that contain my roots. . . . My identity is established by my beginning. It has been suggested [by Kripke, according to Adams] that no one who was not produced from the same individual egg and sperm cells as I was could have been me. . . . If so, the identity of those gametes presumably depends in turn on their beginnings and on the identity of my parents, which depends on the identity of the gametes from which they came, and so on.[10]

If our identities are established by our beginnings, Adams takes it that "a multiplicity of interacting chances, including evils great and small, affect which people mate, which gametes find each other, and which children come into being."[11]

It does not take much to affect procreation history. Any actions that have a significant effect on the movement of matter will, given enough time, have an effect on who comes to exist. This is because over time a butterfly effect—which can be readily demonstrated in our best weather prediction models—will exponentially multiply the amount of matter that has its movements and thus locations changed by even very slight variations in initial conditions, and eventually this will affect the movement of people enough to influence who conceives with whom, when they conceive, and therefore by which sperm and egg they conceive, and thus who subsequently comes to exist.

"The farther we go back in history," writes Adams, "the larger the proportion of evils to which we owe our being; for the causal nexus relevant to our individual genesis widens as we go back in time. We almost certainly would never have existed had there not been just about the same evils as actually occurred in a large part of human history."[12] This will include both moral evils (lying, stealing, cheating, and killing) and so-called natural evils (earthquakes, tornadoes, diseases, and droughts). It will also include the history relevant to the coming to be of the human race. The truth of any hypothesis about human origins—the gradual emergence of full humanity through evolutionary means, the raising of hominoids to full humanity as described by Plantinga, or the direct miraculous creation of the original humans—would have a major effect on the causal history of the world and therefore on the procreative history of the world. Whatever the truth about human origins, it

10. Adams, "Existence, Self-Interest," 67–68. Adams and I use "world" in the technical sense of a maximal state of affairs.

11. Adams, "Existence, Self-Interest, and the Problem of Evil," 66.

12. Adams, "Existence, Self-Interest, and the Problem of Evil," 66.

is very likely that none of us would have existed had the truth about human origins been significantly different.[13]

This is why, when Gottfried Leibniz considers in *Confessio philosophi* whether we should be indignant that God did not respond to Adam and Eve's fall by replacing them with better creatures who would not have transmitted sin and its consequent suffering down through the generations, he answers that

> if God had done that, sin having been taken away, an entirely different series of things, entirely different combinations of circumstances, persons, and marriages, and entirely different persons would have been produced and, consequently, sin having been taken away or extinguished, they themselves would not have existed. They therefore have no reason to be indignant that Adam and Eve sinned and, much less, that God permitted sin to occur, since they must rather credit their own existence to God's tolerance of those very sins.[14]

Leibniz goes on to compare those who hold such indignation with a half-noble son who is "irritated with his father because he had married a woman unequal in rank . . . not thinking that if his father had married someone else, not he, but some other man, would have come into the world."[15]

An objection surfaces at this point: not everyone will accept the claim that we could not have existed had the events preceding our physical origination been significantly different. There is at least one theory of personal identity that rejects *any* connection between personal identity and physical origination. This is a creationist theory according to which human persons are immaterial souls that exist logically (and in some versions temporally) prior to their embodiment.[16] On some versions of this view, not only is the immaterial soul the individuating feature of persons, but God can join any soul to any or no lump of matter as he likes, in any universe that he chooses to create.

If a theory of this sort is correct, then it is not true that suffering (let alone the precise suffering of the actual world) is essential for the existence of the specific community of actual-world human inhabitants (nor, for that matter, for the existence of any other human persons God could have created); God

13. None of this implies that we cannot one day live in an eternal state where there will be "no more death or mourning or crying or pain" (Rev. 21:4 NIV). It is an individual's *origin* that establishes his identity. Once he comes to exist, however, his *future* can take many different forms while maintaining personal identity.

14. Gottfried W. Leibniz, "The Confession of a Philosopher," in *Confessio Philosophi: Papers concerning the Problem of Evil, 1671–1678*, ed. and trans. Robert C. Sleigh Jr., with contributions from Brandon Look and James Stam (New Haven: Yale University Press, 2005), 107.

15. Leibniz, "The Confession of a Philosopher," 107.

16. This theory has been endorsed in various forms by Plato, René Descartes, Joseph Butler, Thomas Reid, Roderick Chisholm, and Richard Swinburne, among others.

could have gotten the very same individuals in possible worlds with significantly less evil and suffering or even with no evil and suffering at all.

However, even if God could have created us in a very different universe with a very different physical origination, it is another question whether his doing so would have been good *for us*. What we value in life is not just our metaphysical identity but the specific projects, relationships, commitments, experiences, memories, hopes, and aspirations that constitute the concrete content of our lives and in which we have found meaning. Adams suggests that because of the way the potential for evil and suffering is inextricable from so much of what we value in life, a significant alteration in God's policy of evil allowance would have made our lives in such alternative universes radically and fundamentally different from our actual lives. It would have made our lives so different with respect to what we care about that, plausibly, we lack a rational self-interest in those alternative lives.[17] William Hasker reflects, on similar grounds, that if we are glad that we exist (or glad that those we love exist), then "preferring [an alternative] life to one's actual life might be nearly as difficult as preferring not to have lived at all."[18] These thoughts raise questions about whether and to what extent God could have wronged us by his current policy of evil and suffering allowance if under a different policy the concrete content of our lives would have been so different that to wish for one of those alternative lives is to wish away most of what we actually care about and are glad about.

This response requires further development before it can be properly assessed, and I plan to return to it elsewhere. But it suggests that something akin to non-identity theodicy may remain plausible even if the independence of personal identity from physical origination is affirmed and (1) is denied.

That said, most people *do* accept the claim that physical origination affects personal identity. This claim will be plausible to many who deny the existence of an immaterial soul and to those who hold that a human person consists essentially of both a specific body and a specific soul. It may also be plausible to some who believe human persons *are* immaterial souls—for example, to some holding a traducian view (according to which the soul is generated from the specific souls of the parents during the reproductive process) or to some

17. See Adams, "Existence, Self-Interest," 74–75. A related challenge to non-identity theodicy is that if human persons are immaterial souls, and souls are featureless—as they are sometimes thought to be—it is hard to see what reasons God could have for loving that would be particular to specific individuals. But God's motivating love should be understood as tracking more than bare metaphysical identity. Adams reminds us that "to love a person . . . is not just to care about a bare metaphysical identity"; it is also to care for her "projects" and "aspirations," finding hope and value in particular "actions" and "experiences" ("Love and the Problem of Evil," 246).

18. Hasker, *Providence, Evil and the Openness of God*, 21. Hasker attributes this point to Robert Rosenthal.

holding an emergent view (according to which the soul results in some way from the structure and/or functioning of the human organism). This claim may even be plausible to some who believe human persons are immaterial souls and hold creationist views of the soul. Hasker notes that "Thomists, for instance, hold that the soul, as a form, is individuated by the matter which it informs; the soul is created as the soul of *this particular body*."[19]

The many who agree that significant changes in the causal history of the world would result in changes in the physical origins of human persons and therefore in the identities of which persons come to exist might reasonably conclude, then, that God has not wronged us by creating a universe in which we are offered a great eternal life rather than creating one in which we never would have lived.

We might wish that God would discontinue his policy of evil allowance once *we* come to exist, but Adams suggests that no person or generation has the right to special pleading.[20] By enabling our existence, the policy has been good for us on the whole, and so morality does not seem to require that in our lifetimes it should be discontinued.[21]

This brings us to condition (3) of non-identity theodicy. Even if God does not *wrong* anyone by allowing evil to occur, whether creating and sustaining an evil-producing universe reveals a defect in character is another question. Perhaps in creating a universe that includes great evil and suffering God displays a vice.[22] Perhaps, for instance, his motivation for creating an evil-prone universe is so that he can play hero or because he finds violence entertaining: "As flies to wanton boys are we to th' gods. They kill us for their sport."[23]

Non-identity theodicy resists this suggestion by claiming that God is motivated in creating by the virtue of grace. Adams identifies a gracious person as one with "a disposition to love which is not dependent on the merit of the person loved," one who "sees what is valuable in the person he loves, and does not worry about whether it is more or less valuable than what could be found in someone else he might have loved."[24]

God's primary creative choice, according to non-identity theodicy, is of a group of particular persons whom God finds lovable. Because God is gracious, his desire to love us is not on the condition that we are more valuable than other creatures he could have created or that our existence allows for

19. Hasker, *Providence, Evil and the Openness of God*, 11 (emphasis original).

20. Adams, "Existence, Self-Interest," 70–71.

21. Hasker affirms a similar point in *Providence, Evil and the Openness of God*, 19.

22. Adams ("Must God Create the Best?," 323) notes that Plato suggests the vice of envy in *Timaeus* 29e–30a.

23. William Shakespeare, *King Lear*, act 4, scene 1.

24. Adams, "Must God Create the Best?," 324.

the maximization of overall world value. Understanding God as gracious in this way is consonant with the tendency of religious worshippers to express gratitude to God for taking a particular interest in them despite their comparative deficiencies—"What are human beings that you are mindful of them, mortals that you care for them?" (Ps. 8:4).[25] The virtue of grace may be foreign to some ethical sensitivities (to those of Plato and Leibniz, for instance), but if it is accepted as a component of the ethical ideal, then desiring to create and love persons vulnerable to significant evil and suffering can be just as fitting with the abundance of divine generosity as desiring to create and love the most valuable, most useful, or most well-off persons God could create.[26]

Adams likens God's decision to create the actual universe to Adams's own unabashed preference for "the preservation of the human race . . . to its ultimate replacement by a more excellent species,"[27] to human parents preferring to procreate a normal child rather than a genetically enhanced superchild, to an activist's preference for a free society even if a totalitarian one would be better overall, and to a person breeding goldfish rather than more excellent beings. All of these examples are most naturally construed as including preferences not aimed at value maximization, and the first three examples can be naturally construed as including preferences not aimed at minimizing suffering. Intuitions are controversial here, but I join Adams in not thinking that he, the parents, the activist, or the goldfish breeder have—under otherwise normal circumstances—displayed a vice.

Conjoining the belief that God has not wronged those he has created with the claim that God's world choice is motivated by the virtue of grace rather than by a defect in character, we have the outline of a full theodicy. In sum, the postulated justifying goods of non-identity theodicy are individual human persons, and accepting evil and suffering as an inevitable consequence of attaining these goods is consistent with God's ethical perfection so long as the human persons are brought into existence because God desires to love them,[28] they could not have existed without the actual divine policy of evil and suffering allowance, and they are offered very worthwhile lives overall.

25. Adams uses this verse to make a related point in Adams, "Must God Create the Best?," 324–25.

26. Non-identity theodicy is noncommittal regarding whether God has created or will create beings other than or even better than those whose existence we are aware of. This provides an additional way that non-identity theodicy can resist objections claiming that God should have created better beings or beings who suffer less; for all we know, he has.

27. Adams, "Existence, Self-Interest," 71.

28. Because I claim that God is motivated in creating by a *desire* to love individuals rather than by love for them per se, I am not committed to the possibility of loving nonexistent objects. In *The Triumph of God over Evil: Theodicy for a World of Suffering* (Downers Grove, IL: IVP

Non-Identity Theodicy and Free Will

As I have outlined non-identity theodicy to this point, God aims to produce specific persons. But for God to will a cosmic system because it will produce these rather than those specific persons, God would have to have strong reason to believe in advance of creation that it will in fact produce these rather than those. Given the extreme sensitivity of procreation history, God could only have such knowledge by deterministic control or Molinist control.[29] If the cosmic system includes only natural causes, then God could have the requisite knowledge by deterministically controlling the history of the world. If the system includes libertarian voluntary causes as well, then God would need middle knowledge; the combination of middle knowledge and a deterministic control of natural causes would allow God to guide the unfolding of history with the precision necessary to produce specific persons.

However, on libertarian non-Molinist assumptions (i.e., the assumptions that we have undetermined free will and God does not have middle knowledge),[30] God could not know enough in advance about the future free and contingent choices of persons to ensure—or even make probable—that he would wind up with the specific community of human persons he was motivated to bestow grace on in the first place.[31] Even seemingly trivial free choices—for example, to take the scenic route to work or to stop to pick up a piece of trash—are enough to significantly alter which sperm and eggs join in conception, when they do so, and the circumstances under which their joining proceeds.[32] This

---

Academic, 2008), Hasker raises a concern about this when he writes, "Prior to [God] making the decision, there *are no* creatures for God to love; there is only a set of abstract possibilities" (84, emphasis original).

29. Molinism is the view that there is a true counterfactual corresponding to every possible situation in which a possible free creature is faced with a free decision, and that God knows the truth values of all of these counterfactuals. (In other words, although our actions are free and undetermined, God knew prior to creation how we would freely act in any circumstance he could have put us in.) Such counterfactuals are allegedly contingent truths God has to work with when deciding whether and which universe to create. God's knowledge of the truth values of these counterfactuals is referred to as middle knowledge.

30. Some think God does not have middle knowledge because there are no truths to be known about how someone would freely act in a given situation prior to their actually freely acting in that situation.

31. Even if (without deterministic or Molinist control) God could not have this knowledge in advance, it may be that he has this knowledge timelessly. Nevertheless, because this timeless knowledge would be logically posterior to the free human choices in question, this knowledge would not be of use to God in deciding which universe to create.

32. If human persons are the first inhabitants of earth with non-Molinist free will, then maybe God still could have aimed individually for some of the first human persons. Even so, the suffering of countless subsequent generations could not be plausibly justified by God's intention to create a relatively small number of human individuals at the commencement of the species.

exposes that the version of non-identity theodicy I have outlined to this point is logically committed to either theological determinism or Molinism, whereby God chooses at the point of creation among fully determinate possible worlds.

That non-identity theodicy sits well with theological determinism is a significant result. Richard Swinburne seems to speak on behalf of many contemporary theodicists in asserting that "it would . . . be very difficult to construct a satisfactory theodicy which did not rely on the doctrine of human free will"[33] and that "the central core of any theodicy must . . . be the 'free-will defence.'"[34] William Hasker is in unequivocal agreement: "Theological determinism is emphatically rejected, not least because of the difficulty—the insuperable difficulty, as I believe—it creates for any attempt to deal constructively with the problem of evil."[35] If a non-identity approach to theodicy has anywhere near the promise I have suggested it has, this calls into serious question the widespread supposed wedlock of theodicy with libertarianism.[36]

This loosing of theodicy from libertarian free will also guards against extreme forms of anthropocentrism. As Adams suggests, "The perspective of omniscience must be less bound to the human than ours, and the creator of a universe of which humanity occupies so small a part may be presumed interested in other things in it besides us."[37] Unlike free-will-based theodicies, non-identity theodicy can without theoretical complication spread its net of divine interest as widely as it likes. Whereas plausibly only human persons (among earthly beings) have the sort of significant libertarian free will that takes central place in most theodicies, fairly narrow origin constraints on identity are as plausible for stars, mountains, plants, and animals as they are for human persons.

Animal suffering, therefore, including any prehuman animal suffering, can be accounted for not only by the particular human persons it allows to exist but also by the particular animals God desires to exist. Returning to the three conditions of non-identity theodicy, animal suffering affects which human persons come to exist (condition [1]), but it also affects which animals come to

33. Richard Swinburne, *Providence and the Problem of Evil* (Oxford: Clarendon, 1998), 241.

34. Richard Swinburne, *Is There a God?*, rev. ed. (Oxford: Oxford University Press, 2010), 86.

35. Hasker, *Triumph of God*, 93.

36. The theist committed to theological determinism will face a challenge in meeting condition (2) of non-identity theodicy. But she is not without options. She will have to argue either that there is a morally significant sense in which someone can be *offered* a great eternal life even if they are determined to reject that offer, or that God ensures that even those who are determined to reject him nevertheless have lives that are worth living overall, or that ultimately no one will reject God, or that condition (2) should be weakened so that not every person needs to be offered a great life in order for non-identity theodicy to be successful.

37. Robert M. Adams, *Finite and Infinite Goods* (Oxford: Oxford University Press, 1999), 148.

exist. Even if there is a special form of love God can share with human persons as free beings (condition [3]), God nevertheless has affection for animals and creates them out of a desire to appreciate and bestow value on them. It is a disputed point among Christians and other theists whether the animals that exist in the present age will partake in an afterlife, but it is plausibly within the vast resources of omnipotence for God to give each animal a life worth living (or even very worth living) on the whole (condition [2]). One may object that some animals perish from starvation or other forms of suffering very early in life. However, even the short lives of these animals will have an effect on the movement of matter and, therefore, over time, on which humans come to exist. Perhaps it is a great good *for an animal* if that animal is used by God for his purpose of bringing human persons into existence. But if some animals have earthly lives that are not worth living, God can ensure that they exist after death in a long enough and good enough state for condition (2) to be satisfied. This suggests that with no more than slight amendments, the three conditions of non-identity theodicy can account plausibly for animal suffering. If you believe that animals can enjoy an afterlife, then the conditions of non-identity theodicy can account for animal suffering even without making reference to human persons (or any other nondivine beings, such as angels). This may be attractive to anyone concerned for animals to be treated as ends in themselves (as opposed to mere means to benefit others) in the context of theodicy.

A Second Version of Non-Identity Theodicy

If one has arguments that favor the existence of non-Molinist libertarian free will or thinks that determinism or even Molinism would make God too directly involved in the bringing about of evil for him to be perfectly good, then that person will be inclined to reject the version of non-identity theodicy I have presented. However, I believe non-identity theodicy can be reformulated to be made plausible on non-Molinist libertarian assumptions about free will. If I am correct, some version of non-identity theodicy will be available to theists regardless of their assumptions about free will.

Without middle knowledge or deterministic control of the universe, God's motivation in creating cannot be love for specific individuals. But even if (on non-Molinist libertarian assumptions) God cannot aim for specific individuals, perhaps he can nonetheless aim for specific being-*types*, and perhaps this too can be a loving motivation consonant with having a flawless character and not wronging those he creates. Moreover, because plausibly the individuals who actually exist could not have originated as other being-types, this remains for God a non-identity choice—one that brings into existence people who otherwise could not have existed. Condition (1) of non-identity theodicy is therefore satisfied.

Likewise, the assumption of non-Molinist libertarianism will not impede non-identity theodicy's ability to meet condition (2). The denial of theological determinism may even make it easier for those who believe in certain theories of hell to maintain that condition (2) is satisfied.[38]

That leaves condition (3). On this second version of non-identity theodicy, God can be likened to human procreators. Choices to procreate are non-identity choices. However, even in cases of well-informed and fully voluntary human procreation, parents cannot know enough about their future children to aim for specific individuals. Nevertheless, they can aim for a being of a certain type—for a human child or for their biological child—with the determination to love whichever individual of that type they end up procreating.

Intuitions suggest that there is a morally significant sense in which human parents can procreate out of a desire to love their future children, despite only aiming in procreating for a being-type. They recognize what is valuable in the type they aim for and act out of a desire to love whichever individual of that type they ultimately produce. Analogously, so long as God has control enough to aim for specific types of beings,[39] then even without deterministic or Molinist control God can be motivated in creating by a desire to love the unspecified individuals of one or more being-types, irrespective of whether those being-types are better or worse than other being-types God could have created. I take it that if there is a God, human persons are among the being-types he has aimed for in creating and sustaining the universe.

The remaining question is whether evil comparable to the evil of the actual world is necessary for us to be the type of being we are. Condition (3) is only satisfied if a universe prone to evil and suffering is a necessary condition of producing beings of our type. I believe that it is. Three of the most significant aspects of human persons as a being-type are human psychology, human biology, and the narrative of humanity,[40] and without a universe prone to evil and suffering, each of these would look very different.

38. Cf. n. 36 above.

39. I take it that most religious traditions that attribute to God the power to create universes and perform miracles will be happy to attribute to him a level of control sufficient for directing the unfolding of history to include certain being-types.

40. This is affirmed by the fact that three of the most prominent theories of personal identity are psychological, biological, and narrative theories, reflecting that what human persons value about themselves as individuals are—among other things—their psychological states such as memories, beliefs, intentions, desires, hopes, and faith, the biological organisms that they are

It strains the imagination to think of what human psychology would be like if we lived in a world without serious evils. Part of what it is to be us is to be the fragile beings that we are, vulnerable to violation and destruction. So much of our meaning-making systems—what we value, desire, participate in, and invest in—depends on our living in an environment prone to much evil. Resultantly, so much of our psyche is dominated by denying, worrying about, preventing, responding to, and dealing with actual evils that any beings born into and maturing in a world with much less evil would be radically psychologically different from us.

Likewise, for us to be the type of being we are under a narrative description, that narrative would have to include stories of false motives and bad decisions that have been at the root of many of the major turns in human history. It would also have to include external destruction such as natural disasters, human diseases, and wars.[41] This is not to say that God loves these aspects of the human narrative; he may regret and even hate them. Rather, God loves beings of our type, and being our type is deeply interwoven with the narrative of human history. This is evidenced by the tendency of all human cultures to identify themselves by, and set up manifold structures and practices for, the remembrance and commemoration of events, objects, and individuals important to the history of our race. No narrative that did not include many of the sorts of things that would be key features of any good documentary on the human race could plausibly be considered the narrative of our being-type.

Finally, is the extent of actual evil necessary for us to be the type of being we are under a biological description? Technically, perhaps not. Human persons seem uniquely capable (among earthly creatures) of perpetrating and suffering some of the worst forms of actual evil. Only human persons have been capable of sex trafficking children, for instance, or of feeling prolonged hatred toward oneself. Any processes or events that helped produce and hence preceded our biological type could not have included suffering that is conditional on the concurrent existence of our type. Moreover, with the resources of omnipotence, perhaps God could have miraculously protected our biological type from suffering once we came to exist. Therefore, it may be within the power of God both to produce and to sustain beings of our biological type without allowing some of the worst forms of evil and suffering.

---

continuous with, and the integrated stories running through their lives. Moreover, good lovers seek to help their beloveds to see and appreciate what is lovable in them, so our valuing of these aspects of humanity is some evidence for God's valuing of them.

41. This does not entail that God created a universe that would inevitably produce these forms of external destruction. See footnote 42 for further discussion of this point.

However, this would be to get our being-type under one description at the expense of the other two. Perhaps such persons would be the same species in a biological sense, but if they were continuously supernaturally protected from evil from the commencement of our species, they would not share the psychology or narrative of our being-type. Moreover, even if human suffering is not necessary for our biological type to exist, plausibly the natural processes out of which that suffering emerges are. Our biological lineage and makeup would not look nearly the same without the laws of thermodynamics having underlain physical systems as they have and therefore without our world having had the natural threats to survival that it has had. Maybe God could have eradicated these processes once human persons came to exist, but there is good reason to think he would not have.

Many women value pregnancy intensely. Part of their love for their children is valuing the processes and events out of which their children came to be. Likewise, the natural processes that God cares about in caring for us may be much richer than we are apt to assume. Part of God's love for our type would be valuing the natural world out of which we came, and this is reason to think he would be resistant to discarding major features of that world as soon as human life had commenced.

Even if non-Molinist human free will means that God could not aim for specific human persons in creating and sustaining this universe, he could nonetheless aim for specific being-types, and one side effect of aiming for our being-type under psychological, narrative, and biological descriptions would be evil and suffering similar to that of the actual world. That one day we may exist in an evil-free environment does not undermine these conclusions, because part of what it is to be of our type is to be headed for redemption in various respects.[42]

42. Some theists may worry that God could not be aiming for our being-type, not because they believe things will be different in the end but because they believe things were different in the beginning. If humanity has fallen from some form of original righteousness, this could be taken to imply that, insofar as God aimed for a human being-type, he aimed for it under a prefall suffering-free description and not under the current description we have freely fallen into. But I think this conclusion is avoidable. Even if God did not desire for humanity to fall, one reason he could be taken to have *allowed* a fall and its consequences is that he desired to bring into existence and to love beings of our biological, psychological, and narrative description. God can love many different beings under many different descriptions. He could love the first human persons in their condition of original righteousness and subsequent human persons in their fallen condition.

I also take a fall of humanity to be reconcilable with the Molinist or deterministic version of non-identity theodicy. A fall of humanity, as a significant event in history, would affect which individuals come to exist subsequently. God therefore could be taken to have allowed a fall in part in order to aim for specific individuals that he desired to create and love.

My conclusion, therefore, is that if God creates out of a holistic love for beings of our type, we should expect his creation to have the suffering-producing tendencies of the actual world. As we have seen, all three conditions of a successful non-identity theodicy can be met even on non-Molinist libertarian assumptions about free will.

Divine Creation and Human Procreation

The plausibility of the justification offered by non-identity theodicy is aided by an analogy between divine creation and human procreation. In both cases, we have creators choosing to bring beings into existence when they know those beings will suffer significantly. Human parents who voluntarily have children do something that they know will result in serious suffering because serious suffering accompanies even the most fortunate of human lives. Even more than that, they procreate knowing full well that one day their child will suffer death. Arguably, death (or the dying process) is one of the worst evils. Despite this, most people believe that voluntary human procreation is not uncommonly morally permissible. The question is on what grounds they believe this. In other words, how does human procreation fare with respect to the conditions of morally acceptable creation recommended by non-identity theodicy?

Procreation meets condition (1). If my parents had chosen not to procreate, I never would have existed. And indeed this does seem important to the morality of procreation. If parents had the option—all things being equal—of having their very same children without them suffering severely and ultimately dying, and they didn't take it, this would call into serious question the morality of their procreative act. That the one who suffers as a result of a given action would not exist had that action not been performed can have a very significant effect on the morality of bringing human persons into existence.[43]

Procreation does not fare as well as divine creation with respect to justificatory condition (2). Only God can offer to each person an eternity in which any evil endured will be infinitely outweighed. The best human procreators can offer to a new child is a probably worthwhile life. Because I don't think morally permissible procreation relies on certain theistic beliefs about the afterlife, I believe that the good of a merely natural human existence—limited in its duration, with the risks of misery that accompany it, and with death as

43. That the good of worthwhile human life has this marked justificatory power also helps to make sense of the intuition that wrongful-life lawsuits are only morally compelling in exceptional circumstances.

its bad end—is sometimes sufficient for justifying human procreation. With omniscience and omnipotence, God is capable of offering to each person a life such that physical death is not the end it appears to be and such that all but the earliest fraction of human life will be spent in great happiness and fulfillment. God is in a more favorable position than human procreators both for the afterlife that only he can give and for the burden of final death that only he can take away.

This leaves us with how human procreation fares with respect to condition (3). Again, it fares not nearly as well as divine creation. According to non-identity theodicy, God creates out of a desire to love those who come to exist and to offer them a great eternal life. One of God's primary reasons for creating is a desire for the good of the specific persons who will come to exist. But even in morally favorable cases of human procreation, the reasons human persons have for procreating are complex, and a concern for the good of the one who will come to exist is not always central. Sometimes human persons procreate for selfish reasons, and a concern for the good of the one who will come to exist is absent altogether or considered only as an afterthought. As David Benatar recognizes, parental motivations for procreating are often at least partly self-serving: to "satisfy biological desires," to "find fulfillment," to ensure "an insurance policy for old age" and an influence beyond the grave.[44] Indeed, many times parents don't initially intend to procreate at all; procreation can be an unintended side effect of physical desire or relationship bonding. Yet human procreation is in general morally permissible despite faring significantly worse than divine creation with respect to non-identity theodicy's proposed conditions for the morally acceptable creation of beings vulnerable to significant suffering.

Someone might object that a morally relevant distinction favoring human procreation over divine creation is that human persons are not responsible for the reproductive system within which they procreate and that it may be unfair to expect human persons to renounce their natural functions. However, even if being stuck with a certain frame makes acts of human procreation more understandable, I doubt this diminishes human responsibility so far as to account for the extent of the moral freedom to procreate that many find strongly intuitive. For most of us, the frame we inherit makes lying, cheating, stealing, and a host of other bad acts come just as naturally as procreation, perhaps now even more naturally in places of readily available contraception. Just as our natural inclinations to such acts do little to diminish their

44. David Benatar, "Why It Is Better Never to Come into Existence," *American Philosophical Quarterly* 34, no. 3 (1997): 351.

immorality, our natural tendency to procreate cannot morally excuse us from the harm resulting from procreation.

Moreover, God may be working with a similar frame. It is consonant with non-identity theodicy that God's desire to create the actual-world inhabitants is as strong as or stronger than any human desires resulting in procreation. Non-identity theodicy suggests that it is a necessary truth that creating those inhabitants would result in grave suffering. The divine case is then much like the human procreation case with the exception that God has significant moral advantages at both the beginning of human life (where he can create out of pure motivations) and the end of human life (where he can offer an eternity of fulfillment beyond the grave).

A second objection claims that human procreation per se is not the appropriate analogy, that divine creation of this evil-prone universe is more like a parent intentionally conceiving a child with a congenital disease than like a normal case of procreation. However, there are a number of reasons to be morally suspicious of this sort of abnormal procreation that don't easily transfer to its divine analogue. Parents' desire to aim for a disease-affected child may reflect questionable motives for bringing a child into existence and therefore may call into further question their fulfillment of condition (3). The parents may be using the child as a means to an end—say fame, or the chance to play hero, or fulfilling some other psychological or financial need of theirs—rather than valuing the child for her own sake. This concern about an immoral instrumentalism helps explain why many would have a similar aversion to the intentional conception of children with Down syndrome, despite the fact that children with this condition arguably suffer no more on average than normal children.[45] Moreover, in cases of intentionally conceiving a child with a disease that causes great suffering, the parents may have good reason to doubt that the child's natural life will be worthwhile for her, all things considered—that is, they may have less reason to be confident that they can meet condition (2). With God, though, we need not have concerns about suspect motivations, and, furthermore, we can be confident that he can offer even those born into serious suffering eternal lives that will be tremendous goods to them overall.[46]

45. Likewise, a concern about an immoral instrumentalism may help explain why some have intuitions that it is more plausibly morally permissible to intentionally procreate in a particularly dangerous part of the world than to intentionally procreate a deaf child, even if it is probable that the deaf child will suffer less overall than the child born in dangerous circumstances. The most common ways of imagining the details of such cases may leave the parents who procreate a deaf child more prone to a charge of immoral instrumentalism.

46. A third reason that someone might be morally suspicious of the intentional conception of a child with a congenital deficiency is if they take human beings to have a moral obligation

If the much more limited good of probably worthwhile natural human life is sufficient to justify the serious human suffering and death that accompanies human procreation, then I find it reasonable to think that the good of God-given human life—with its substantial moral advantages at both the beginning and the end of life—is sufficient for justifying divine permission of actual evils.

In sum, if you think human procreation is permissible, all the more so should you think divine creation of our universe is permissible. If you think God has acted immorally by creating human persons into an environment that produces suffering, then you have even more reason to think that human parents who procreate voluntarily are acting immorally (and therefore that many people would be justified in bringing wrongful-life lawsuits against their parents).

Conclusion: Distinctive Features of Non-Identity Theodicy

Non-identity theodicy is distinct as a theodicy in a number of ways. First, unlike most theodicies, it does not suggest that evil and suffering (or the possibility of evil and suffering) allow those who exist to live more valuable or more meaningful lives than the lives they would have lived without evil and suffering. Rather, it suggests that without evil and suffering those who exist could not have lived at all. The primary justificatory good proposed by non-identity theodicy is not some benefit to life but life itself; it is not some form of human existence but human persons themselves and their status as objects of divine love. Human persons are thereby treated not as means to something else but as ends in themselves.

Second, non-identity theodicy is distinct in that it is available to the theist regardless of her assumptions about the existence and nature of free will. Even the assumption of theological determinism does not undermine non-identity theodicy in any obvious way.

Third, the plausibility of non-identity theodicy is unaffected by one's assumptions about God's method of producing the human species. Whichever processes or events have led to the existence of the human race, those processes or events will have significantly affected the causal history and therefore the procreative history of the world. Whichever method God chose, therefore, can be explained by his desire to create and love the individuals or being-types made possible by that method. In particular, as I have discussed, this allows

to respect God's purposes for human life by not engineering human life in certain ways. Again, God is not vulnerable to this objection, for he has no creator to whom he is obligated. For further discussion of this point, see Adams, "Must God Create the Best?," 330–32.

the non-identity theodicist to account for animal suffering (including any prehuman animal suffering) without theoretical complication.

Finally, non-identity theodicy is available to the theist regardless of her appraisal of most other theodicies, including other theodicies represented in this book. Non-identity theodicy suggests that the goodness of God can be defended because God creates and sustains the universe out of a desire to love and offer eternal life to people who otherwise could not have existed. But perhaps it is also true, as Michael Lloyd suggests, that God permits rather than causes suffering and that God has greater moral reason not to cause suffering than not to permit it. Or perhaps Richard Swinburne is correct that God only allows evil to occur when it serves greater goods such as the opportunity to freely form our character and to be of help to others. More good reasons for performing an action generally make it more likely that one has morally sufficient reason for performing that action. If you think the reasons proffered by non-identity theodicy are sufficient to justify God's allowance of suffering, then the cumulative reason provided by multiple theodicies may provide God with overdetermined justification. If you think the reasons recommended by non-identity theodicy are morally significant but not sufficient, they may nevertheless contribute to a successful cumulative-case theodicy. Thinking that none of the individual theodicies represented in this book or elsewhere are sufficient to maintain the goodness of God in the face of evil and suffering is not sufficient to defeat the project of theodicy, for it would not be at all surprising if an infinitely wise and omniscient God had more than one reason for a decision as complex and significant as which universe to create and sustain.

CONCLUSION TO PART 3

Michael Lloyd

The contributors to part 3 have offered different—and at times seemingly contradictory—theodicies in response to the violence inherent within, and the pain resulting from, the evolutionary processes. In this conclusion, however, I want to suggest that these theodicies may have more in common than might at first appear—in at least four ways. First, all the contributors seem to believe that the current state of evolutionary biology and modern genetics leaves us plenty of space in which to do theodicy. The very diversity of the contributions makes that point quite strikingly—and, if we had unlimited pages, there are many more (significantly different) approaches that we could include.[1] And however much the contributors may disagree with one another, their very engagement with one another on this topic is an implicit testimony to the spaciousness of that field and its amenity to multiple interpretations and meaningful exploration. To take seriously the tenets of modern evolutionary biology leaves plenty of room for passionate and rational commitment to the goodness of God.

Second, all the contributors acknowledge the raw seriousness of the problem of evil in relation to the evolutionary processes, and they all reject those approaches that deny the problem by, for example, refusing to acknowledge the reality or moral significance of animal suffering.[2] Richard Swinburne does

1. See, for example, Neil Messer, "Natural Evil after Darwin," in *Theology after Darwin*, ed. Michael S. Northcott and R. J. Berry (Milton Keynes, UK: Paternoster, 2009), 139–54.

2. For an example of a writer who denies the reality of animal pain, see Charles Raven, *The Creator Spirit* (London: Hopkinson, 1927), 120. For an example of a writer who denies the moral significance of animal pain, see Peter Geach, *Providence and Evil* (Cambridge: Cambridge University Press, 1977), 77–79.

ask whether the larger prefrontal cortex in humans increases human capacity for pain, but he also concludes that "the only reasonable assumption is that many animals do suffer." And Michael Lloyd argues that predation would be a moral problem even in the absence of animal pain. None of the contributors takes the easy way out of denying or belittling the problem.

Third, all the contributors recognize that what they have presented in this volume falls far short of a full theodical narrative. Christopher Southgate, for instance, accepts that his only way argument is "inadequate unless incorporated into a compound theodicy." Indeed, I suggest that there would be significant agreement between the contributors regarding the contours of that compound theodicy, of which we can identify five common components.

The first component might be an affirmation of creaturely freedom. Richard Swinburne suggests that "it would . . . be very difficult to construct a satisfactory theodicy which did not rely on the doctrine of human free will."[3] Such an affirmation is logically necessary as a foundation for Swinburne's Irenaean account and for all fall accounts, including the free-process defense. The aspect of Augustine's thought on which Stanley Rosenberg draws in his chapter is more the tendency of finite matter toward nonbeing than the freedom of the human will, but anyone who believes in the fall of both Adam and Satan, as Augustine did, arguably requires a doctrine of creaturely free will if they are to avoid attributing the sin of the creature to the agency of the Creator. And while Vince Vitale suggests that one version of non-identity theodicy is compatible with theological determinism, he also offers a version of non-identity theodicy that affirms both free will and the significance for theodicy of creaturely fallenness.

The second component might be an affirmation of the cross as an important ingredient in any overall theodicy, both as the beginning of God's redemption of the created order and as God's assumption in Christ of the pain of the created order. Indeed, the former depends on the latter since "that which is not assumed is not healed."[4] As Christopher Southgate writes, "That atonement—however understood—makes possible the eschatological phase of God's work, the 'new creation' (Isa. 65:17; 2 Cor. 5:17)." That atoning and eschatologically transforming assumption of the pain of creation is also read as inferring "the cosuffering of God with the suffering of all creatures," which Southgate considers to be "a vital element in an evolutionary theodicy." As

3. Richard Swinburne, *Providence and the Problem of Evil* (Oxford: Clarendon, 1998), 241.

4. "That which was not assumed is not healed" was a widespread patristic dictum. (See, for instance, Gregory of Nazianzus, Epistle 101.) It asserts that, because nothing can be restored or fulfilled without being brought into contact with God, that which is not taken up in some way into the human nature of Christ is not healed.

Mitchell concludes, "either all of this relates to the suffering God in Christ—who groans with his suffering creation and, by taking its suffering into himself, defuses it of any power to frustrate his loving purposes for his world and enables it to share in his resurrection—or we are of all people most miserable indeed (1 Cor. 15:19)."

The third component of a compound and more complete theodicy, which leads directly from the second, might be an affirmation of the theodical importance of eschatology. Just as the ethics of a just war demand a reasonable prospect of success before political leaders could be warranted in exposing soldiers and civilians to the threat and horror of war, so the ethics of theodicy require the hope of a renewed world in which sufferings are ended, wrongs are righted, the grieving and grieved-for are reunited, and remade persons are so compensated for what they have endured that it is "not worth comparing with the glory about to be revealed" to them (Rom. 8:18). Only with such a *telos* to creation could God be warranted in exposing his creatures to such suffering as has racked them. All the contributors seem to recognize this eschatological necessity. Swinburne accepts that "if any life on earth is still on balance bad, God has an obligation to compensate for that bad in the afterlife so that the total life of such an individual will be on balance good. That, in his omnipotence, he can do. Christianity teaches that humans live again in a new world after their death, and clearly God can compensate any persons whose lives on earth are on balance bad with a good afterlife." Vitale assumes that "God offers to every person an eternal life that would be a great good to them overall." And Southgate expresses his belief that the atonement "leads ultimately to a dimension of existence in which there is no more suffering."

The fourth component of a compound theodicy might be the common belief that eschatological hope is grounded, and has been glimpsed, in the resurrection of Jesus Christ. As Michael Lloyd writes, "It is on the cross that the fundamental divisions of creation are ultimately healed, and it is in the resurrection that we see the firstfruits of the renewed and restored creation"; it would be hazardous to believe in the reality of eschatological hope if our forebears in the faith had not seen with their own eyes the reality of the resurrection and declared to us what they had seen with their eyes and touched with their hands. Only on the basis of such reported revelation may we believe that God is light and in him there is no darkness at all (i.e., in the utter goodness of God); and only on the basis of such reported revelation, therefore, may our joy be complete (cf. 1 John 1:1–4).

The fifth component of a compound theodicy would be the shared view of all the contributors that, given God's action against evil, suffering, and death in the ministry, death, resurrection, and return of Jesus Christ, humans are called to work with their Creator against all that mars and defaces his world, in whatever ways are realistically open to us—to work against injustice, as a glimpse of the justice of God's coming kingdom; to work medically and compassionately and economically and prayerfully against suffering, as a glimpse of the day when mourning and crying and pain will be no more (see Rev. 21:4). The best theodical argument is a human life given to compassionate cooperation with the redemptive work of God.

Finally, the fourth way in which the contributors are perhaps closer than might at first appear is that they all seem to accept that their positions still have challenges to face and work to do. Rosenberg's exploration of Augustine and evolution would be strengthened (and could, perhaps, become a full-blown theodicy) if it could be explained why, if God is committed to the ultimate overcoming of suffering and death, he did not intervene to prevent the natural tendency of finite being to decay. Lloyd's fall-of-the-angels hypothesis, like all fall-based theodicies, needs to give an account of how a fully aware declension from a truly perceived Deity, experienced as the source of all love and the quintessence of beauty, could be anything other than inexplicable and arbitrary. Give the angels too much reasonable ground for falling, and evil gets rooted in the ontology of creation; give them too little ground for falling, and evil is not accounted for at all. Swinburne's Irenaean theodicy has to address the apparent tension between any attempt to justify the way things are and the suffering that pertains, on the one hand, and the divine assault on suffering and the divine movement to change the way things are so that they come to conform to the kingdom of God, on the other. Southgate's only way theodicy, like all inevitable accounts of creaturely suffering, could usefully do further work on the nature of that inevitability and give further support for the view that the currently pain-ridden natural order is the only way in which God could have created a physical world containing free creatures such as ourselves. Vitale could do more either to argue that personal identity is in fact tied to physical origination or to show how his approach could accommodate the rejection of this claim. His theodicy is also vulnerable to a concern about suffering in one person's life being allowed not primarily for the good of that person but for the good of future people.

In May 1832 John Constable's painting *The Opening of Waterloo Bridge* was exhibited beside J. M. W. Turner's latest seascape. After both paintings had been hung, Turner returned with his paintbrush and palette and added a single blob of red paint in the middle of his green sea. When Constable revisited the exhibition, he is reported to have exclaimed, "Turner has been here, and has fired a cannon!" Works of art do not just sit mutely beside each other: they interact, they interrogate each other, they highlight problems in each other, and they reveal new insight in one another. So do academic writings. Inevitably, the publication of our different theodical positions side by side in this volume will cause us to revisit and revise our own work. The essays in part 3 are therefore works in progress, but the authors hope that they give both inspiration and confidence in the project of theodicy.

Further Reading

Berry, R. J., and Michael Northcott, eds. *Theology after Darwin*. Milton Keynes, UK: Paternoster, 2009.

Edwards, Denis. *The God of Evolution: A Trinitarian Theology*. New York: Paulist Press, 1999.

Friesenhahn, Jacob. *The Trinity and Theodicy: The Trinitarian Theology of Von Balthasar and the Problem of Evil*. New York: Routledge, 2016.

Griffin, David Ray. *God, Power and Evil: A Process Theodicy*. Philadelphia: Westminster, 1976.

Kropf, Richard W. *Evil and Evolution: A Theodicy*. Eugene, OR: Wipf & Stock, 2004.

Mathewes, Charles T. *Evil and the Augustinian Tradition*. Cambridge: Cambridge University Press, 2007.

McGrath, Alister. *Darwinism and the Divine: Evolutionary Thought and Natural Theology*. Malden, MA: Wiley-Blackwell, 2011.

Messer, Neil. *Selfish Genes and Christian Ethics: Theological and Ethical Reflection on Evolutionary Biology*. London: SCM, 2007.

Nowak, Martin A., and Sarah Coakley. *Evolution, Games, and God: The Principle of Cooperation*. Cambridge, MA: Harvard University Press, 2013.

Rist, John. *Augustine: Ancient Thought Baptized*. Cambridge: Cambridge University Press, 1994.

Ruse, Michael. *Can a Darwinian Be a Christian? The Relationship between Science and Religion*. Cambridge: Cambridge University Press, 2001.

———. *The Evolution-Creation Struggle*. Cambridge, MA: Harvard University Press, 2006.

Walton, John. *The Lost World of Adam and Eve: Genesis 2–3 and the Human Origins Debate*. Downers Grove, IL: IVP Academic, 2015.

———. *The Lost World of Genesis One: Ancient Cosmology and the Origins Debate*. Downers Grove, IL: IVP Academic, 2009.

BIBLIOGRAPHY

Adams, Marilyn McCord, and Robert Merrihew Adams, eds. *The Problem of Evil.* Oxford: Oxford University Press, 1990.

Adams, Robert M. "Existence, Self-Interest, and the Problem of Evil." *Noûs*, 1979. Reprinted with corrections in Robert Merrihew Adams, *The Virtue of Faith, and Other Essays in Philosophical Theology*, 65–76. Oxford: Oxford University Press, 1987.

———. *Finite and Infinite Goods*. Oxford: Oxford University Press, 1999.

———. "Love and the Problem of Evil." *Philosophia* 34, no. 3 (2006): 243–51.

———. "Must God Create the Best?" *Philosophical Review* 81 (1972): 317–32.

Alexander, Denis R. *Creation or Evolution: Do We Have to Choose?* 2nd ed. Oxford: Monarch, 2014.

Alvarez, Sara, Anthony Di Fiore, Jane Champion, Mary Susan Pavelka, Johanna Páez, and Andrés Link. "Male-Directed Infanticide in Spider Monkeys (*Ateles* spp.)." *Primates* 56 (2015): 173–81.

Andrews, Kristin. *The Animal Mind: An Introduction to the Philosophy of Animal Cognition*. New York: Routledge, 2015.

"Animal Odd Couples." *Nature* PBS video, 53:20. Premiered on November 7, 2012. http://www.pbs.org/wnet/nature/animal-odd-couples-full-episode/8009/.

Aquinas. *See* Thomas Aquinas.

Aristotle. *Complete Works of Aristotle*. Vol. 2, *The Revised Oxford Translation*. Edited by Jonathan Barnes. Bollingen Series. Princeton: Princeton University Press, 1984.

———. *Metaphysics*. Translated by Hugh Lawson-Tancred. New York: Penguin, 1998.

Arnold, Bill T. *Genesis*. New Cambridge Bible Commentary. Cambridge: Cambridge University Press, 2008.

Atkins, Peter. "Atheism and Science." In *Oxford Handbook of Religion and Science*, edited by Philip Clayton and Zachary Simpson, 124–36. Oxford: Oxford University Press, 2006.

Atran, Scott. *In Gods We Trust: The Evolutionary Landscape of Religion*. New York: Oxford University Press, 2012.

Attfield, Robin. *Creation, Evolution and Meaning*. Burlington, VT: Ashgate, 2006.

Augustine. *The Augustine Catechism: Enchiridion on Faith, Hope and Charity*. In *Works of St. Augustine for the Twenty-First Century*, translated by Bruce Harbert, edited and introduced by Boniface Ramsey. Hyde Park, NY: New City Press, 1999.

———. *City of God*. Translated by Henry Bettenson. New York: Penguin, 1972.

———. *The City of God against the Pagans*. Translated by R. W. Dyson. New York: Cambridge University Press, 1998.

———. *Confessions*. Translated by Henry Chadwick. Oxford: Oxford University Press, 1991.

———. *Confessions and Enchiridion*. Translated by Albert Cook Outler. Library of Christian Classics 7. London: SCM, 1955.

———. *Confessions of St. Augustine, Books I–X*. Translated by Francis J. Sheed. New York: Sheed & Ward, 1942.

———. *Expositions of the Psalms*. 6 vols. Translated by Maria Boulding. Hyde Park, NY: New City, 2000–2004.

———. *The Literal Meaning of Genesis*. Translated by John H. Taylor, SJ. Ancient Christian Writers 41 and 42. New York: Paulist Press, 1982.

———. *On Christian Teaching*. Translated by R. P. H. Green. Oxford: Oxford University Press, 1999.

———. *On the Free Choice of the Will*. In *The Problem of Free Choice*, translated by Dom Mark Pontifex. New York: Newman, 1955.

———. *Propositions from the Epistle to the Romans*. In *Augustine on Romans*, translated by Paula Fredriksen Landes, 2–49. Chico, CA: Scholars Press, 1982.

———. *Saint Augustine: Anti-Pelagian Writings*. Edited by Philip Schaff. Translated by Peter Holmes. *The Nicene and Post-Nicene Fathers of the Christian Church*, series 1, vol. 5. New York: Christian Literature, 1887.

———. *Sermons*. 11 volumes. Translated by Edmund Hill. Works of Saint Augustine III/1–III/11. Hyde Park, NY: New City, 1990–97.

Austin, J. L. *How to Do Things with Words*. Cambridge, MA: Harvard University Press, 1962.

Axelrod, Robert. *The Evolution of Cooperation*. New York: Basic Books, 1984.

Ayala, Francisco J. *Darwin's Gift to Science and Religion*. Washington, DC: Joseph Henry, 2007.

———. "Molecular Biology: Darwin's Precious Gift." In *The Cambridge Encyclopedia of Darwin and Evolutionary Thought*, edited by Michael Ruse, 397–404. Cambridge: Cambridge University Press.

Baker, Mark C., and Goetz Stewart, eds. *The Soul Hypothesis: Investigations into the Existence of the Soul*. New York: Continuum, 2011.

Balcombe, Jonathan. *Second Nature: The Inner Lives of Animals*. New York: Palgrave Macmillan, 2010.

Balfour, Arthur James. *Theism and Humanism*. New York: Hodder & Stoughton, 1915.

Barnard, Alan. *Genesis of Symbolic Thought*. Cambridge: Cambridge University Press, 2012.

Barr, James. *The Garden of Eden and the Hope of Immortality*. Minneapolis: Fortress, 1992.

Barrett, Matthew, and Ardel B. Caneday, eds. *Four Views on the Historical Adam*. Grand Rapids: Zondervan, 2013.

Barth, Karl. *Christ and Adam*. Translated by T. A. Smail. New York: Collier, 1952.

———. *Church Dogmatics* III/1. *The Doctrine of Creation*. Edited by G. Bromiley and T. F. Torrance. Edinburgh: T&T Clark, 1958.

Bartlett, Jamie. *The Dark Net: Inside the Digital Underworld*. Portsmouth, NH: William Heinemann, 2014.

Bauckham, Richard. *Bible and Ecology: Rediscovering the Community of Creation*. Sarum Theological Lectures. Waco: Baylor University Press; London: Darton, Longman and Todd, 2010.

Benatar, David. "Why It Is Better Never to Come into Existence." *American Philosophical Quarterly* 34, no. 3 (1997): 345–55.

Berkhof, Hendrikus. *Christian Faith: An Introduction to the Study of the Faith*. Grand Rapids: Eerdmans, 1979.

———. *Introduction to the Study of Dogmatics*. Grand Rapids: Eerdmans, 1985.

Bimson, John J. "Doctrines of the Fall and Sin after Darwin." In *Theology after Darwin*, edited by Michael S. Northcott and R. J. Berry, 106–22. Milton Keynes, UK: Paternoster, 2009.

———. "Reconsidering a Cosmic Fall." *Science & Christian Belief* 18, no. 1 (2006): 63–81.

Blocher, Henri. *Original Sin: Illuminating the Riddle*. Grand Rapids: Eerdmans, 1999.

Boehm, Christopher. *Moral Origins: The Evolution of Virtue, Altruism, and Shame*. New York: Basic Books, 2012.

Botha, Rudolf. "Constraining the Arbitrariness of Exaptationist Accounts of the Evolution of Language." *Lingua* 121 (2011): 1552–63.

———. "Inferring Modern Language for Ancient Objects." In *The Oxford Handbook of Language Evolution*, edited by Maggie Tallerman and Kathleen R. K. Gibson, 303–12. Oxford: Oxford University Press, 2012.

———. "Protolanguage and the 'God Particle.'" *Lingua* 122 (2012): 1308–24.

Botha, Rudolf, and Martin Everaert, eds. *The Evolutionary Emergence of Language: Evidence and Inference*. Oxford: Oxford University Press, 2013.

———. "Introduction: Evidence and Inference in the Study of Language Evolution." In *The Evolutionary Emergence of Language: Evidence and Inference*, edited by Rudolf Botha and Martin Everaert, 1–17. Oxford: Oxford University Press, 2013.

Bowler, Peter J. *Monkey Trials and Gorilla Sermons: Evolution and Christianity from Darwin to Intelligent Design*. Cambridge, MA: Harvard University Press, 2007.

Bretzke, James T. *Consecrated Phrases: A Latin Theological Dictionary; Latin Expressions Commonly Found in Theological Writings*. 3rd ed. Collegeville, MN: Liturgical Press, 2013.

Brink, Gijsbert van den. *See* van den Brink, Gijsbert.

Brooke, John Hedley. *Science and Religion: Some Historical Perspectives*. Cambridge: Cambridge University Press, 1991.

———. *Science and Religion: Some Historical Perspectives*. Cambridge: Cambridge University Press, 2014.

Brown, Robert F. "On the Necessary Imperfection of Creation: Irenaeus' *Adversus Haereses* iv, 38." *Scottish Journal of Theology* 28 (1975): 17–25.

Brown, William P. *The Seven Pillars of Creation: The Bible, Science, and the Ecology of Wonder*. New York: Oxford University Press, 2010.

Brunner, Emil. *Christian Doctrine of Creation and Redemption*. Translated by Olive Wyon. Philadelphia: Westminster, 1952.

Burdett, Michael S. *Eschatology and the Technological Future*. New York: Routledge, 2015.

———. "The Image of God and Human Uniqueness: Challenges from the Biological and Information Sciences." *Expository Times* 127, no. 1 (2015): 3–10.

Burhoe, Ralph Wendell. "The Source of Civilization in the Natural Selection of Coadapted Information in Genes and Culture." *Zygon* 11, no. 3 (1976): 263–302.

Caird, George B. *Principalities and Powers: A Study in Pauline Theology*. Oxford: Clarendon, 1956.

Calcagno, James M., and Agustín Fuentes. "What Makes Us Human? Answers from Evolutionary Anthropology." *Evolutionary Anthropology* 21 (2012): 182–94.

Cann, Rebecca L., Mark Stoneking, and Allan C. Wilson. "Mitochondrial DNA and Human Evolution." *Nature* 325 (January 1987): 31–36. doi:10.1038/3225031a0.

Carruthers, Peter. *The Architecture of the Mind*. Oxford: Oxford University Press, 2006.

Cartmill, Matt, and Kaye Brown. "Being Human Means That 'Being Human' Means Whatever We Say It Means." *American Journal of Physical Anthropology* 144 (2011): 106.

Catechism of the Catholic Church. New York: Doubleday, 1995.

Catechism of the Catholic Church: Revised in Accordance with the Official Latin Text Promulgated by Pope John Paul II. 2nd ed. Vatican: Libreria Editrice Vaticana, 2000.

Chapman, Allan. *Slaying the Dragons: Destroying Myths in the History of Science and Faith*. Oxford: Lion Hudson, 2013.

———. *Stargazers: Copernicus, Galileo, the Telescope and the Church*. Oxford: Lion Hudson, 2014.

Chesterton, G. K. *Orthodoxy*. New York: Dodd, Mead, 1908. Reprint, Milwaukee: Cavalier, 2015.

Clayton, Philip, and Jeffrey Schloss, eds. *Evolution and Ethics: Human Morality in Biological and Religious Perspective*. Grand Rapids: Eerdmans, 2004.

Clines, D. J. A. "The Image of God in Man." *Tyndale Bulletin* 19 (1968): 53–103.

Clottes, Jean, and David Lewis-Williams. *The Shamans of Prehistory: Trance and Magic in the Painted Caves*. New York: Abrahams, 1998.

Coakley, Sarah. "Sacrifice Regained: Evolution, Cooperation and God." Lecture given at The Gifford Lectures, University of Aberdeen, Aberdeen, Scotland, 2012. http://www.giffordlectures.org/lectures/sacrifice-regained-evolution-cooperation-and-god.

Collins, C. John. "Adam and Eve in the Old Testament." In *Adam, the Fall, and Original Sin*, edited by Michael Reeves and Hans Madueme, 3–32. Grand Rapids: Baker Academic, 2014.

———. *Did Adam and Eve Really Exist? Who They Were and Why You Should Care*. Wheaton: Crossway, 2011.

———. "Echoes of Aristotle in Romans 2:14–15; or, Maybe Abimelech Was Not So Bad after All." *Journal of Markets and Morality* 13, no. 1 (2010): 123–73.

———. *Genesis 1–4: A Linguistic, Literary, and Theological Commentary*. Phillipsburg, NJ: P&R, 2006.

———. "Historical Adam (Old Earth)." In *Four Views on the Historical Adam*, edited by Matthew Barrett and Ardel B. Caneday, 143–75. Grand Rapids: Zondervan, 2013.

———."A Peculiar Clarity: How C. S. Lewis Can Help Us Think about Faith and Science." In *The Magician's Twin: C. S. Lewis on Science, Scientism, and Society*, edited by John G. West, 69–106. Seattle: Discovery Institute Press, 2012.

———. "Reading Genesis 1–2 with the Grain: Analogical Days." In *Reading Genesis 1–2: An Evangelical Conversation*, edited by J. Daryl Charles, 73–92. Peabody, MA: Hendrickson, 2013.

Collins, Francis S. *The Language of God*. New York: Free Press, 2006.

Cooper, John. *Body, Soul and Life Everlasting: Biblical Anthropology and the Monism-Dualism Debate*. Grand Rapids: Eerdmans, 1989.

Cortez, Marc. *Theological Anthropology: A Guide for the Perplexed*. London: T&T Clark, 2010.

Crisp, Oliver. "A Christological Model of the *Imago Dei*." In *The Ashgate Research Companion to Theological Anthropology*, edited by Joshua R. Farris and Charles Taliaferro, 217–32. Farnham, UK: Ashgate, 2015.

———. "On Original Sin." *International Journal of Systematic Theology* 17 (2015): 252–66.

Crouch, C. L. "Genesis 1:26–7 as a Statement of Humanity's Divine Parentage." *Journal of Theological Studies* 61 (2010): 1–15.

Cruz, Helen De, and Yves De Maeseneer. "The *Imago Dei*: Evolutionary and Theological Perspectives." *Zygon* 49, no. 1 (March 2014): 135–56.

Cunningham, Conor. *Darwin's Pious Idea: Why Ultra-Darwinists and Creationists Both Get It Wrong*. Grand Rapids: Eerdmans, 2010.

Darwin, Charles. "Letter no. 2814." Charles Darwin to Asa Gray, May 22, 1860. Darwin Correspondence Project. http://www.darwinproject.ac.uk/DCP-LETT-2814.

———. "A Low & Lewd Nature." In *Darwin: The Life of a Tormented Evolutionist*, edited by Adrian Desmond and James Moore, 441–50. New York: Norton, 1991.

———. *The Origin of Species by Means of Natural Selection*. 6th ed. Harvard Classics. New York: Collier, 1909. First published 1872 by John Murray (London).

Dawkins, Richard. *The Blind Watchmaker*. London: Penguin, 1986.

———. *The Selfish Gene*. London: Granada, 1978. Reprinted, New York: Oxford University Press, 1989.

———. "Universal Darwinism." In *Evolution from Molecules to Men*, edited by D. S. Bendall, 403–25. Cambridge: Cambridge University Press, 1983.

Deacon, Terrence William. "Language." In *Encyclopedia of Science and Religion*, edited by J. Wentzel Vrede van Huyssteen, 504–8. New York: Macmillan, 2003.

———. *The Symbolic Species: The Co-evolution of Language and the Human Brain*. New York: Norton, 1997.

Deane-Drummond, Celia E. *Creation through Wisdom: Theology and the New Biology*. Edinburgh: T&T Clark, 2000.

———. *The Wisdom of the Liminal: Evolution and Other Animals in Human Becoming*. Grand Rapids: Eerdmans, 2014.

Delitzsch, Franz. *A New Commentary on Genesis*. Edinburgh: T&T Clark, 1888.

Dembski, William. *The End of Christianity: Finding a Good God in an Evil World*. Nashville: B&H Academic, 2009.

Domning, Daryl P. *Original Selfishness: Original Sin and Evil in the Light of Evolution*. Burlington, VT: Ashgate, 2006.

Donald, Merlin. *A Mind So Rare: The Evolution of Human Consciousness*. New York: Norton, 2001.

———. *Origins of the Modern Mind: Three Stages in the Evolution of Culture and Cognition*. Cambridge, MA: Harvard University Press, 1991.

Dougherty, Trent. *The Problem of Animal Pain: A Theodicy for All Creatures Great and Small*. New York: Palgrave Macmillan, 2014.

Downes, Stephen, and Edouard Machery, eds. *Arguing about Human Nature*. New York: Routledge, 2013.

Duffy, Stephen J. "Our Hearts of Darkness: Original Sin Revisited." *Theological Studies* 49 (1988): 597–622.

Dugatkin, Lee Alan. *Cheating Monkeys and Citizen Bees: The Nature of Cooperation in Animals and Humans*. Cambridge, MA: Harvard University Press, 1999.

———. *Cooperation among Animals: An Evolutionary Perspective*. Oxford: Oxford University Press, 1997.

Dunn, James D. G. *Romans*. Word Biblical Commentary. Dallas: Word, 1988.

Dupre, John. *Humans and Other Animals*. Oxford: Clarendon, 2002.

Durham, William H. *Coevolution: Genes, Culture, and Human Diversity*. Stanford, CA: Stanford University Press, 1991.

Eastman, Susan. "The Shadow Side of Second-Person Engagement: Sin in Paul's Letter to the Romans." *European Journal for Philosophy of Religion* 5, no. 4 (2013): 125–44.

Edwards, Denis. "Every Sparrow That Falls to the Ground: The Cost of Evolution and the Christ-Event." *Ecotheology* 11, no. 1 (2006): 103–23.

———. *The God of Evolution: A Trinitarian Theology*. New York: Paulist Press, 1999.

Enns, Peter. *The Evolution of Adam: What the Bible Does and Doesn't Say about Human Origins*. Grand Rapids: Brazos, 2012.

———. *Inspiration and Incarnation*. Grand Rapids: Baker Academic, 2005.

Farris, Joshua. "A Substantive (Soul) Model of the *Imago Dei*: A Rich Property View." In *The Ashgate Research Companion to Theological Anthropology*, edited by Joshua R. Farris and Charles Taliaferro, 165–78. Farnham, UK: Ashgate, 2015.

Farris, Joshua, and Charles Taliaferro, eds. *The Ashgate Research Companion to Theological Anthropology*. Farnham, UK: Ashgate, 2015.

Farrow, Douglas. *Ascension and Ecclesia: On the Significance of the Doctrine of the Ascension for Ecclesiology and Christian Cosmology*. Grand Rapids: Eerdmans, 1999.

———. "St. Irenaeus of Lyons: The Church and the World." *Pro Ecclesia* 4 (1995): 333–55.

Feinberg, John S. *Where Is God? A Personal Story of Finding God in Grief and Suffering*. Nashville: Broadman & Holman, 2004.

Fergusson, David. "Humans Created according to the *Imago Dei*: An Alternative Proposal." *Zygon* 48 (2012): 439–53.

Fern, Richard L. *Nature, God and Humanity: Envisioning an Ethics of Nature*. Cambridge: Cambridge University Press, 2002.

Feuerbach, Ludwig. *The Essence of Christianity*. Translated by George Eliot. Buffalo: Prometheus Books, 1989.

Formby, C. W. *The Unveiling of the Fall*. London: Williams and Norgate, 1923.

Fowler, Chris. *The Archaeology of Personhood: An Anthropological Approach*. New York: Routledge, 2004.

Frei, Hans. "The 'Literal Reading' of Biblical Narrative in Christian Tradition: Does It Stretch or Will It Break?" In *The Bible and Narrative Tradition*, edited by Frank McConnell, 36–77. Oxford: Oxford University Press, 1986.

Fretheim, Terence. *God and World in the Old Testament: A Relational Theology of Creation*. Nashville: Abingdon, 2005.

———. *The Suffering of God: An Old Testament Perspective*. Philadelphia: Fortress, 1984.

Fuentes, Agustín. *Evolution of Human Behavior*. New York: Oxford University Press, 2009.

———. "Human Evolution, Niche Complexity, and the Emergence of a Distinctly Human Imagination." *Time and Mind* 7, no. 3 (2014): 241–57.

———. "A New Synthesis: Resituating Approaches to the Evolution of Human Behaviour." *Anthropology Today* 25, no. 3 (2009): 12–17.

———. "On Nature and the Human: Introduction." *American Anthropologist: Vital Forum* 112, no. 4 (2010): 512.

———. "On Nature and the Human: More than a Human Nature." *American Anthropologist: Vital Forum* 112, no. 4 (2010): 519.

———. *Race, Monogamy, and Other Lies They Told You: Busting Myths about Human Nature*. Berkeley: University of California Press, 2012.

Fuentes, Agustín, and Aku Visala. *Conversations on Human Nature*. Walnut Creek, CA: Left Coast, 2015.

Garr, W. Randall. "'Image' and 'Likeness' in the Inscription from Tell Fakhariyeh." *Israel Exploration Journal* 50 (2000): 227–34.

Gauger, Ann, Douglas Axe, and Casey Luskin. *Science and Human Origins*. Seattle: Discovery Institute Press, 2012.

Gazzaniga, Michael. *Human: The Science behind What Makes Your Brain Unique*. New York: HarperCollins, 2009.

Geach, Peter. *Providence and Evil*. Cambridge: Cambridge University Press, 1977.

Gehlen, Arnold. *Der Mensch: Seine Natur und seine Stellung in der Welt*. Vol. 12. Wiesbaden: AULA-Verlag, 1978. Translated by Clare McMillan and Karl Pillemer as *Man, His Nature and Place in the World* (New York: Columbia University Press, 1988).

Geisler, Norman L. *The Roots of Evil*. Grand Rapids: Zondervan, 1978.

Gergely, G., and G. Csibra. "Sylvia's Recipe: The Role of Imitation and Pedagogy in the Transmission of Cultural Knowledge." In *Roots of Human Sociality: Culture, Cognition and Interaction*, edited by N. J. Enfield and Stephen C. Levinson, 229–55. New York: Berg, 2006.

Giberson, Karl, and Francis Collins. *The Language of Science and Faith: Straight Answers to Genuine Questions*. Downers Grove, IL: InterVarsity, 2011.

Gingerich, Owen. *God's Planet*. Cambridge, MA: Harvard University Press, 2014.

Göcke, Benedikt Paul, ed. *After Physicalism*. Notre Dame, IN: University of Notre Dame Press, 2012.

Gould, Stephen Jay, and Niles Eldredge. "Punctuated Equilibria: An Alternative to Phyletic Gradualism." In *Models in Paleobiology*, edited by Thomas J. M. Schopf, 82–115. San Francisco: Freeman Cooper, 1972.

Green, Joel. *Body, Soul, and Human Life: The Nature of Humanity in the Bible.* Bletchley, UK: Paternoster, 2008.

Green, Peter. *The Problem of Evil.* London: Longmans, Green, 1920.

Gregersen, Niels H. "The Cross of Christ in an Evolutionary World." *Dialog: A Journal of Theology* 40, no. 3 (2001): 192–207.

———. "Deep Incarnation: Why Evolutionary Continuity Matters in Christology." *Toronto Journal of Theology* 26, no. 2 (2010): 173–82.

———. "The Naturalness of Religious Imagination and the Idea of Revelation." *Ars Disputandi: The Online Journal for Philosophy of Religion* 3 (2003). www.arsdisputandi.org.

Grenz, Stanley. *The Social God and the Relational Self: A Trinitarian Theology of the Imago Dei.* Louisville: Westminster John Knox, 2001.

Griffin, David Ray. *God, Power and Evil: A Process Theodicy*. Philadelphia: Westminster, 1976.

Griffiths, Paul, and Kim Sterelny. *Sex and Death: An Introduction to the Philosophy of Biology*. Chicago: University of Chicago Press, 1999.

Guinagh, Kevin. "Saint Augustine and Evolution." *Classical Weekly* 40, no. 4 (1946): 26–31.

Gunton, Colin. *The Triune Creator*. Grand Rapids: Eerdmans, 1998.

Hamilton, Victor P. *The Book of Genesis: Chapters 1–17*. New International Commentary on the Old Testament. Grand Rapids: Eerdmans, 1990.

Hamilton, W. D. "The Evolution of Altruistic Behavior." *American Naturalist* 97, no. 896 (1963): 354–56.

Harent, Stéphane. "Original Sin." *Catholic Encyclopedia*. New York: Appleton, 1911. http://www.newadvent.org/cathen/11312a.htm.

Harlow, Daniel. "After Adam: Reading Genesis in an Age of Evolutionary Science." *Perspectives on Science and Christian Faith* 62, no. 3 (2010): 179–95.

Harris, Mark. *The Nature of Creation: Examining the Bible and Science*. Durham: Acumen, 2013.

Harrison, Peter. *The Bible, Protestantism, and the Rise of Natural Science*. Cambridge: Cambridge University Press, 2001.

———. *The Fall of Man and the Foundations of Science*. Cambridge: Cambridge University Press, 2009.

———. *The Territories of Science and Religion*. Chicago: University of Chicago Press, 2015.

Hasker, William. *The Emergent Self*. Ithaca, NY: Cornell University Press, 1999.

———. *Providence, Evil and the Openness of God*. New York: Routledge, 2004.

———. "Souls Beastly and Human." In *The Soul Hypothesis: Investigations into the Existence of the Soul*, edited by Mark C. Baker and Stewart Goetz, 202–21. New York: Continuum, 2011.

———. *The Triumph of God over Evil: Theodicy for a World of Suffering*. Downers Grove, IL: IVP Academic, 2008.

Haught, John F. *Deeper than Darwin*. Boulder, CO: Westview, 2003.

———. "Science, Teilhard and Vatican II." *Lumen: A Journal of Catholic Studies* 2, no. 1 (2014): 1–12.

Hauke, Manfred. *Heilsverlust in Adam: Stationen griechischer Erbsündenlehre; Irenäus—Origenes—Kappadozier*. Paderborn, Germany: Bonifatius, 1993.

Hays, Christopher B. *Hidden Riches: A Sourcebook for Comparative Study of the Hebrew Bible and Ancient Near East*. Louisville: Westminster John Knox, 2014.

Hays, Christopher M. "Towards a Faithful Criticism." In *Evangelical Faith and the Challenge of Historical Criticism*, edited by Christopher M. Hays and Christopher B. Ansberry, 1–23. Grand Rapids: Baker Academic, 2013.

Hays, Christopher M., and Christopher B. Ansberry, eds. *Evangelical Faith and the Challenge of Historical Criticism*. Grand Rapids: Baker Academic, 2013.

Hays, Christopher M., and Stephen Lane Herring. "Adam and the Fall." In *Evangelical Faith and the Challenge of Historical Criticism*, edited by Christopher M. Hays and Christopher B. Ansberry, 24–54. Grand Rapids: Baker Academic, 2013.

Hefner, Philip J. "Biocultural Evolution and the Created Co-Creator." In *Science and Theology: The New Consonance*, edited by Ted Peters, 162–73. Boulder, CO: Westview, 1998.

———. "Biological Perspectives on Fall and Original Sin." *Zygon* 28, no. 1 (1993): 77–101.

———. "Culture Is Where It Happens." *Zygon* 40, no. 3 (2005): 523–27.

———. *The Human Factor: Evolution, Culture, and Religion*. Minneapolis: Fortress, 1993.

Hick, John. *Evil and the God of Love*. 3rd ed. New York: Palgrave Macmillan, 2010. First published 1966.

———. "An Irenaean Theodicy." In *Encountering Evil: Live Options in Theodicy*, edited by Stephen T. Davis, 38–72. New ed. Louisville: Westminster John Knox, 2001.

Hoekema, Anthony A. *Created in God's Image*. Grand Rapids: Eerdmans, 1994.

Holloway, Richard. Review of *The Face of God: The Gifford Lectures*, by Roger Scruton. *New Statesman*, March 29, 2012. http://www.newstatesman.com/books/2012/03/face-god-gifford-lectures.

Holsinger-Friesen, Thomas. *Irenaeus and Genesis: A Study of Competition in Early Christian Hermeneutics*. Winona Lake, IN: Eisenbrauns, 2009.

Horner, Victoria, and Andrew Whiten. "Causal Knowledge and Imitation/Emulation Switching in Chimpanzees (*Pan troglodytes*) and Children (*Homo sapiens*)." *Animal Cognition* 8, no. 3 (2005): 164–81.

Howell, Nancy R. "Relations between *Homo sapiens* and Other Animals: Scientific and Religious Arguments." In *The Oxford Handbook of Religion and Science*, edited by Philip Clayton and Zachary Simpson, 945–61. Oxford: Oxford University Press, 2006.

Hrdy, Sarah. *Mothers and Others: The Evolutionary Origins of Mutual Understanding.* Cambridge, MA: Harvard University Press, 2009.

Hudson, Hud. *The Fall and Hypertime.* Oxford: Oxford University Press, 2014.

Huijgen, Arnold. *Divine Accommodation in John Calvin: Analysis and Assessment.* Göttingen: Vandenhoeck & Ruprecht, 2011.

Hume, David. *Dialogues concerning Natural Religion.* 2nd ed. Indianapolis: Hackett, 1998 (1779).

Hünermann, Peter. "Experience of 'Original Sin'?" *Concilium* 1 (2004): 108–14.

Huyssteen, J. Wentzel van. *See* van Huyssteen, J. Wentzel.

Ingold, Tim. "On Nature and the Human: What Is a Human Being?" *American Anthropologist: Vital Forum* 112, no. 4 (2010): 513–14.

Irenaeus of Lyons. *Against Heresies.* Translated by Dominic Unger. Ancient Christian Writers 55–57. New York: Paulist Press, 1992.

Jablonka, Eva, and Marion J. Lamb. *Evolution in Four Dimensions: Genetic, Epigenetic, Behavioral, and Symbolic Variation in the History of Life.* Cambridge, MA: MIT Press, 2005.

Jacobsen, Anders-Christian. "The Importance of Genesis 1–3 in the Theology of Irenaeus." *Zeitschrift für antikes Christentum* 8, no. 2 (2005): 299–316.

Jenson, Robert. *Systematic Theology.* Vol. 2, *The Works of God.* New York: Oxford University Press, 1999.

John of Damascus. *On the Orthodox Faith.* In *Hilary of Poitiers, John of Damascus,* ed. Philip Schaff and Henry Wace, trans. S. D. F. Salmond, *The Nicene and Post-Nicene Fathers of the Christian Church,* series 2, vol. 9. Oxford: James Parker, 1899.

Johnson, Elizabeth A. *Ask the Beasts: Darwin and the God of Love.* London: Bloomsbury, 2014.

Jong, Jonathan, and Aku Visala. "Three Quests for Human Nature: Some Philosophical Reflections." *Philosophy, Theology and the Sciences* 1 (2014): 146–71.

Karmin, Monika, et al. "A Recent Bottleneck of Y Chromosome Diversity Coincides with a Global Change in Culture." *Genome Research* 25, no. 4 (April 2015): 459–66. doi:10.1101/gr.186684.114.

Kaufman, Gordon D. *In the Beginning . . . Creativity.* Philadelphia: Fortress, 2004.

Kearney, Richard. *On Paul Ricoeur: The Owl of Minerva.* Aldershot, UK: Ashgate, 2004.

Kelly, Douglas. *Creation and Change: Genesis 1.1–2.4 in the Light of Changing Scientific Paradigms.* Ross-shire, UK: Christian Focus, 1997.

Kelly, Joseph F. *The Problem of Evil in the Western Tradition: From the Book of Job to Modern Genetics.* Collegeville, MN: Liturgical Press, 2002.

Kidner, Derek. *Genesis*. Tyndale Old Testament Commentary. Leicester, UK: Inter-Varsity, 1967.

Kilner, John F. *Dignity and Destiny: Humanity in the Image of God*. Grand Rapids: Eerdmans, 2015.

King, Barbara. *Evolving God: A Provocative View on the Origins of Religion*. New York: Doubleday, 2007.

King, Peter. "Damaged Goods: Human Nature and Original Sin." *Faith and Philosophy* 24, no. 3 (July 2007): 247–67.

Kirkpatrick, Lee A. *Attachment, Evolution, and the Psychology of Religion*. New York: Guilford, 2005.

Kluger, Jeffrey. "Scientists Rush to Understand the Murderous Mamas of the Monkey World." *Time*, June 15, 2011. http://content.time.com/time/health/article/0,8599,2076786,00.html.

Korsmeyer, Jerry D. *Evolution and Eden: Balancing Original Sin and Contemporary Science*. New York: Paulist Press, 1998.

Kreeft, Peter. *Making Sense out of Suffering*. Ann Arbor, MI: Servant, 1986.

Kripke, Saul A. "Naming and Necessity." In *Semantics of Natural Language*, edited by Donald Davidson and Gilbert Harman, 312–14. Dordrecht, Netherlands: Reidel, 1972.

Kuhn, Thomas S. *The Structure of Scientific Revolutions*. 2nd ed. Chicago: University of Chicago Press, 1970.

Laland, K. N., J. Odling-Smee, and M. W. Feldman. "Cultural Niche Construction and Human Evolution." *Journal of Evolutionary Biology* 14, no. 1 (January 8, 2001): 22–33.

Lamoureux, Denis O. "Beyond Original Sin: Is a Theological Paradigm Shift Inevitable?" *Perspectives on Science and Christian Faith* 67 (2015): 35–49.

———. *Evolutionary Creation: A Christian Approach to Evolution*. Eugene, OR: Wipf & Stock, 2008.

———. *Evolution: Scripture and Nature Say Yes!* Grand Rapids: Zondervan, 2016.

———. *I Love Jesus & I Accept Evolution*. Eugene, OR: Wipf & Stock, 2009.

———. "Lessons from the Heavens: On Scripture, Science and Inerrancy." *Perspectives in Christian Faith and Science* 60 (2008): 4–15.

———. "No Historical Adam: Evolutionary Creation View." In *Four Views on the Historical Adam*, edited by Matthew Barrett and Ardel B. Caneday, 37–65. Grand Rapids: Zondervan, 2013.

Lane, A. N. S. "Irenaeus on the Fall and Original Sin." In *Darwin, Creation and the Fall*, edited by R. J. Berry and T. A. Noble, 130–42. Nottingham, UK: Inter-Varsity, 2009.

Leftow, Brian. "Souls Dipped in Dust." In *Soul, Body and Survival: Essays on the Metaphysics of Human Persons*, edited by Kevin Corcoran, 120–38. Ithaca, NY: Cornell University Press, 2001.

Leibniz, Gottfried W. "The Confession of a Philosopher." In *Confessio Philosophi: Papers concerning the Problem of Evil, 1671–1678*, edited and translated by Robert C. Sleigh Jr., 26–109. New Haven: Yale University Press, 2005.

———. *Theodicy: Essays on the Goodness of God, the Freedom of Man, and the Origin of Evil*. Translated by E. M. Huggard. Hartford, CT: Yale University Press, 1952 (1709).

Lewin, Roger. *The Origins of Modern Humans*. New York: Scientific American Library, 1993.

Lewis, C. S. *The Discarded Image: An Introduction to Medieval and Renaissance Literature*. Cambridge: Cambridge University Press, 1964.

Lewis-Williams, David. *The Mind in the Cave: Consciousness and the Origins of Art*. New York: Thames & Hudson, 2002.

Lewontin, R. C. "Gene, Organism and Environment." In *Evolution from Molecules to Men*, edited by D. S. Bendall, 273–86. Cambridge: Cambridge University Press, 1983.

Lindbeck, George A. "Doctrinal Standards, Theological Theories and Practical Aspects of the Ministry in the Lutheran Churches." In *Evangelium-Welt-Kirche: Schlussbericht und Referate der römisch-katholisch/evangelisch-lutherischen Studienkommission "Das evangelium und die Kirche," 1967–1971*, 263–83. Frankfurt am Main: Lembeck and Knecht, 1975.

———. *The Nature of Doctrine: Religion and Theology in a Postliberal Age*. Philadelphia: Westminster, 1984.

Lindberg, David C., and Ronald L. Numbers, eds. *God and Nature: Historical Essays on the Encounter between Christianity and Science*. Berkeley: University of California Press, 1986.

Livingstone, David N. *Dealing with Darwin: Place, Politics, and Rhetoric in Religious Engagements with Evolution*. Baltimore: Johns Hopkins University Press, 2014.

Lloyd, Michael. "Are Animals Fallen?" In *Animals on the Agenda*, edited by Andrew Linzey and Dorothy Yamamoto, 147–60. London: SCM, 1997.

———. "The Cosmic Fall and the Free Will Defence." DPhil thesis, Oxford University, 1997.

———. "Fall." In *Dictionary of Ethics, Theology and Society*, edited by Paul Barry Clarke and Andrew Linzey, 368–70. New York: Routledge, 1996.

Longman, Tremper, III. "What Genesis 1–2 Teaches (and What It Doesn't)." In *Reading Genesis 1–2: An Evangelical Conversation*, edited by J. Daryl Charles, 103–28. Peabody, MA: Hendrickson, 2013.

Luther, Martin. "Heidelberg Disputation." In *Luther's Works*, vol. 31, *Career of the Reformer I*, edited by Harold J. Grimm and Helmut T. Lehmann, 35–70. Minneapolis: Fortress, 1957.

Lutheran World Federation and the Catholic Church. "Joint Declaration on the Doctrine of Justification." October 31, 1999. www.ewtn.com/library/curia/pccujnt.htm.

Lycan, William. "Giving Dualism Its Due." *Australasian Journal of Philosophy* 87 (2009): 551–63.

MacKay, Donald M. *The Open Mind, and Other Essays: A Scientist in God's World.* Edited by Melvin Tinker. Leicester, UK: Inter-Varsity, 1988.

Madueme, Hans, and Michael Reeves, eds. *Adam, the Fall, and Original Sin: Theological, Biblical, and Scientific Perspectives.* Grand Rapids: Baker Academic, 2014.

Mahlmann, Theodor. "Articulus Stantis et (Vel) Cadentis Ecclesiae." In *Religion Past & Present: Encyclopedia of Theology and Religion*, edited by Hans Dieter Betz, Don S. Browning, Bernd Janowski, and Eberhard Jüngel, 167–271. Leiden: Brill, 2007.

Manson, William. Review of *Principalities and Powers: A Study in Pauline Theology*, by G. B. Caird. *Scottish Journal of Theology* 11, no. 2 (June 1958): 202–4.

Marks, Jonathan. "On Nature and the Human: Off Human Nature." *American Anthropologist: Vital Forum* 112, no. 4 (2010): 513.

———. *Tales of the Ex-Apes: How We Think about Human Evolution.* Oakland: University of California Press, 2015.

———. *What It Means to Be 98% Chimpanzee: Apes, People, and Their Genes.* Berkeley: University of California Press, 2003.

———. "You Are Not an Ape." Guest lecture. TEDxEast, August 23, 2012. http://global.oup.com/us/companion.websites/fdscontent/uscompanion/us/static/companion.websites/9780190210847/pdf/17.pdf.

Markus, R. A. *Saeculum: History and Society in the Theology of St. Augustine.* Rev. ed. Cambridge: Cambridge University Press, 1988.

Marmodoro, Anne, and Jonathan Hill, eds. *The Metaphysics of the Incarnation.* New York: Oxford University Press, 2011.

Marrou, Henri I. *St. Augustine and His Influence through the Ages.* Translated by Patrick Hepburne-Scott. London: Longmans, Green, 1957.

Marx, Karl. "The Secret of Primitive Accumulation." Chap. 26 in *Capital*, vol. 1, *Economic Manuscripts.* Translated by Samuel Moore and Edward Aveling. First published in German in 1867. https://www.marxists.org/archive/marx/works/1867-c1/ch26.htm.

Mascall, Eric L. *Christian Theology and Natural Science.* London: Longmans, Green, 1956.

Mawson, Tim. "The Problem of Evil and Moral Indifference." *Religious Studies* 35, no. 3 (1999): 323–45.

McCoy, Andrew M. "Becoming Who We Are Supposed to Be: An Evaluation of Schneider's Use of Christian Theology in Conversation with Genetic Science." *Calvin Theological Journal* 49 (2014): 63–84.

McDaniel, Jay B. *Of God and Pelicans: A Theology of Reverence for Life.* Louisville: Westminster John Knox, 1989.

McFarland, Ian A. *In Adam's Fall: A Meditation on the Christian Doctrine of Original Sin*. Oxford: Wiley-Blackwell, 2010.

McGrath, Alister. "Augustine's Origin of Species: How the Great Theologian Might Weigh In on the Darwin Debate." *Christianity Today*, May 8, 2009, 38–41.

———. *The Foundations of Dialogue in Science and Religion*. New ed. Malden, MA: Blackwell, 1999.

———. *The Genesis of Doctrine: A Study in the Foundations of Doctrinal Criticism*. Cambridge, MA: Blackwell, 1990.

———. *A Scientific Theology*. Vol. 3, *Theory*. New York: T&T Clark, 2006.

McKenzie, Steven L. *How to Read the Bible: History, Prophecy, Literature—Why Modern Readers Need to Know the Difference and What It Means for Faith Today*. Oxford: Oxford University Press, 2005.

McLaughlin, Ryan. *Preservation and Protest: Theological Foundations for an Eco-Eschatological Ethics*. Minneapolis: Fortress, 2014.

Mellars, Paul. "Cognitive Changes and the Emergence of Modern Humans in Europe." *Cambridge Archeological Journal* 1, no. 1 (1991): 136–38.

———. "Major Issues in the Emergence of Modern Humans." *Current Anthropology* 30, no. 3 (1989): 349–85.

Meltzoff, Andrew N. "Infant Imitation after a 1-Week Delay: Long-Term Memory for Novel Acts and Multiple Stimuli." *Developmental Psychology* 24, no. 4 (1988): 470–76.

Messer, Neil. "Natural Evil after Darwin." In *Theology after Darwin*, edited by Michael S. Northcott and R. J. Berry, 139–54. Milton Keynes, UK: Paternoster, 2009.

Middleton, J. Richard. *The Liberating Image: The* Imago Dei *in Genesis 1*. Grand Rapids: Brazos, 2005.

Millard, A. R., and P. Bordreuil. "A Statue from Syria with Assyrian and Aramaic Inscriptions." *The Biblical Archaeologist* 45, no. 3 (1982): 135–41.

Miller, J. Maxwell. "In the 'Image' and 'Likeness' of God." *Journal of Biblical Literature* 91 (1972): 289–304.

Mitchell, Terence. "Eden, Garden of." In *New Bible Dictionary*, edited by I. Howard Marshall et al., 289–90. Downers Grove, IL: InterVarsity, 1996.

Mithen, Steven. *The Prehistory of the Mind: A Search for the Origins of Art, Religion and Science*. London: Thames & Hudson, 1996.

———. *The Singing Neanderthals: The Origins of Music, Language, Mind, and Body*. Cambridge, MA: Harvard University Press, 2006.

Moltmann, Jürgen. *God in Creation: A New Theology of Creation and the Spirit of God*. Minneapolis: Fortress, 1993.

Moreland, J. P. *The Recalcitrant* Imago Dei*: Human Persons and the Failure of Naturalism*. London: SCM, 2009.

Moritz, Joshua. "Animal Suffering, Evolution, and the Origins of Evil." *Zygon* 49, no. 2 (2014): 348–80.

———. "Evolution, the End of Human Uniqueness, and the Election of the *Imago Dei*." *Theology and Science* 9, no. 3 (2011): 307–39.

Mühling, Markus. *Resonances: Neurobiology, Evolution and Theology; Evolutionary Niche Construction, the Ecological Brain and Relational-Narrative Theology*. Göttingen: Vandenhoeck & Ruprecht, 2014.

Murphy, George L. "Roads to Paradise and Perdition: Christ, Evolution, and Original Sin." *Perspectives on Science and Christian Faith* 58 (2006): 109–18.

Murphy, Nancey. "Science and the Problem of Evil: Suffering as a By-Product of a Finely-Tuned Cosmos." In *Physics and Cosmology: Scientific Perspectives on the Problem of Evil*, edited by Nancey Murphy, Robert J. Russell, and William R. Stoeger, SJ, 131–51. Berkeley: Vatican Observatory and Center for Theology and the Natural Sciences, 2007.

Murray, Michael J. *Nature Red in Tooth and Claw: Theism and the Problem of Animal Suffering*. Oxford: Oxford University Press, 2008.

Nagel, Thomas. *Mind and Cosmos: Why the Materialist Neo-Darwinian Conception of Nature Is Almost Certainly False*. New York: Oxford University Press, 2012.

Newbigin, Lesslie. *Proper Confidence: Faith, Doubt, and Certainty in Christian Discipleship*. Grand Rapids: Eerdmans, 1995.

Newlands, George. *Christ and Human Rights*. Aldershot, UK: Ashgate, 2006.

———. *The Transformative Imagination*. Aldershot, UK: Ashgate, 2004.

Niebuhr, Reinhold. *Man's Nature and His Communities*. New York: Charles Scribner's Sons, 1965.

"No Adam, No Eve, No Gospel." *Christianity Today*, June 2011, 61.

Noble, T. A. "Original Sin and the Fall: Definitions and a Proposal." In *Darwin, Creation and the Fall*, edited by R. J. Berry and T. A. Noble, 101–12. Nottingham: Inter-Varsity, 2009.

Noble, William, and Iain Davidson. *Human Evolution, Language and Mind: A Psychological and Archaeological Inquiry*. Cambridge: Cambridge University Press, 1996.

Norenzayan, Ara. *Big Gods: How Religion Transformed Cooperation and Conflict*. Princeton: Princeton University Press, 2013.

Odling-Smee, F. John, Kevin N. Laland, and Marcus W. Feldman. *Niche Construction: The Neglected Process in Evolution*. Princeton: Princeton University Press, 2003.

Office of the General Assembly—Presbyterian Church (USA). *The Book of Confessions*. Louisville: Westminster John Knox, 2007.

O'Halloran, Nathan W., SJ. "Cosmic Alienation and the Origin of Evil: Rejecting the 'Only Way' Option." *Theology and Science* 13, no. 1 (2015): 43–63.

Olson, Eric. *What Are We? A Study in Personal Ontology*. Oxford: Oxford University Press, 2007.

Oord, Thomas Jay. *Defining Love: A Philosophical, Scientific, and Theological Engagement*. Grand Rapids: Brazos, 2010.

———. *The Nature of Love: A Theology*. St. Louis: Chalice, 2010.

———. *The Science of Love: The Wisdom of Well-Being*. Philadelphia: Templeton, 2005.

———. *The Uncontrolling Love of God: An Open and Relational Theory of Providence*. Downers Grove, IL: IVP Academic, 2015.

O'Regan, Cyril. *Gnostic Return in Modernity*. Albany, NY: SUNY Press, 2001.

Ostling, Richard N. "The Search for the Historical Adam." *Christianity Today*, June 2011, 23.

Page, Ruth. *God and the Web of Creation*. London: SCM, 1996.

Pagels, Elaine. *Adam, Eve, and the Serpent*. New York: Random House, 1988.

Parfit, Derek. *Reasons and Persons*. Oxford: Oxford University Press, 1984.

Park, Clara Claiborne. *The Siege: The First Eight Years of an Autistic Child; With an Epilogue, Fifteen Years Later*. Boston: Little, Brown, 1982.

Pascal, Blaise. *Pensées*. Translated by A. J. Krailsheimer. New York: Penguin, 1995.

Patterson, Sue M. *Realist Christian Theology in a Postmodern Age*. New York: Cambridge University Press, 1999.

Peacocke, Arthur. "Biological Evolution—A Positive Theological Appraisal." In *Evolutionary and Molecular Biology: Scientific Perspectives on Divine Action*, edited by Robert J. Russell, William R. Stoeger, SJ, and Francisco J. Ayala, 357–76. Berkeley: Vatican Observatory and Center for Theology and the Natural Sciences, 1998.

———. "The Cost of New Life." In *The Work of Love: Kenosis as Creation*, edited by John Polkinghorne, 21–42. Grand Rapids: Eerdmans, 2001.

Peters, Ted, and Martinez Hewlett. *Can You Believe in God and Evolution?* Nashville: Abingdon, 2009.

———. *Evolution from Creation to New Creation: Conflict, Conversation, and Convergence*. Nashville: Abingdon, 2003.

Pinker, Steven. *The Blank Slate: The Modern Denial of Human Nature*. New York: Penguin, 2002.

———. *How the Mind Works*. London: Penguin, 1997.

Pinsent, Andrew. *The Second-Person Perspective in Aquinas's Ethics: Virtues and Gifts*. New York: Routledge, 2012.

Pius XII, Pope. "Humani Generis, Concerning Some False Opinions Threatening to Undermine the Foundations of Catholic Doctrine (Encyclical)," *Libreria Editrice Vaticana*. August 12, 1950. http://w2.vatican.va/content/pius-xii/en/encyclicals/documents/hf_p-xii_enc_12081950_humani-generis.html.

Plantinga, Alvin. *God, Freedom, and Evil*. Grand Rapids: Eerdmans, 2002. First published 1974.

———. "Historical Adam: One Possible Scenario." *Think Christian* (blog), February 14, 2013. http://thinkchristian.reframemedia.com/historical-adam-one-possible-scenario.

———. *Warrant and Proper Function*. New York: Oxford University Press, 1993.

———. *Where the Conflict Really Lies: Science, Religion, and Naturalism*. New York: Oxford University Press, 2011.

Polkinghorne, John. *Belief in God in an Age of Science: The Terry Lectures*. New Haven: Yale University Press, 1998.

———. *Exploring Reality: The Intertwining of Science and Religion*. London: SPCK, 2005.

———. *The God of Hope and the End of the World*. London: SPCK, 2002.

———. *Living with Hope: A Scientist Looks at Advent, Christmas, and Epiphany*. Louisville: Westminster John Knox, 2003.

———. *Reason and Reality: The Relationship between Science and Theology*. Philadelphia: Trinity Press International, 1991.

———. "Reflections of a Bottom-Up Thinker." In *God and the Scientist: Exploring the Work of John Polkinghorne*, edited by Fraser Watts and Christopher Knight, 1–12. Aldershot, UK: Ashgate, 2012.

———. *Rochester Roundabout: The Story of High Energy Physics*. New York: Freeman, 1989.

———. *Science and Providence: God's Interaction with the World*. London: SPCK, 1989.

———. *Science and Providence: God's Interaction with the World*. Philadelphia: Templeton Foundation Press, 2005.

———. *Science and the Trinity: The Christian Encounter with Reality*. New Haven: Yale University Press, 2006.

Polkinghorne, John, and M. Welker, eds. *The End of the World and the Ends of God: Science and Theology on Eschatology*. Harrisburg, PA: Trinity Press International, 2000.

Potts, Richard. "Environmental and Behavioral Evidence Pertaining to the Evolution of Early *Homo*." *Current Anthropology* 53, supp. 6 (2012): S299–S317.

———. *Humanity's Descent*. New York: Morrow, 1996.

———. "Sociality and the Concept of Culture in Human Origins." In *The Origins and Nature of Sociality*, edited by Robert W. Sussman and Audrey R. Chapman. New York: Walter de Gruyter, 2004.

Poythress, Vern. "Adam versus Claims from Genetics." *Westminster Theological Journal* 75 (2013): 65–82.

Putz, Oliver. "Moral Apes, Human Uniqueness, and the Image of God." *Zygon* 44, no. 3 (2009): 613–24.

Rad, Gerhard von. *Genesis: A Commentary*. Translated by John H. Marks. Rev. ed. Louisville: Westminster John Knox, 1973.

Rahner, Karl. *Basic Christian Ethics*. Louisville: Westminster John Knox, 1993.

———. "Current Problems in Christology." In *Theological Investigations*, vol. 1. London: Darton, Longman and Todd, 1974.

———. "The Theological Concept of Concupiscentia." In *Theological Investigations*, 1:347–82. London: Darton, Longman and Todd, 1974.

Ramsey, Paul. *Basic Christian Ethics*. Louisville: Westminster John Knox, 1993.

Raven, Charles. *The Creator Spirit*. London: Hopkinson, 1927.

Reeves, Michael, and Hans Madueme. "Threads in a Seamless Garment: Original Sin in Systematic Theology." In *Adam, the Fall, and Original Sin: Theological, Biblical, and Scientific Perspectives*, edited by Hans Madueme and Michael Reeves, 209–24. Grand Rapids: Baker Academic, 2014.

Ricoeur, Paul. *Oneself as Another*. Chicago: University of Chicago Press, 1992.

Rizzolatti, Giacomo. "Imitation: Mechanisms and Importance for Human Culture." *Rendiconti Lincei: Scienze Fisiche E Naturali* 25, no. 3 (2014): 285–89.

Roberts, Jason. "'Fill and Subdue?' Imaging God in New Social and Ecological Contexts." *Zygon* 50, no. 1 (March 2015): 42–63.

Robinson, Andrew. *God and the World of Signs: Trinity, Evolution, and the Metaphysical Semiotics of C. S. Peirce*. Boston: Brill, 2010.

Robinson, Dominic. *Understanding the* "Imago Dei"*: The Thought of Barth, von Balthasar and Moltmann*. Farnham, UK: Ashgate, 2011.

Rolston, Holmes, III. "Disvalues in Nature." *Monist* 75 (1992): 250–75.

———. *Science and Religion: A Critical Survey*. Philadelphia: Templeton Foundation Press, 2006.

Rosenberg, Stanley P. "Forming the *Saeculum*: The Desacralization of Nature and the Ability to Understand It in Augustine's *Literal Commentary on Genesis*." In *Studies in Church History*, vol. 46, edited by P. Clarke and T. Claydon, 1–14. Woodbridge, UK: Ecclesiastical History Society, 2010.

———. "Not So Alien and Unnatural after All: The Role of Deification in Augustine's Sermons." In *Visions of God and Ideas on Deification in Patristic Thought*, edited by M. Edwards and Elena Ene D-Vasilescu, 89–117. London: Routledge, 2016.

Roth, G., and U. Dicke. "Evolution of the Brain and Intelligence." *Trends in Cognitive Sciences* 9 (2005): 250–57.

Rowley, H. H. *The Faith of Israel*. London: SCM, 1956.

Ruse, Michael. *Can a Darwinian Be a Christian? The Relationship between Science and Religion*. Cambridge: Cambridge University Press, 2001.

———. *The Philosophy of Human Evolution*. Cambridge: Cambridge University Press, 2012.

Russell, Bertrand. *Why I Am Not a Christian, and Other Essays on Religion and Other Subjects*. New York: Simon & Schuster, 1957.

Russell, Robert John. *Cosmology, Evolution, and Resurrection Hope: Theology and Science in Creative Mutual Interaction*. Edited by Carl S. Helrich. Kitchener, ON: Pandora, 2006.

———. *Cosmology: From Alpha to Omega*. Minneapolis: Fortress, 2008.

———. *Time in Eternity*. Notre Dame, IN: University of Notre Dame Press, 2012.

Ryken, Philip G. "We Cannot Understand the World or Our Faith without a Real, Historical Adam." In *Four Views on the Historical Adam*, edited by Matthew Barrett and Ardel B. Caneday, 267–79. Grand Rapids: Zondervan, 2013.

Sala, Nohemi, et al. "Lethal Interpersonal Violence in the Middle Pleistocene." *PLOS ONE* 10, no. 5 (2015): e0126589. doi:10.1371/journal.pone.0126589.

Sawyer, John F. A. "The Meaning of בְּצֶלֶם אֱלֹהִים ('in the Image of God') in Genesis I–XI." *Journal of Theological Studies*, n.s., 25 (1974): 418–26.

Schaff, Philip, and David Schaff. *The Creeds of Christendom*. New York: Harper & Row, 1931.

Schloss, Jeffrey P. "Evolutionary Theory and Religious Belief." In *Oxford Handbook of Religion and Science*, edited by Philip Clayton, 187–206. Oxford: Oxford University Press, 2008.

Schneider, John R. "Recent Genetic Science and Christian Theology on Human Origins: An 'Aesthetic Supralapsarianism.'" *Perspectives on Science and Christian Faith* 62 (2010): 196–212.

Schrag, Calvin. *The Resources of Rationality: A Response to the Postmodern Challenge*. Bloomington: Indiana University Press, 1992.

Scruton, Roger. *The Face of God: The Gifford Lectures 2010*. New York: Continuum, 2012.

Seebohm, Frederic. *The Oxford Reformers*. London: Longmans, Green, 1869.

Shantz, Colleen. *Paul in Ecstasy: The Neurobiology of the Apostle's Life and Thought*. Cambridge: Cambridge University Press, 2009.

Sheets-Johnstone, Maxine. *The Roots of Morality*. University Park: Pennsylvania State University Press, 2008.

———. *The Roots of Thinking*. Philadelphia: Temple University Press, 1990.

Sherlock, Charles. *The Doctrine of Humanity*. Downers Grove, IL: InterVarsity, 1996.

Skinner, John. *A Critical and Exegetical Commentary on Genesis*. Edinburgh: T&T Clark, 1930.

Smith, James K. A. *The Fall of Interpretation: Philosophical Foundations for a Creational Hermeneutic*. Downers Grove, IL: InterVarsity, 2000.

———. "What Stands on the Fall? A Philosophical Exploration." In *Evolution and the Fall*, edited by William T. Cavanaugh and James K. A. Smith, 48–64. Grand Rapids: Eerdmans, 2017.

Smith, Quentin. "An Atheological Argument from Evil Natural Laws." *International Journal for Philosophy of Religion* 29, no. 3 (June 1991): 159–74.

Sober, Elliot, and David Sloan Wilson. *Unto Others: The Evolution and Psychology of Unselfish Behavior*. Cambridge, MA: Harvard University Press, 1998.

Sollereder, Bethany Noël. "Animal Suffering in an Unfallen World: A Theodicy of Non-Human Evolution." PhD diss., University of Exeter, 2014.

Sosis, Richard. "The Adaptationist-Byproduct Debate on the Evolution of Religion: Five Misunderstandings of the Adaptationist Program." *Journal of Cognition and Culture* 9 (2009): 315–32.

Southgate, Christopher. "Cosmic Evolution and Evil." In *The Cambridge Companion to the Problem of Evil*, edited by Chad Meister and Paul Moser, 147–64. Cambridge: Cambridge University Press, 2017.

———. "Creation as 'Very Good' and 'Groaning in Travail': An Exploration in Evolutionary Theodicy." In *The Evolution of Evil*, edited by Gaymon Bennett, Martinez Hewlett, Ted Peters, and Robert John Russell, 53–85. Göttingen: Vandenhoeck & Ruprecht, 2008.

———. "Does God's Care Make Any Difference? Theological Reflection on the Suffering of God's Creatures." In *Christian Faith and the Earth: Current Paths and Emerging Horizons in Ecotheology*, edited by Ernst M. Conradie, Sigurd Bergmann, Celia Deane-Drummond, and Denis Edwards, 97–114. London: Bloomsbury, 2014.

———. "God's Creation Wild and Violent, and Our Care for Other Animals." *Perspectives on Science and Christian Faith* 67 (2015): 245–53.

———. *The Groaning of Creation: God, Evolution, and the Problem of Evil*. Louisville: Westminster John Knox, 2008.

———. "Re-reading Genesis, John, and Job: A Christian's Response to Darwinism." *Zygon* 46, no. 2 (2011): 370–95.

Southgate, Christopher, and Andrew Robinson. "Varieties of Theodicy: An Exploration of Responses to the Problem of Evil Based on a Typology of Good-Harm Analyses." In *Physics and Cosmology: Scientific Perspectives on the Problem of Evil*, edited by Nancey Murphy, Robert J. Russell, and William R. Stoeger, SJ, 67–90. Berkeley: Vatican Observatory and Center for Theology and the Natural Sciences, 2007.

Sparks, Kenton L. *God's Word in Humans Words: An Evangelical Appropriation of Critical Biblical Scholarship*. Grand Rapids: Baker Academic, 2008.

Spencer, Nick, and Robert White. *Christianity, Climate Change, and Sustainable Living*. London: SPCK, 2007.

Steenberg, Matthew C. *Irenaeus on Creation: The Cosmic Christ and the Saga of Redemption*. Vigiliae Christianae Supplements. Leiden: Brill, 2008.

Stenmark, Mikael. "Is There a Human Nature?" *Zygon* 47 (2012): 890–902.

Sterelny, Kim. *The Evolved Apprentice: How Evolution Made Humans Unique*. Cambridge, MA: MIT Press, 2012.

Stump, Eleonore. "Non-Cartesian Substance Dualism and Materialism without Reductionism." *Faith and Philosophy* 12 (1995): 505–31.

———. "The Problem of Evil." *Faith and Philosophy* 2, no. 4 (October 1985): 392–424.

Surin, Kenneth. *Theology and the Problem of Evil*. Oxford: Blackwell, 1986.

Swinburne, Richard. *The Evolution of the Soul*. 2nd ed. Oxford: Oxford University Press, 1997.

———. *Is There a God?* Rev. ed. Oxford: Oxford University Press, 2010.

———. *Mind, Brain, and Free Will*. Oxford: Oxford University Press, 2013.

———. *Providence and the Problem of Evil*. Oxford: Clarendon, 1998.

Tanner, Kathryn. "Eschatology without a Future?" In *The End of the World and the Ends of God: Science and Theology on Eschatology*, edited by John Polkinghorne and Michael Welker, 222–37. Harrisburg, PA: Trinity Press International, 2000.

Tattersall, Ian. *Becoming Human: Evolution and Human Uniqueness*. New York: Harcourt Brace, 1998.

———. *The Monkey in the Mirror: Essays on the Science of What Makes Us Human*. New York: Harcourt, 2002.

———. "Origins of the Human Sense of Self." In *In Search of Self: Interdisciplinary Perspectives on Personhood*, edited by J. Wentzel van Huyssteen and Erik P. Wiebe, 33–49. Grand Rapids: Eerdmans, 2011.

Thomas Aquinas. *On Evil*. Edited by Brian Davies. Translated by Richard Regan. Oxford: Oxford University Press, 2003.

———. *Summa contra Gentiles*. Translated by the English Dominican Fathers. 2 vols. London: Burns, Oates and Washbourne, 1923–1924.

———. *Summa Theologica*. Translated by the English Dominican Fathers. 5 vols. Westminster, MD: Christian Classics, 1948.

Tinker, Melvin. "Language, Symbols and Sacraments: Was Calvin's View of the Lord's Supper Right?" *Churchman* 112, no. 2 (1998): 131–49.

Tomasello, Michael. "The Human Adaptation for Culture." *Annual Review of Anthropology* 28 (1999): 509–29.

———. *A Natural History of Human Thinking*. Cambridge, MA: Harvard University Press, 2014.

Tomasello, Michael, Sue Savage-Rumbaugh, and Ann Cale Kruger. "Imitative Learning of Actions on Objects by Children, Chimpanzees, and Enculturated Chimpanzees." *Child Development* 64, no. 6 (1993): 1688–705.

Toren, Benno van den. *See* van den Toren, Benno.

Torrance, T. F. *Divine and Contingent Order*. Edinburgh: T&T Clark, 1998.

Towes, John E. *The Story of Original Sin*. Eugene, OR: Wipf & Stock, 2013.

Towner, W. Sibley. "Interpretations and Reinterpretations of the Fall." In *Modern Biblical Scholarship: Its Impact on Theology and Proclamation*, edited by Francis A. Eigo, 53–85. Villanova, PA: Villanova University Press, 1984.

Trivers, Robert L. "The Evolution of Reciprocal Altruism." *Quarterly Review of Biology* 46, no. 1 (1971): 35–37.

Vainio, Olli-Pekka. "*Imago Dei* and Human Rationality." *Zygon* 49, no. 1 (2014): 121–34.

van den Brink, Gijsbert. "Are We Still Special? Evolution and Human Dignity." *Neue Zeitschrift für systematische Theologie und Religionsphilosophie* 53, no. 3 (2011): 318–32.

———. "Should We Drop the Fall? On Taking Evil Seriously." In *Strangers and Pilgrims on Earth: Essays in Honour of Abraham van de Beek*, edited by E. Van der Borght and P. van Geest, 761–77. Leiden: Brill, 2012.

van den Toren, Benno. *Christian Apologetics as Cross-Cultural Dialogue*. London: T&T Clark, 2011.

———. "Distinguishing Doctrine and Theological Theory: A Tool for Exploring the Interface between Science and Faith." *Science and Christian Belief* 28, no. 2 (2016): 55–73.

———. "Human Evolution and a Cultural Understanding of Original Sin." *Perspectives on Science and Christian Faith* 68, no. 1 (March 2016): 12–21.

VanGemeren, Willem A., ed. *New International Dictionary of Old Testament Theology and Exegesis*. Vol. 2. Carlisle, UK: Paternoster, 1996.

Vanhoozer, Kevin J. *The Drama of Doctrine: A Canonical-Linguistic Approach to Christian Theology*. Louisville: Westminster John Knox, 2005.

van Huyssteen, J. Wentzel. *Alone in the World? Human Uniqueness in Science and Theology*. Grand Rapids: Eerdmans, 2006.

———. "Coding the Nonvisible: Epistemic Limitations and Understanding Symbolic Behavior at Çatalhöyük." In *Religion in the Emergence of Civilization: Çatalhöyük as a Case Study*, edited by Ian Hodder, 99–121. Cambridge: Cambridge University Press, 2010.

———. "From Empathy to Embodied Faith: Interdisciplinary Perspectives on the Evolution of Religion." In *Evolution, Religion, and Cognitive Science: Critical and Constructive Essays*, edited by Fraser Watts and Léon P. Turner, 132–51. Oxford: Oxford University Press, 2014.

———. "The Historical Self: Memory and Religion at Çatalhöyük." In *Religion at Work in a Neolithic Society: Vital Matters*, edited by Ian Hodder, 109–31. Cambridge: Cambridge University Press, 2013.

———. "Interdisciplinary Perspectives on Human Origins and Religious Awareness." In *Becoming Human: Innovation in Prehistoric Material and Spiritual Culture*, edited by Colin Renfrew and Iain Morley, 235–52. Cambridge: Cambridge University Press, 2009.

———. "Post-Foundationalism and Human Uniqueness: A Reply to Responses." *Toronto Journal of Theology* 27, no. 1 (2011): 73–86.

———. "What Makes Us Human? The Interdisciplinary Challenge to Theological Anthropology and Christology." *Toronto Journal of Theology* 26, no. 2 (2010): 143–60.

———. "When Were We Persons? Why Hominid Evolution Holds the Key to Embodied Personhood." *Neue Zeitschrift für systematische Theologie und Religionsphilosophie* 52 (2010): 329–49.

Venema, Dennis R. "Genesis and the Genome: Genomics Evidence for Human-Ape Common Ancestry and Ancestral Hominid Population Sizes." *Perspectives on Science and Christian Faith* 62, no. 3 (2010): 166–78.

———. "Neanderthals, Denisovans and Human Speciation." *Letters to the Duchess* (blog), BioLogos Forum, September 23, 2011. http://biologos.org/blogs/dennis-venema-letters-to-the-duchess/understanding-evolution-neanderthals-denisovans-and-human-speciation.

Venema, Dennis R., and Scot McKnight. *Adam and the Genome: Reading Scripture after Genetic Science*. Grand Rapids: Brazos, 2017.

Visala, Aku. "*Imago Dei*, Dualism and Evolutionary Psychology." *Zygon* 49, no. 1 (2014): 101–20.

———. "Persons, Minds, and Bodies: Christian Philosophy on the Relationship of Persons and Their Bodies, Part I." *Philosophy Compass* 9 (2014): 713–22.

Waal, Frans B. M. de. *The Age of Empathy: Nature's Lessons for a Kinder Society*. New York: Harmony, 2009.

———. *Primates and Philosophers: How Morality Evolved*. Edited by Stephen Macedo and Josiah Ober. Princeton: Princeton University Press, 2006.

Wahlberg, Mats. "Was Evolution the Only Possible Way for God to Make Autonomous Creatures? Examination of an Argument in Evolutionary Theodicy." *International Journal of Philosophy and Religion* 77 (2015): 37–51.

Walsh, James, and P. G. Walsh, eds. *Divine Providence and Human Suffering*. Message of the Fathers of the Church. Wilmington, DE: Glazier, 1985.

Walton, John H. *Ancient Near Eastern Thought and the Old Testament: Introducing the Conceptual World of the Hebrew Bible*. Grand Rapids: Baker Academic, 2006.

———. *The Lost World of Adam and Eve: Genesis 2–3 and the Human Origins Debate*. Downers Grove, IL: IVP Academic, 2015.

Ward, Keith. "Freedom and the Irenaean Theodicy." *Journal of Theological Studies* 20 (1969): 249–54.

———. *God, Faith and the New Millennium: Christian Belief in an Age of Science*. Oxford: Oneworld, 1998.

———. *Religion and Human Nature*. Oxford: Oxford University Press, 1998.

Weaver, David. "The Exegesis of Romans 5:12 among the Greek Fathers and Its Implication for the Doctrine of Original Sin: The 5th–12th Centuries (Part II)." *St. Vladimir's Theological Quarterly* 27, no. 4 (1983): 133–59.

———. "The Exegesis of Romans 5:12 among the Greek Fathers and Its Implication for the Doctrine of Original Sin: The 5th–12th Centuries (Part III)." *St. Vladimir's Theological Quarterly* 28, no. 1 (1984): 231–57.

Webb, Stephen. *The Dome of Eden: A New Solution to the Problem of Creation and Evolution*. Eugene, OR: Wipf & Stock, 2010.

Weinandy, Thomas. "St. Irenaeus and the *Imago Dei*: The Importance of Being Human." *Logos* 6, no. 4 (2003): 35–50.

Welsch, Wolfgang. *Vernunft: Die Zeitgenössische Vernunftkritik und das Konzept der Transversalen Vernunft*. Frankfurt am Main: Suhrkamp Taschenbuch, 1996.

Wenham, Gordon J. *Genesis 1–15*. Word Biblical Commentary. Waco: Word, 1987.

———. *Story as Torah: Reading Old Testament Narrative Ethically*. Grand Rapids: Baker Academic, 2000.

Westermann, Claus. *Genesis 1–11: A Commentary*. Translated by John J. Scullion. Minneapolis: Augsburg, 1984.

Whitehead, Alfred North. *Process and Reality: An Essay in Cosmology*. Edited by David Ray Griffin and Donald W. Sherburne. Corrected ed. New York: Free Press, 1978. First published 1929.

Whiten, Andrew, et al. "Emulation, Imitation, Over-Imitation and the Scope of Culture for Child and Chimpanzee." *Philosophical Transactions of the Royal Society B: Biological Sciences* 364, no. 1528 (2009): 2417–28.

Wildman, Wesley. *Science and Religious Anthropology*. Farnham, UK: Ashgate, 2009.

Wiley, Tatha. *Original Sin: Origins, Developments, Contemporary Meanings*. Mahwah, NJ: Paulist Press, 2002.

Wilkinson, Michael B., with Hugh N. Campbell. *Philosophy of Religion: An Introduction*. New York: Continuum, 2010.

Williams, Norman P. *The Ideas of the Fall and of Original Sin: A Historical and Critical Study*. London: Longmans, Green, 1927.

Williams, Patricia A. *Doing without Adam and Eve: Sociobiology and Original Sin*. Minneapolis: Fortress, 2001.

———. "Sociobiology and Original Sin." *Zygon* 35, no. 4 (2000): 783–812.

Williams, Stephen N. "*Adam, the Fall, and Original Sin*: A Review Essay." *Themelios* 40 (2015): 203–17.

Wilson, Edward O. *On Human Nature*. 1978. Reprint, Cambridge, MA: Harvard University Press, 2004.

Wingren, Gustaf. *Man and the Incarnation: A Study in the Biblical Theology of Irenaeus*. Edinburgh: Oliver & Boyd, 1959.

Wolters, Albert. *Creation Regained: Biblical Basics for a Reformational Worldview*. Grand Rapids: Eerdmans, 1985.

Wright, Christopher. *Old Testament Ethics for the People of God*. Downers Grove, IL: InterVarsity, 2004.

Wright, N. T. *Evil and the Justice of God*. London: SPCK, 2006.

———. *Surprised by Scripture: Engaging Contemporary Issues*. New York: HarperCollins, 2014.

Wuketits, Franz M. *Evolutionary Epistemology and Its Implications for Humankind*. Albany, NY: SUNY Press, 1990.

Zimmerman, Dean. "From Experience to Experiencer." In *The Soul Hypothesis: Investigations into the Existence of the Soul*, edited by Mark C. Baker and Stewart Goetz, 168–201. New York: Continuum, 2011.

———. "Three Introductory Questions." In *Persons: Human and Divine*, edited by Dean Zimmerman and Peter van Inwagen, 1–34. Oxford: Oxford University Press, 2007.

CONTRIBUTORS

Michael Burdett, DPhil (University of Oxford), is a theologian who holds degrees in theology, engineering, and physics and whose work focuses on theological anthropology, eschatology, and science and technology. He is a research fellow at Wycliffe Hall, Oxford, and director of studies in religion, science, and technology at Scholarship and Christianity in Oxford (SCIO), and an editor for the Routledge Science and Religion book series.

C. John ("Jack") Collins, PhD (University of Liverpool), is professor of Old Testament at Covenant Theological Seminary, St. Louis. With degrees from MIT (SB, SM) and the University of Liverpool (PhD), he has been a research engineer, a church planter, and, since 1993, a teacher. In addition to his early focus on Hebrew and Greek grammar, he also studies science and faith, how the New Testament uses the Old, and biblical theology. During the 2016–17 academic year, he was a senior research fellow at the Carl Henry Center for Theological Understanding, Trinity International University, Deerfield, IL.

Mark Harris, PhD (University of Cambridge), is a condensed-matter physicist who also trained in academic theology while preparing for ordained ministry. He is especially interested in the relationship between biblical studies and the natural sciences and now combines these interests by leading the University of Edinburgh's graduate programs in science and religion.

Christopher M. Hays, DPhil (University of Oxford), is a scholar of New Testament studies and early Christianity. Formerly a British Academy postdoctoral fellow at the University of Oxford, he is currently a professor of New Testament at the Biblical Seminary of Colombia, Medellín.

Michael Lloyd, DPhil (University of Oxford), is principal at Wycliffe Hall, Oxford. He has been a chaplain and has taught theology at both Oxford University and Cambridge University. His academic work has focused on the problem of evil, and he is also interested in the theology of George Frideric Handel.

Andrew M. McCoy, PhD (University of St. Andrews), is a theologian who studies contemporary cultural concerns and Christian spiritual formation. He is director of the Center for Ministry Studies and assistant professor of ministry studies at Hope College, Holland, MI. He has also previously served as a scholar-in-residence with the Calvin Institute of Christian Worship at Calvin College, Grand Rapids, MI.

C. Ben Mitchell, PhD (University of Tennessee, Knoxville), is provost and vice president for academic affairs at Union University, where he also serves as Graves Professor of Moral Philosophy. He was a fellow of the John Templeton Oxford Seminars on Science and Christianity from 2003 to 2005.

Thomas Jay Oord, PhD (Claremont Graduate University), is a theologian, philosopher, and scholar of multidisciplinary studies. He is professor at Northwest Nazarene University and the author or editor of more than twenty books. Oord is an award-winning author and lecturer and serves in leadership roles for a number of academic societies.

Ted Peters, PhD (University of Chicago), is a systematic theologian who concentrates on Reformation theology as well as the dialogue between faith and science. His current area of research centers on astrotheology, cosmology, and divine action. He coedits the journal *Theology and Science* and is author of a number of leading texts in bioethics, Christian doctrine, and science and faith. He serves on the Standards Working Group (SWG) of the California Institute of Regenerative Medicine (CIRM), which sets standards for stem cell line derivation, oocyte donation, and related practices.

Andrew Pinsent, DPhil and PhD (University of Oxford and Saint Louis University), is Research Director of the Ian Ramsey Centre for Science and Religion at Oxford University. He was formerly a high energy physicist on the DELPHI experiment at CERN and has pontifical degrees in philosophy and theology in addition to one doctorate in particle physics and another doctorate in philosophy. He has publications on virtue ethics, neurotheology, science and religion, the philosophy of the person, divine action, and the nature of evil. He has given public lectures in many countries, contributed to a wide variety of catechetical materials, and appeared on the BBC, EWTN, Channel 4, and a wide range of other media on science and faith issues.

Stanley P. Rosenberg, PhD (Catholic University of America), is a historian of late antiquity and early Christianity focusing particularly on Augustine, early Christian cosmology, and the reception of Genesis 1–3. He is the executive director of Scholarship and Christianity in Oxford (SCIO), on the Wycliffe Hall academic staff, a member of the University of Oxford's Faculty of Theology and Religion, associate member of the Ian Ramsey Centre for Science and Religion, and a research member of the Oxford Centre for Late Antiquity.

Christopher Southgate, PhD (University of Cambridge), is associate professor in interdisciplinary theology at the University of Exeter. He gained his PhD in biochemistry from Cambridge and has taught the science-religion debate at Exeter since 1993. He also has ongoing interests in the impact of trauma on congregations and the science of the origin of life.

Richard Swinburne, DPhil (University of Oxford), was professor of the philosophy of religion at Oxford University from 1985 until 2002. In addition to his many books on the existence of God and the internal coherence of theism, and on the mind-body problem, he has also written a tetralogy on the meaning and justification of the doctrines that distinguish Christianity from other religions. He was elected a fellow of the British Academy in 1993.

Gijsbert van den Brink, PhD (Utrecht University), holds the university research chair of theology and science at the Faculty of Theology, Vrije Universiteit Amsterdam, and is head of its Department of Beliefs and Practices. He previously held teaching positions at the universities of Groningen, Utrecht, and Leiden and served for a year at the Center for Theological Inquiry, Princeton, NJ. His most recent research focuses on the incorporation of the findings of evolutionary biology within Reformed theology.

Benno van den Toren, PhD (Kampen), taught theology at the Faculté de Théologie Evangélique de Bangui (Central African Republic) and Wycliffe Hall, Oxford, and is currently professor of intercultural theology at the Protestant Theological University, Groningen, The Netherlands. His current research interests include the relationship between science and religion in Africa and the nature of intercultural theology.

J. Wentzel van Huyssteen, PhD (Free University of Amsterdam), is a philosophical theologian and the James I. McCord Professor of Theology and Science Emeritus at Princeton Theological Seminary. Since moving to Cape Town, South Africa, in retirement, he has been appointed extraordinary professor of theology at the University of Stellenbosch. Van Huyssteen's academic interests focus on theological anthropology, epistemology, and evolution. His books have received numerous awards and have been translated into many languages, including Russian and Swedish.

Aku Visala, PhD (University of Helsinki), is a philosopher of religion whose work is located at the intersection of analytic philosophy, theological anthropology, and the cognitive sciences. He is currently an adjunct professor in philosophy of religion and research fellow of the Finnish Academy at the University of Helsinki, Finland. He has held postdoctoral positions at the universities of Oxford, Princeton, and Notre Dame and has authored many leading publications on human nature and philosophy of religion.

Vince Vitale, DPhil (University of Oxford), is associate tutor in philosophy at Wycliffe Hall and a member of the Faculty of Theology and Religion at the University of Oxford. He was formerly lecturer in philosophy at Princeton University and team director of the Oxford Centre for Christian Apologetics, and he is currently director of the Zacharias Institute.

SCRIPTURE AND ANCIENT WRITINGS INDEX

Old Testament

Genesis

NAME INDEX

SUBJECT INDEX